GLOBALISM, LOCALISM AND IDENTITY

Globalism, Localism and Identity
Fresh Perspectives on the Transition
to Sustainability

Edited by Tim O'Riordan

Earthscan Publications Ltd, London and Sterling, VA

First published in the UK and USA in 2001 by
Earthscan Publications Ltd

Copyright © Tim O'Riordan, 2001

ISBN: 1 85383 732 6 paperback
      1 85383 731 8 hardback

Typesetting by JS Typesetting, Wellingborough, Northamptonshire
Printed and bound by Creative Print and Design, Ebbw Vale
Cover design by Yvonne Booth

For a full list of publications please contact:

Earthscan Publications Ltd
120 Pentonville Road
London, N1 9JN, UK
Tel: +44 (0)20 7278 0433
Fax: +44 (0)20 7278 1142
Email: earthinfo@earthscan.co.uk
http://www.earthscan.co.uk

22883 Quicksilver Drive, Sterling, VA 20166–2012, USA

Earthscan is an editorially independent subsidiary of Kogan Page Ltd and
publishes in association with WWF-UK and the International Institute for
Environment and Development

A catalogue record for this book is available from the British Library

Library of Concgress Cataloging-in-Publication Data

O'Riordan, Timothy.
    Globalism, localism and identity : fresh perspectives on the transition to
    sustainability / edited by Tim O'Riordan.
        p. cm.
    Includes bibliographical references and index.
    ISBN 1-85383-731-8 (hardcover) – ISBN 1-85383-732-6 (pbk.)
        1. Sustainable development.   2. International economic relations.
    3. Central-local government relations.   I. Title.

HC79.E5 O763 2000
338.9'27—dc21

                                                                00-046643

This book is printed on elemental chlorine-free paper

CONTENTS

LIST OF ACRONYMS AND ABBREVIATIONS

ADEPE	Association for the Development of Peniche (Portugal)
AIDS	acquired immune deficiency syndrome
AIMinho	Associação Industrial do Minho (Minho Industrial Association, Portugal)
AIPortuense	Associação Industrial Portuense (Oporto Industrial Association, Portugal)
AMAP	Associção Mútua dos Armadores de Peniche (Mutual Association of Peniche Shipowners, Portugal)
AMAVE	Associação dos Municípios do Vale do Ave (Association of Vale do Ave Municipalities, Portugal)
ANPED	Northern Alliance for Sustainability
APTV	Associação Portuguesa dos Têxteis e do Vestuário (Portuguese Association of Textiles and Clothing Industries)
ATE	Agricultural Bank of Greece
CAP	Common Agricultural Policy
CCRN	Comissão de Coordenação da Região Norte (Coordination Commission of the North Region, Portugal)
CEEETA	Centro de Estudos em Economia da Energia, dos Transportes e do Ambiente (Portugal)
CEMR	Council for European Regions and Municipalities
CFP	Common Fisheries Policy
CPF	Community Power Forum
CSF	community support framework
CO$_2$	carbon dioxide
CP	Community Power Initiative
CSERGE	Centre for Social and Economic Research on the Global Environment
DGDR	Direcção-Geral do Desenvolvimento Regional (Directorate General for Regional Development, Portugal)
DGP	Direcção-Geral das Pescas (Directorate General for Fisheries, Portugal)
EC	European Community
ecu	European currency unit
EEC	European Economic Community
EFTA	European Free Trade Association

EMAS	European Eco-Management and Audit Scheme
EMS	environmental management system
EMU	European Monetary Union
EU	European Union
EUR15	15 member states of the EU
FESETE	Federação dos Sindicatos dos Trabalhadores Têxteis, Lanifícios, Vestuário, Calçado e Peles de Portugal (Federation of the Portuguese Labour Unions of Textiles, Woollen Goods, Clothing and Leather Workers)
FGM	focus-group meeting
FOA	Defence Research Organization (Sweden)
FORPESCAS	Training programme set up in 1986 by the Portuguese government to develop professional training courses and to increase the qualification of the human resources present in the Portuguese fisheries sector
GAA	Greater Athens Area
GAV	gross-added value
GDP	gross domestic product
GMO	genetically modified organism
GO	governmental organization
GREIF	Graz Energy Information (Austria)
HBC	Hackney Borough Council
ICLEI	International Council for Local Environmental Initiatives
ILO	International Labour Organization
IAPMEI	Instituto de Apoio às Pequenas e Médias Empresas e ao Investimento (Portuguese Institute for Support to SMEs and to Investment)
IPAMB	Institute of Environmental Promotion (Portugal)
IPIMAR	Portuguese Institute for Sea Research
IPM	integrated pest management
IT	information technology
KEDKE	Central Union of Local Governments in Greece
LA21	Local Agenda 21
Mecu	10^6 ecu
MPAT	Ministério do Planeamento e da Administração do Território (Portuguese Ministry of Planning and Territory Administration)
MQE	Portuguese Ministry for Qualification and Employment
MSSS	Portuguese Ministry of Solidarity and Social Security
N21	Norwich 21
NAs	Greek prefectures or counties
NATO	North Atlantic Treaty Organization
NCP	Norwich Community Power
NCSD	National Council for the Environment and Sustainable Development
NEPP	National Environmental Policy Plan
NGO	non-governmental organization
Nimby	not in my backyard

ÖC	*Östgöta Correspondenten* (Sweden)
OECD	Organization for Economic Cooperation and Development
OTAs	Greek communities and municipalities
PASEGES	Panhellenic Confederation of Unions of Agricultural Cooperatives (Greece)
PROAVE	Programa de Desenvolvimento Integrado do Vale do Ave (Integrated Programme for the Development of Vale do Ave, Portugal)
RDP	regional development plan
SIDVA	Sistema de Despoluição do Vale do Ave (Vale do Ave Clearing from Pollution System, Portugal)
SINDAVE	Sistema de Incentivos à Diversificação do Vale do Ave (System of Incentives for the Economic Diversification of Vale do Ave, Portugal)
SINDETEX	Sindicato Democrático dos Têxteis (Textile's Democratic Labour Union, Portugal)
SME	small- and medium-sized enterprise
SODC	Strategic Options for the Development of the Country
SRB	single regeneration budget
SRN	Swedish Council for Planning and Coordination of Research
SUN	Sustainable Urban Neighbourhood Initiative
SWOT	strengths, weaknesses, opportunities, threats
TEU	Treaty of the European Union
UK	United Kingdom
UN	United Nations
UNCED	United Nations Conference on Environment and Development
UNED-UK	United Nations Environment and Development-UK
US	United States
VA	voluntary agreement
WTO	World Trade Organization
WWF	World Wide Fund for Nature
YPEHODE	Greek Ministry of Environment, Physical Planning and Public Works

List of Contributors

Tim O'Riordan

Tim O'Riordan is Associate Director of the Centre for Social and Economic Research on the Global Environment and Professor of Environmental Sciences at the University of East Anglia, Norwich, NR4 7TJ. E-mail: t.oriordan@uea.ac.uk

Chris Church

Chris Church is a consultant to the Community Development Foundation and UNED-UK, specializing in work on local sustainability and socio-environmental issues. He chairs the Board of ANPED, the Northern Alliance for Sustainability, a network of NGOs working in all parts of Europe. C Church PO Box 893, London, E5 9RU. E-mail: cjchurch@geo2.poptel.org.uk

Heather Voisey

Heather Voisey was formerly a Senior Research Associate in the Centre for Social and Economic Research on the Global Environment at the University of East Anglia, Norwich, and is now a postgraduate student at the University of Glasgow. She can be contacted at the following e-mail address: sian.pearce@uea.ac.uk

Uno Svedin

Uno Svedin is Professor of Environmental Policy Studies at the University of Linköping, Tema, and Director of Research at the Swedish Council for Planning and Coordination of Research (SRN). E-mail: uno.svedin@frn.se

ANDREW JORDAN

Andrew Jordan is a Lecturer in Environmental Politics in the School of Environmental Sciences, University of East Anglia, Norwich, NR4 7TJ. E-mail: a.jordan@uea.ac.uk

JUDITH CHERNI

Judith Cherni can be contacted at Imperial College of Science, Technology and Medicine, Environmental Policy and Management Group, 48 Prince's Gardens, London, SW7 2PE. E-mail: j.cherni@ic.ac.uk

MARIA KOUSIS

Maria Kousis is Associate Professor at the Department of Sociology, University of Crete, Gallos Campus, Rethimno 74100, Greece. E-mail: kousis@social.soc.uoc.gr

GEOFFREY GOOCH

Geoffrey Gooch is Senior Lecturer in Political Science, Jean Monnet Lecturer in European Political Integration, and Jean Monnet Lecturer in Europe in a Regional Perspective. Department of Political Science, Tema Institute, Linköping University, S-58183 Linköping, Sweden. E-mail: GeoGo@tema.liu.se

ANDERS HJORT AF ORNÄS

Anders Hjort af Ornäs is Director of Environmental Policy and Society Network Department of Water and Environmental Studies at Linköping Universitet, S-581 83 Linköping, Sweden. E-mail: Anders.Hjort@tema.liu.se

ULRIK LOHM

Ulrik Lohm can be contacted at Tema V, Linköping Universitet, 5-533 81 Linköping, Sweden. E-mail: UlrLo@tema.liu.se

ANDREA GRABHER

Andrea Grabher can be contacted at JOINTS, Joanneum Research Institut fur Nachhaltige Techniken und Systeme, Joanneum Research, Maritzener

Hauptstrasse 3, A-8130 Frohnleiten, Austria. E-mail: andrea.grabher@ joanneum.ac.at

MICHAEL NARODOSLAWSKY

Michael Narodoslawsky is Professor at the Institut fur Grundlagen der Verfahrenstechnik und Anlagentechnik Technische, Universitaet Graz, Inffeldgasse 25, A-8010 Graz, Austria. E-mail: Braunegg@glvt.tu-graz.ac.at

VALDEMAR RODRIGUES

Valdemar Rodrigues is a Senior Research Associate in the Environmental Economics and Management Department, CEEETA (Centro de Estudos em Economia da Energia, dos Transportes e do Ambiente), R Dr António Cândido, 10, 4º 1050 Lisbon, Portugal. E-mail: vjrodrigues@mail.telepac.pt

FÁTIMA DIREITINHO

Fátima Direitinho is Senior Researcher Associated Environmental Economics and Management Group, CEEETA, Portugal. E-mail: fad@mail.telepac.pt

EUGENIA PETROPOPOLOU

Eugenia Petropopolou is a Researcher in the Department of Sociology, University of Crete, Rethimno 74100, Crete, Greece. E-mail: bm-cwtdfx@ otenet.gr

ANDREW WALTERS

Andrew Walters is Community Development Officer for the Tidy Britain Group in Norwich. E-mail: andreww@tidybritain.org.uk

LIST OF TABLES, FIGURES AND BOXES

TABLES

FIGURES

BOXES

PREFACE

If there is one word that describes the departed 20th century, surely it is 'globalization'. Two world wars, the onset of television and the long-haul jet, the advent of the Internet, and the outreach of the multinational have helped to create what Marshall McLuhan elegantly described as the 'global village'. In all probability, the next century will bring the 'local globe', namely the localization of globalization. The trend of hugely facile communication allows local democracy to flourish just as much an intercontinental e-mail traffic. The themes of identity and distinctiveness that pervade the text that follows, are being translated into multilayered governance. This is the capability of connecting public to private sectors of the economy at various scales of responsibility, accountability and evaluation. It is possible to run a commune locally, be funded from multinational sources, implement a global environmental agreement, and be regulated by a national organization responsive to global and local needs. Locality, therefore, can evolve in a globalizing world, and global outcomes are nothing but the accumulation of countless local actions. To tackle global environmental change, there will have to be resonant and interconnected local action. This book also, therefore, enquires into social connectedness: namely the bonds that keep people in communities, and encourage them to take a citizenship perspective into their household behaviour.

In a previous volume (O'Riordan and Voisey, *The Transition to Sustainability*, 1998), sustainability was described as an evolutionary, creative and revelatory exploration. Sustainability can never be achieved, for it defines itself by its own pathways. Each stage is a reflection of its predecessor and a prognosis for the next. There is no collective memory of the past in the sustainability transition, for we all have our own interpretations of the previous, non-sustainable, age. Nor can there be any predictions of the future: the future is only what we collectively make it. And as we create it, so we become more or less connected, and more or less sustainable. Each stage only defines the circumstances for the next – not for the next but one.

The Transition to Sustainability also indicated clearly why the notion of sustainability is both paradoxical and beguilingly ambiguous. Like so many contradictory concepts, such as fairness, justice or equity, sustainability eludes a common definition. That is the nature of democratic debate and resolution. Every individual and social network will perceive sustainability in the context of its history, its aspirations, its power relations, and its response to opportunities to reveal its local identities. We therefore introduce in this volume a multilayered interpretation of sustainability, governance and identity so that the reader can observe the social, economic and political circumstances through which these concepts evolve. Doubtless, in years to come, many, much richer, interpretations of these notions will appear. That is as it should be.

The framework for this book is the changing relationship of globalization and localization as played out through the medium of ten case studies in five member states of the European Union (EU). Each case study has its own history of relationships and networks; each has its own unique combinations of actors, leaders, followers and the disenchanted. But each does display the touching of two great spheres, global and local, through patterns of self-esteem and social identity, and interconnecting governance. Hence the title of this volume.

We conclude that sustainability is not a pathway devoid of histories and futures. Nor can sustainability be approached only through its own policy envelope. When sustainability is touched, there are new sets of losers. At the very least are those who are advantaged by non-sustainable practices and policies. Because the very notion of sustainability is so ambiguous and contradictory, it is not even possible to identify obvious groups of losers in any sustainability transition. For example, German brown-coal miners are notoriously subsidized to continue to produce lignite, one of the highest sources of carbon per unit of heat created. If a carbon tax were to be imposed, some would surely lose their jobs. Are they losing out to sustainable development? Or would such an outcome be a product of market rationalization, arguably long overdue.

The issue here is not so much that there are losers and gainers in any transformed policy arena attempting to be sustainable. What counts is how such policies are conceived, and how various interests are treated as a consequence. How individuals respond to a policy shift in favour of sustainability therefore depends on identity and democracy, at least as they see these patterns. And how managers and policy-makers respond involves a combination of reactions, only a few of which have sustainability stamped on them. The sustainability transition is supported by networks of policy innovations and rigidities, all of which apply to connectivities of governance and patterns of identity. One should be wary of attempting to standardize that transition. There is no best practice or benchmark. There is only the memory of learning and the excitement of prognosis.

In this book, no great case is made for sustainability. In *The Transition to Sustainability* (p281) a deliberately optimistic note was struck. This was written in the teeth of evidence that the old order was always in the ascendant, even under the guise of 'modernization'. This position was held because there are discernible moves towards environmental well-being and social justice in a period of modern change, even though it is not obviously driven by the sustainability engine. Here, the case studies reveal the same frustrating contradiction: a lot of turbulence, plenty of 'old-order' survival, but glimmers of hope.

The case studies selected have four important characteristics:

- (Graz, Linköping, Perniche) Some explicitly seek to promote sustainable outcomes for peoples and ecosystems, and to create wealth in the process. We ask how they do this, who loses, and who identifies the winners and losers. We also examine how installing identity in community can empower losers and move the collective towards sustainability.
- (Vale do Ave, Åtvidaberg) Some are the victims of global economic change, but are deploying fascinating reinterpretations of social–local identity in their move towards a sustainability trackway.
- (Timbaki, Feldbach) Some have experienced the failure of EU agricultural and structural policies and look to a combination of governments to help them solve their plight. Their success depends on visionary leadership and skilful diplomacy, in both cases born of social–local identity.
- (Aegaleo, Mile Cross in Norwich, Hackney in London) There are urban communities in the midst of economic and social flux where sustainability has yet to appear in a recognizable form, but where social–local identify could provide the basis for the transition.

The ten case studies each have a story and a lesson. Chapter 1 summarizes the lessons and the implications both for theory-building and thoroughly pragmatic policy-making. The following four chapters explore the theory in more detail: global–local relationships and the new spatial order; multilayered governance and the new a-hierarchy of authority; social–local identities and the new patterns of empathy and apathy; and methods of conduct, especially the value of exploratory and intuitive inquiry. Each of these chapters suggests that novel ways of examining multiple levels of relationships and interpretations required a fresh approach to recording and concluding the evidence. Research may have to become increasingly adaptable and path-dependent, not fixed by initiating hypothesis and predetermined frames of examination. Such an approach may be conventional. But it could strangle novelty and the analysis of progressive sequences of accommodation, where each stage can only be interpreted in the context of its predecessor. This is why intuitive methodology may begin to find its niche in the conduct of research inquiry.

Intuitive methodology is a combination of ordered and wholly responsive approaches to soliciting information. The task is to sense the occasion; to be fully empathetic to the mood and the qualities of knowledge and emotion in respondents; and to allow opportunities to be created and seized. Intuitive research applies as a sensitive and exploratory process to the discovery and interpretations of documents as much as it does to associating with the inner psyche of human contact. The formal approach to social science research is still vital, however. This involves developing propositions for existing studies, and analysing the comparative and unique elements of the inquiry to be undertaken, while always being prepared to explore a journey of theoretical and methodological discovery without being bound to established research principles. The exploratory element is equally essential, as this enables the richness of experiences to be fully opened up and incorporated. Intuitive methodology is also an active resource in that it promotes the scope for the researcher to be an agent in the pattern of change. This approach must not be exploited: the trick is to ensure that active engagement is persuasive and constructive, not manipulative.

For intuitive methodology to flourish, however, the researcher will have to draw upon reserves of courage and sensitivity. Intuitive research ought to be harder to do well than programmed research. This is because it is so sensitive to what is happening at each moment of examination and reflection. Intuition is engaged by the active and creative observer who becomes a participant insofar as interaction reveals the insights that strict detachment can never uncover. This is a fascinating world of inquiry, not new to ethnographers and many people-centred social scientists, but unfamiliar to those social scientists trained to observe, record and assess against predetermined frameworks of conduct.

Finally, we take a look at the implications of all this work on the future of subsidiarity and localism in the European Union. As the European family of member states expands, so the playing out of conformity and distinctiveness through the transition to sustainability will become increasingly a test of the European ideal's durability. Europe has a demos, but not a polis. It has a democratic allegiance, spurred by accountability and the delivery of greater fairness and justice. But it has no political homogeneity. Maybe it should not have a collective political identity; instead, it should have thousands of local identities that share common political and economic aspirations. Create the large by acting through the small. We have yet to learn this lesson in Europe.

ACKNOWLEDGEMENTS

Every research project is a family experience. Researchers form bonds that generate humour as well as bestow learning. The group of scholars that formed this 'family' visited and existed in a variety of configurations. The personnel were never all the same at any of the five meetings; but the spirit of a family united in the excitement of inquiry never waned. So my first cheer of gratitude is to all my colleagues, each of whom appears as an author in the text that follows.

The European Commission provided a research context that may not be repeated. This is the uniting of social science researchers in an inter-disciplinary format looking at similar phenomena across cultures and experiences. What was particularly valuable about this research was the effort each team put in to enable us all to meet with actors and citizens and policy-makers and various points in the patterns of governance. All of this enriched our understanding and, we hope, enriched, in turn, their own outlooks. The Science and Research Directorate of the Commission, formerly DG XII, made this possible. So, to Andrew Sors, Jonathan Parker and Angela Liberatore for their huge goodwill goes a second cheer for supportive understanding in our endeavour.

No manuscript comes without a human word processor. Ann Dixon in CSERGE is wonderfully tolerant and cheerful, so the passage of ideas to text was a matter of personal goodwill as well as electronic wizardry. A mighty third cheer to her.

Uno Svedin, Tim O'Riordan and Andrew Jordan wish to thank Geoffrey Gooch, Andrea Grabher and Michael Narodoslawsky for important con-tributions to Chapter 3.

In Chapter 8, the authors Valdemar Rodrigues and Fátima Direitinho deeply acknowledge IPAMB, IAPMEI and the municipalities of Peniche and Guimarães for the support provided during the various stages of their project. In particular, to Jorge Gonçalves, the mayor of Peniche, and to Manuel Ferreira (coordinator of PROAVE) and Martins Soares (AMAVE) a word of gratitude is due for their active involvement and cooperation. To the local NGOs Sol do Ave (Guimarães) and ADEPE (Peniche), as well as to the team of the Arco Íris Project, the authors are grateful for the collab-oration provided during the field surveys. The lead author is also grateful to Fundação para a Ciência e Tecnologia (FCT) for its financial support through the concession, in 1998, of a doctoral research scholarship for a period of two years.

The authors of Chapter 8 would also like to express their sincere gratitude to Ana Batalha and José dos Loios (Peniche local collaborators); to Graça Guedes and Teresa Amorim from the University of Minho, who contributed invaluably to the selection of companies to be surveyed; to Susana Dias and José João Dias, Ana Oleirinha, Ana Catarina, Mário Machado (local inquirers); and to Alice Ferreira and Graça Gonçalves, who prepared, tested and analysed the questionnaires. For the valuable comments made during the course of the project, thanks are due to Carlos Pimenta and Professor Maria do Rosário Partidário. To the local populations of Peniche and Guimarães (Barco and Pevidém), a word of appreciation is given for their availability, without which nothing but generic ideas could have been obtained in the study. A last word of sincere admiration goes to Teresa Ribeiro.

Tim O'Riordan
Norwich
September 2000

PART 1: PROVIDING PERSPECTIVE

1   Synthesis and Context

Tim O'Riordan and Chris Church

Perspective

Globalization and localization unite at all spatial scales. There is little, and maybe nothing, that is global that does not have some sort of a local manifestation. And each local manifestation changes the global context. Place-centredness is the amalgam of global change and local identity. Every place reveals itself at a variety of scales. Local perceptions are shaped by global influences, the combinations of which process local actions. These in turn are fuelled by local aspirations, many of which are the product of global images and expectations. All of these local activities accumulate to create chaotic but global outcomes.

In the text that follows, we distinguish between globalization and localization, and globalism and localism. *Globalization* and *localization* are processes of change that impact on economies, cultures and environments in ways that are both global and local. Such changes may take place at any scale and at any level of social organization. *Globalism* and *localism* are socially and politically framed interpretations of these changes that have meaning through processes of personal experience, patterns of trust, connectivities of reciprocity, and social networks of interest and bias. These two discourses entwine to form social identity, the basis for self-actualization and the bedrock of any transition to sustainability. Globalism and localism are processes of responsiveness and adaptability that are mediated and defined by various institutional arrangements and swirling patterns of social expectations. For example, in the Portuguese fishing town of Peniche, the EU Common Fisheries Policy (CFP) has constrained local fishermen in terms of catching fish in offshore international waters. That is one institutional arrangement. But another is that Moroccan fishermen can operate in these waters beyond the CFP reach. So the local Portuguese and the obliging Moroccans have struck a deal. Fishing goes on, unsustainably, while supported by the holes in the institutional netting.

Global and local are neither 'good' nor 'bad' for democracy and sustainability. It is the opportunities that they provide, and the mechanisms

Box 1.1 *Principal objectives of this book*

1 Develop a theory of globalism and localism in the transition to sustainability, taking into account their shifting cultural, political and social meanings.
2 Develop a theory of social–local identity in the framing of this analysis, and relate this theory to the scope for governance to be more flexible and adaptable in targeting social–local intelligence and economic opportunity through the sustainability transition.
3 Test this theory as it applies to concepts of insecurity, vulnerability, empowerment and revelation with a series of case studies. Each case study would take as its cue some externally framed pressure on a locality, where that pressure is directed towards, or away from, sustainability.
4 Develop and extend methods of examination of global–local relationships as these are played out through the centredness of place. Enquire how various social networks in transition respond to these changes. Assist this response through a combination of intuitive and participatory research.
5 Examine the findings from the case studies in the framework of European integration, European expansion, subsidiarity politics and citizen perceptions on the role of a more pervasive EU at the local level.

The case studies were selected on the following criteria (see text for more details):

1 EU integrationist and competitive policies create local economic and social change (Timbaki; Feldbach; Åtvidaberg).
2 Migration and disempowerment degrade opportunities for sustainability (Aegaleo; Timbaki).
3 Integrationist transport networks leave local communities economically disadvantaged (Graz; Timbaki; Vale do Ave).
4 Searching for sustainability policies creates local hardships and opportunities (Peniche).
5 There are opportunities for social advance through sustainability strategies (UK studies; Atvidaberg; Graz; Linköping).

through which democracy and identity reveal themselves, that ultimately determine their value. Consider the decision of McDonald's to follow The Natural Step in Sweden. The Natural Step is a concept that seeks to avoid depleting the planet of non-replaceable resources. This means, in effect, using replaceable materials, renewable energy and non-toxic or persistent substances. A global corporation makes a local gesture. But are the consequences any good for the diets of Swedish fast-food addicts? The Natural Step says nothing about the sustainability of the product, only the process. And could the beef not come from local organic cooperatives? What is good or bad about any of this?

Take two further illustrations from the case studies that follow, namely Feldbach in eastern Austria, and Timbaki in Crete. Both have experienced the disturbing hand of the Common Agricultural Policy (CAP). In Feldbach, the outcome was the restructuring of small farms into bigger, more intensive operations, and the release of some 6000 families into the pool of locally unemployed. To find jobs the families had to commute to regional centres, disrupting the rhythms of their intimate lives and adding to the burdens of transport. The local mayor, assisted by the research team, found ways in which to create a regional visioning process named *Leitbild*, in cooperation with the province of Styria. During mid-1999, five *Leitbild* workshops were held involving some 30 participants, each of whom was selected because of their connections to social–local networks. The *Leitbild* were built on social identity and gave confidence to all participants. They recognized the strength of their culture, their people, their leisure opportunities, their heritage, their capacity for innovative, small-scale business enterprise and the scope for generating wealth through locally distinctive 'gentle tourism'. The weaknesses were lack of connecting routeways, variable educational and training skills, and a failure to realize the strength of their common cause once their collective identity had been tapped. Now the residents of Feldbach have reached out to Brussels for structural funds to create income-generating capacities that they can coordinate through sustainability, and through the capture of the enlarged EU. The capacity to innovate is spurred by a renewed sense of collective purpose and the opportunity to link the local to the new Europe.

In Timbaki, on the other hand, the CAP reforms and the subsequent cuts in state subsidies have led to adverse economic and social impacts. In the 1990s, farmers experienced quick increases in the price of inputs while product prices remained stable or declined. At the same time, competition with other Southern EU and developing world countries offering Mediterranean products makes the Timbaki-grown (or Greek-grown) traditional products, such as olives and vegetables, difficult to market both at home and abroad. The strong local agricultural cooperatives envision sustainability as targeting more efficient planning and better marketing of high-quality and simultaneously environmentally-friendly produce. Local political figures also envision a role for agro-tourism or other alternative forms of tourism. The fact is that some farmers have started their own initiatives towards an environment-friendly agriculture, relying on very limited EU support, while others seek their survival outside intensive agriculture. For the majority of those surveyed, however, the sustainability of such initiatives depends on support from the EU and state agencies as well as on local community institutions. The active agricultural cooperatives, the local councils and the producers themselves are considered the driving forces; they are trusted with moving Timbaki into a more sustainable future. These actors have more trust in the EU than in national institutions.

These two vignettes from the case studies that follow reveal some of the central messages of this text:

- No locality is an island of self-sufficiency: external influences impinge in unpredictable ways.
- The unpredictability of global–local relationships can be heightened by the drive towards sustainability when these forces do not take into account the sensitivities to change.

- Where non-sustainable external changes affect local economies and societies, there is no clear line of support and restoration through the chain of governmental response. It is therefore necessary to concoct a response from a tiering of governmental arrangements.
- Such creative responses come from visionary local leaders who seize opportunities from the array of governmental schemes on offer, and who create social solidarities by focusing some of these schemes on local capacity-building and training.
- Communities under pressure from potentially disruptive, externally-induced change can display their resilience through existing social solidarities, which in turn reinforce their identities.

This book assesses changing interpretations of globalization and localization as they apply to new patterns of local–social identity, and through that to democracy at the local level. To do this, we have looked at the intermingling of scales of governance for the management of global–local relationships, and we have also sought to analyse this in the framework of an emerging Europe, as well as in the light of the transition to sustainability. Box 1.1 summarizes the objectives of this book, Box 1.2 explains the reasons for the case studies and Box 1.3 gives an interpretation of the transition to sustainability.

The transition to sustainability may well need to include a search for *social intelligence*. By this we mean the recognition of how networks of support and survival can be connected to programmes of local assistance and capacity-building so that the transition links local–social transformation to the practices of sustainability. The active Timbaki cooperatives and individual farmers could return to the production and marketing of organic vegetables if they were given assistance for the period of adjustment, as well as training in marketing skills and in food handling. They would also require adjustment payments from the EU, as well as from the Greek state. Some of these national payments could come from the proceeds of a pesticides levy, and/or a fertilizer levy. This is the kind of multitiered package of responses that would have to be thought through for a fragment of the transition. But it is symbolic of the global–local patterns of response that pepper the texts that follow.

CRITERIA FOR CASE STUDY SELECTION

The case studies were chosen in the countries of the groups participating in the project, following a set of criteria formulated in the early project meetings. Four sets of criteria were constructed.

1 There should be evidence of where EU competitiveness policies are creating local economic and/or cultural changes that are leading to hardship or serious problems of adjustment.

Examples of this type of area are places where agricultural intensification has increased at the expense of traditional, less 'efficient' forms of agriculture. The case studies conducted by the Greek group in the south of Crete, by the Austrian team in the south of Austria and by the Swedish group in the rural south of Sweden fit into this category. Agricultural intensification can also lead to soil erosion that results in negative effects on local physical environments and public health. Another example in which EU policies have led to changes is in the fishing industry. The case study conducted by the Portuguese team in Perniche on the Atlantic coast of Portugal is an example of the ways in which EU fishing policy has influenced local communities. A third sector where EU policies can affect the move to sustainability is forestry. When competitiveness occurs, more ecologically sound forestry practices often change and become more intensive. As the Swedish case study in the rural areas surrounding the town of Åtvidaberg has shown, developments in forestry can have far-reaching implications for the local population. All of the case studies presented in this book have not, however, met the criteria that primary sectors such as farming, fishing and forestry be affected. Urban areas are also influenced by EU competitiveness policies. Areas such as Hackney in London have seen major changes take place in which traditional forms of employment have disappeared and led to repopulation of the area by new ethnic groups.

As can be seen by the preceding section, the criteria that there should be evidence of EU competitiveness policies creating economic and/or cultural change can be met in many different ways. In fact, it is hard to envisage any region of Europe today that has not been affected by EU policies, and even the relatively wealthy areas of the north of Europe may feel that these policies have led to negative changes. The problems differ from those experienced by the Mediterranean countries, but may be just as intensely perceived by local communities.

2 There should be evidence that EU transport policies, as well as economic competition that has been aimed at generally improving access and people movement, has led to local hardships for disadvantaged communities.

The by-passing of whole sub-regions by new roads, the influx of new economic goods that have removed the market base for formerly viable local economies, and the resistance to new road constructions by communities or nations are examples of how these criteria could be met.

These selection criteria proved difficult to define. Transport and economic competition affect all segments of European society today, and different groups in the same local community may benefit from them or find themselves disadvantaged. Opposition to new roads and railways has become widespread in Europe, and while none of the case studies directly addressed this issue, it formed the background for the studies in a number of the participating countries. The Cretan farmers, for example, have been able to change their production because of new and improved communications with mainland Europe.

3 Are there ways in which the EU, in trying to bring about the sustainable utilization of resources, may be causing local social and economic hardship?

The case study of Peniche in Portugal shows how a medium-sized fishing community can suffer when the EU attempts to develop a more sustainable common fisheries policy. While the preservation of fishing stock in a European perspective is a move towards sustainability, communities such as Peniche have been hit hard by the limitations imposed upon them. The protection of water resources may in a similar way negatively affect local communities that have been dependent upon these for their economies. Restrictions placed on mining concerns also may lead to loss of jobs for the local population.

4 The final criteria is that the case studies should provide examples of areas where EU policies that are specifically geared to promoting a more sustainable or environmentally protective future have been or were being applied.

Examples of these are reformulating the structural cohesion of LIFE funds to bring about environmentally supportive infrastructures in water management, sewage treatment, education and health protection. Other examples are the ways in which measures are being taken to support sustainable tourism.

The ambition of the project was that the selection of localities in each country should reflect the first two points (1 and 2) in one case study and the second two (3 and 4) in another. As can be seen, the criteria fall into two groups. The first two are concerned with the impact of EU economic integration, and the second two with the impact of EU initiatives that are aimed explicitly at increasing sustainable resource utilization and environmental protection.

Box 1.2 *Summary of the case studies covered in this book*

Greece

- Timbaki, Crete: a rural community faces the impacts of a rapid shift to intensive greenhouse agriculture to reach European markets and seeks new ways towards a more sustainable agriculture.
- Aegaleo, Athens: a mixed ethnic working-class suburb has rich social networks but many poor and vulnerable small businesses. These are subject to changing regulations from the EC and to environmental threats from a planned new waste plant.

Austria

- Graz: a thriving city of 250,000 full of excitement about its eco-city marketing label of high-tech, clean industry and environmentally burden-reducing services. However, it suffers from traffic congestion and an incapacity to assist the disempowered.

- Feldbach: a rural community suffers from agricultural change, with deterioration in groundwater quality and rising unemployment and out-migration. It is now embarked on regional transformation for the transition to sustainability by enhancing its social networks.

Portugal

- Vale do Ave: a declining textile region of small- and medium-sized businesses (many of them family tied, closely connected and specialized) suffers from local environmental contamination and tries to restructure itself by seeking to remove its textile dependency.
- Peniche: a small Atlantic fishing town faces the loss of access to offshore fishing grounds on the basis of the CFP. Local fishermen form alliances with each other and with Moroccans to maintain income. Meanwhile, fish stocks are still being depleted.

Sweden

- Linköping: a bustling high-tech town that believes that LA21 will help it to become transformed into a 21st-century eco-city. It tries to use social–local networks to empower its citizens.
- Åtvidaberg: a former mining community experiences economic decline and environmental degradation. Now it revitalizes itself through social–local networks.

UK

- Mile Cross, Norwich: a poor and alienated community contains a variety of social interests who have yet to find a common identity through empowerment.
- Hackney and Shoreditch, London: a multiracial community seeks to use citizen democracy and LA21 to improve its economy and social esteem.

GLOBALISM AND LOCALISM

Globalism is blamed for many ills. The following is an extract from an editorial in the cheerfully radical *Ecologist*, introducing a special issue on *Shifting from Global to Local* in March–April 1999 (vol 29, no 3, p153):

> *At the heart of our problems is an economic system that separates producers from consumers, alienates people from nature, and artificially favours ever larger and more unaccountable institutions over their smaller, and more ecological, competitors ... The global economy is undermining those things on which we truly depend, like community, family, clean air, good security and safe water.*

The *Ecologist* clearly regards globalization as a danger to survival. It looks for solace in 'conserving community, providing children with a sense of security and identity, and renewing our relationship with a natural world'. Attached to these sentiments is a feeling of alienation, of political impotence and a sense that democracy, as it is commonly understood, is dying. In an important sense, therefore, globalism is the touchstone for a growing disillusionment over the state of national governance generally.

In an analysis of 14 mature democracies, Puttnam et al (2000) looked at the responses to questions along the lines of: 'Do you feel that politicians can be trusted? Do you think your political representatives really care about people like you?' In essence, the research teams were assessing citizens' views on the nature of democracy, namely representiveness, accountability and transparency of process. In all but three of the countries surveyed, loss of trust and lack of confidence in the democratic political process is very marked. In the US, for example, 75 per cent of voters placed their faith in Washington in 1960 while fewer than 20 per cent do so today. Nearly two in three believe that the US government is run by big business and powerful lobbies to the point where it is no longer interested in the electorate. Only 12 per cent have 'a great deal of confidence' in the executive branch, while 11 per cent offer the same support to the US Congress. One imagines that the latter two groups are connected to the lobbies.

The picture is similar in Europe. Confidence in Westminster has halved from 48 per cent to 24 per cent since 1985. In Sweden, the confidence slump is even more marked: a 51 per cent confidence in the Swedish parliament was lowered to a mere 19 per cent during the decade of 1985–1995. Faith in the parliamentarians in Germany fell from 55 per cent in 1972 to 34 per cent in 1992, while in Italy, such faith is only 12 per cent.

Such statistics appear alarming. But they may herald a fresh look at the politics of globalization and localization, and offer opportunities for radical rethinking in participatory democracy. Puttnam and his colleagues suggest that the late 20th century has created a set of demands from the state that focus loosely on rights, responsibilities and interests in a more active and varied manner. Equality based on gender, sex, disability and ethnicity is a heady package to deliver through the cumbersome organs of the state. So too are penal reform, adequate health-care provision and the removal of social exclusion from the inner city. The grouping of issues around sustainability (as summarized by O'Riordan and Voisey, 1998, pp44–58), which include policy integration, new forms of national accounting, shifting business–environment relationships, redemocratization of local government and ecotaxation (O'Riordan, 1997), also poses formidable challenges to centralized delivery by established political institutions. So it is hardly surprising that citizens generally want to be critical of their national and local democracies (see, for example, Norris, 1999).

Heather Voisey, in Chapter 2, plays down the theories of economic dominance in the globalization debate as being too single-cause and too simplistic for such a rich and varied set of forces. She holds on to this view, despite the rhetoric of Tony Clarke (1999, p158) who claims that the annual revenues of the biggest 200 corporations are larger than the combined gross domestic product (GDP) of 182 countries in which 80 per cent of the world's populations live. Clarke also quotes David Korten (Clarke, 1999, p161):

> *Each day [currency traders] move more than two trillion dollars around the world in the search for quick profits and safe havens, sending exchange rates and stock markets into wild gyrations wholly unrelated to any underlying economic reality. With abandon, they make and break national economies, buy and sell corporations and hold politicians hostage to their interests.*

Voisey is right to play down this interpretation – not that it is inaccurate or misrepresented, but because it is partial. The rise of the global corporation is to some extent due to a willingness to accept a global consumerist culture, so long as it creates jobs and provides goods that consumers enjoy. Like it or loathe it, McDonald's is popular. But McDonald's also has a habit of providing jobs for the vulnerable so that it can maintain low wages locally.

In a series of essays on a changing Europe edited by Gowan and Anderson (1997), the contributors appeared to agree that the European vision was a bit of a muddle between globalizing subservience and localizing identity. They also tended to accept that the institutions of governance in member states and in the EC itself are not designed for unification of cultural aspirations or a common political cause. In essence, European integration, and a desire for greater accession to the East, stubs against the toe of regional differentiation and local identity, with no obvious means of political expression or legal continuity to accommodate it.

Yet, in a recent survey of public opinion published by *The Economist* (6 November 1999, p4), 44 per cent of the country as a whole felt that the European parliament would have most influence over their lives in 20 years' time. In Scotland 46 per cent thought that the Scottish parliament would be more influential, though the European parliament came second. People identified most with their 'region' and second with their local community. Over two-thirds felt that they did not have 'much say' in the way they were governed – at whatever level of governance.

Voisey regards globalization and localization more as a basis for cultural interpretation through shared meanings, often transmitted through social networks – hence the distinction in this book between globalism and globalization, and localism and localization. Globalism and localism are matters for social discourse, through which citizens gain a sense of understanding and awareness over changes to their economy, identity and political structures. This in turn leads to new concepts of the state and of democracy, which, as we will witness below, is activating citizens into fresh dimensions of participation around the transition to sustainability. This activism, in turn, is emphasized or alienated by patterns of identity. So cultural mediation is a central plank of the economic and the environmental discourses of global change.

Locality is therefore the place-centredness of a variety of arrangements to accommodate globalization and to create new opportunities for social reform and economic revival. We shall see in the case studies that follow that the cities of Graz in Austria and Linköping in Sweden revel in their self-promoted image of environmental innovation, high technology, eco-efficiency, cleanliness and heritage. They exult in doing so in order to publicize the means of 'selling' their cities to inward investors who face huge arrays of similar locations for their attention, as well as for tourism. The eco-city concept is a marketing tactic that propels an elite into a frenzy of collective identity for their own advance. The fact that the excluded are left in their wake is a matter for regret, particularly by those who believe in civic empowerment, as in Mile Cross in Norwich.

Thus locality is the repository of a variety of forces and activities that flourish or disintegrate into patterns of place-centred distinctiveness. In the Athenian suburb of Aegaleo – a working-class and multi-ethnic quarter of an expanding metropolis – local groups have resisted the imposition of a huge new waste transport station on the site of what little communal open space remains. It is likely that this new waste station will be filled by material coming from Athens, not Aegaleo and its neighbours. Will the diverse and community-based network of social–local groupings that sought to use and identify with 'their' open space, affectionately known as 'olive grove', be replaced by a metropolitan authority backed by powerful vested interests? So far the answer appears negative. For the past two years residents as well as other local groups have protested successfully against the siting of the waste transport station. Responding to their calls, the Greek Supreme Court recently annulled the environmental impact study by the Greek Ministry of Environment, Physical Planning and Public Works, asking it to prepare another one. All interested groups and agencies will have a chance to participate in a forthcoming workshop, organized by the municipality and its supporters on the siting of the station. Thus localization becomes a metaphor for disintegration as much as an opportunity for revival (as in Åtvidaberg and Feldbach), depending on the configuration of central and local patterns of locality and democracy. These in turn could be used to ensure both the *social intelligence* and the *institutional intelligence* that influence the capacity to respond to changes in ways that are more sustainable.

Insofar as there is any consensus, localism is 'made aware' of a sense of place that takes into account multiple identities and various social relations and cultural discourses. 'Place', therefore, is both incorporated within communal networks of survival, resistance and expansion, and amalgamated into regional or global outreach through its marketing or image-making. What is clear is that localization is very uneven, as is globalization. Both may exacerbate economic or social vulnerability, or they may release opportunities for sustainable transformation – or any combination in between.

The many transitions to sustainability in Europe

All this, in turn, means that sustainable development, or the move towards sustainability as defined in *The Transition to Sustainability* (O'Riordan and Voisey, 1998; see also Box 1.3 in this chapter), will be interpreted in different ways as the global and the local levels are played out. In *The Transition to Sustainability*, O'Riordan and Voisey gave the appearance of creating a template for the transition that was reasonably similar across countries and cultures. Through subsequent case studies in the book, it became more evident that the transition was anything but comparable, and that a variety of national political and economic factors intervened in the process. Sustainability does have an organizing focus; but its success as a policy arena depends enormously on its capture and metamorphosis of a huge array of other policy developments. These include constitutional reform; tax reform; the changing climate of governance; the integration of policy arenas; the scope for new forms of national accounting and valuation of costs and benefits; new attempts at civic empowerment and local democracy; and the changing business climate towards environmental and social matters.

O'Riordan and Voisey (1998) placed insufficient emphasis on the contradictions between the drivers of modernization in economies and democracies and the failure to capture the sustainability transition in this metamorphosis. In Figure 1.1, there are important developments in the 'domains' summaries, such as in ecotax reform, huge innovations in clean technology and 'Factor 4' efficiency gains, and even in social inclusion strategies. But these important changes are not connected to sustainability, which seems to have missed out in the modernization rhetoric. Despite worthy attempts to create commissions of sustainable development and sustainability indicators, the machinery of governance remains close to the old, non-sustainability trackways. The visionaries are looking in other directions.

Box 1.3 *The transition to sustainability*

The transition to sustainability is characterized by three interlocking relationships, all tightly interconnected (see Figure 1.1 and the introductory text in O'Riordan and Voisey, 1998). The principal driver is the technology and economy domain, which seeks to shift activity to eco-efficiency (creating more wealth for fewer material and energy resources), decoupling consumption for growth, and introducing green accounting into national statistics. Through the latter innovations in data-gathering and interpretation, tax reform in favour of environmental burden levies can now be better calculated. The crucial issues here are:

- the capacity to channel information technology in order to analyse how environmental and social costs occur;
- the capacity to determine what activities are the cause of environmental and social burdens;
- the capacity to determine how any level of tax might affect economic performance and competitiveness generally, and specific sectors in particular.

It will then be possible to target activities and sequentially raise levies in a programmed manner. In addition, it should also be possible to target the revenue from particular social purposes, designed to promote the transition to sustainability.

The legal and institutional domain places an emphasis on networked management that is sensitive to social and ecosystem integrity and well-being. Innovative regulatory practices include strategic and precautionary resource planning for water, soil, fish, biodiversity, forests and coasts. Such planning is capable of generating new integrated policy structures and can pursue more imaginative approaches to regulation. Innovative regulatory practices also include more participatory evaluation, more voluntaristic contracts, more education and guidance, and more scope for civic accountability in the conduct of regulations. Many of these developments are taking place without being associated directly with the transition to sustainability.

The civic society domain embraces civil rights for those disempowered and dispossessed. Innovation in this arena focuses on identifying policy linkages between the social and economic agendas, especially in terms of social exclusion, and also on new ways of improving participation, especially among the marginalized. The overall aim is to improve the conduct of local democracy. This is the essence of much of the text that follows.

Much of this is beginning to happen in a variety of ways in Europe, but the adherence to sustainability is only very slowly beginning to coalesce. Nevertheless, there is movement and much of it is in the 'right' direction.

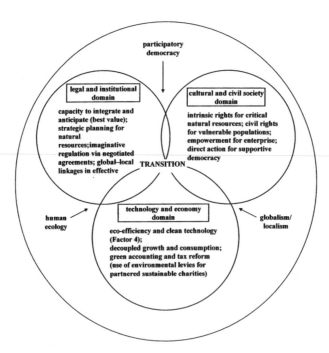

Source: O'Riordan and Voisey (1998, p5)
Note: The linking variables are: the introduction of a more active and inclusive participatory democracy, now being experimented with in LA21; the new configurations of global–local relationships as analysed in Chapter 2; and the first attempts to pursue human ecology, or the creative interrelationships between individuals in themselves as social beings in supportive networks and as stewardship citizens in planetary care. Needless to say, this combination is still elusive.

Figure 1.1 *The domains of sustainability*

This book takes the local differentiation of the sustainability transition a lot further. The evidence for the case studies that follow indicates that the EU is highly ambivalent about both sustainability and subsidiarity. The policy bias remains on economic market integration, the promotion of competition and the facilitation of commerce and transportation. The sensitivity to local and regional identity remains more a matter for member states to monitor and to accommodate. This is rarely the focus for any specific European initiatives. Doubtless, the disposition of structural funds will have an element of bias towards regional identity. But as we shall see in the Vale do Ave and Timbaki case studies, regional structural funds were not tailored either to the vulnerable or, noticeably, to sustainability. This conclusion was also supported by Coffey (1998) in her analysis of the use of cohesion funds by the EC. These funds are designed to pay for much-needed economic infrastructure, notably roads, telecommunications and sewage treatment facilities, but not for intertwining the three domains of sustainability.

The case studies also show that any 'capture' of the transition to sustainability is not set in a national Agenda 21. It is the outcome of particular initiatives, such as civic empowerment, Local Agenda 21 (LA21) as a device for promoting local solidarity, or because of the commercial advantages of investing in eco-efficiency and clean industry.

Another driver for a special focus on sustainability is the radical vision of local movers and shakers who see an opportunity to promote the economic and social advantages of their localities. This happened most obviously in Feldbach. It also occurred in Åtvidaberg and in Mile Cross, and to a lesser extent in Hackney. The role of the 'sustainability entre-preneur' deserves more attention in both research and methodology. The explanatory and intuitive aspects of research design provide means for identifying persons and networks where particular pulses of change are taking place. The interactions between the research teams and local political and social figures were also instrumental in creating these opportunities. All these points are given more prominence in Chapter 5.

LAYERING OF GOVERNANCE

As a reasonable generalization, political scientists have tended to study governance in horizontal 'layers'. This results in comparative studies of similar institutions. Such a tactic helps to illuminate the structure and effectiveness of governance. But it may miss what happens when govern-ance is vertical and discontinuous, since it allows for jumps of policy integration and joint initiatives between various levels of government across national borders. We shall see in the Austrian and Swedish case studies that this layering is particularly apposite in federated national structures with complicated patterns of autonomy and dependence between central, provincial, municipal and local realms of governance, and their various interactions with the EC and other interregional funding sources.

In their analysis of the topic, Uno Svedin and his colleagues (see Chapter 3) suggest that the globalizing patterns referred to by Heather Voisey also contribute to variations in the partnerships of government. They cite three possible drivers:

- technology change in the form of complicated sub-contracting of specialized parts linked across space, based in geographical patterns of emphasis and cooperation;
- organizational change in business and in community structures that favour the patterning of networks rather than hierarchies, again with space as a backdrop;
- new modes of production of knowledge where complex and interactive data analysis can be scavenged into new knowledge forms (one example is the introduction of trial carbon trading in major corporations; another is the pinpointing of environmental burden costs across nations and economic sectors).

According to Svedin, the globalization of economies and the networking of management are leading to the structuring of enterprise-based advantage, not to national sentiment. If, however, local identity (as in Graz and Linköping) creates a productive enterprise that adds value to a product and to an image, then these restructuring forces will capture that spirit. Therefore, multiple layering of government is becoming a factor in recognizing, on the part of opinion formers, how local identity can lead to comparative advantage, marketing image and to international prestige. Should these new partnerships between civic authorities and the new spirit of enterprise endure, then it is possible to see how re-empowered people can become part of the enterprise culture. This is the scope for public–private partnerships in governance that permit the link between sustainability and identity formation. It is multiple-tiering of multigovernmental relations that enables radical combinations to take place in the name of sustainability. This is noticeable most especially in Feldbach and in Åtvidaberg.

Other examples of this combined approach to governance include city associations for climate change, regional groupings of UK local government to create regional resource inventories (for example, water and biodiversity inventories), lobbying exchange networks in Brussels to capture European initiatives for particular interests (chemicals, tourism, conservation), and business associations which pool knowledge in relation to climate-change strategies. At the local level, such coalitions are emerging as part of the loose 'sustainable communities' networks, now evident in a number of European countries. One can look to the creation of local sustainability charities, funded in part by environmental levies, as the basis for future multilayered governmental structures.

A sound theory of multiple tier governance still awaits discovery and presentation. One of the reasons for the delay is the sheer ubiquitousness of new patterns of communication, knowledge focus and political presence that characterizes the structures of European governance in the modern day. It is almost impossible to provide a meaningful typology, let alone a detailed prognosis of how and why such partnerships are formed and how they may evolve. Some points of entry are offered here.

- Institutional intelligence is the pooling of patterns of bias for particular issues and themes as these play through governmental levels. A number of case studies around particular policy arenas would help to unravel these patterns. A start has been made in a series of papers edited by Levidow and Carr (2000). A number of national research teams examined the suite of intergovernmental, regulatory and pressure group relationships that interact concerning the issues of introducing genetically modified organisms (GMOs) into Europe as food products. This fascinating comparative collection showed clearly how science, technology and innovation are perceived and regulated, and how public–private partnerships in policy-making styles have a strong influence on the manner in which the introduction of GMOs is treated. The crucial issues here are the degree of openness in the regulatory process, and the composition of the scientific review committees. The more the process is fully open, and the wider the representation on the assessment panels, the more likely there will be public trust in the outcome.
- Coalitions of influence have enormous scope for flexibility, adding and subtracting according to need, maintaining dialogue through Internet webs and e-mails, and utilizing a host of voice-to-voice communications arrangements to reinforce trust and connectedness. This is particularly pertinent in the climate-change debate, but it is also appearing in the business and sustainability evolution.
- Policy integration through knowledge management allows new groupings of ministries and specialist advisers to form integrated approaches that will address the mix of social and economic circumstances that form civic policy governmental structures. Again, climate change sets the pace. But so too do health policy issues and, more noticeably these days, integrated approaches to managing ageing in European populations.

We conclude this section by urging readers to adopt a variety of innovative approaches to studying the role, structure, effectiveness and evolution of multilayered governance. This is bound to be a highly important political-science arena in the decade to come. It will be especially rewarding to tackle this in the context of the sustainability transition.

SOCIAL–LOCAL IDENTITIES

In Chapter 4 Judith Cherni begins her analysis of social–local identity with a discussion of the relationship between capitalism (which tends to lead to consumerism) and democracy (which tends to lead to citizenship). Identity, at one level, is the expression of citizenship in the form of group distinctiveness, connectedness and capacity to become collectively aware of how neighbours and partners are being treated by various drivers of change.

Through identity, people may become more or less secure, more or less empathetic with their networks, or more or less connected to the general social order.

Cherni focuses on social–local identity as her principal theme. By this she alludes to the situation of 'place' and the connectedness of outlook. The first gives a sense of distinctiveness and of group membership. The second bestows ideology and a belief in collective purpose. The first signals locality. The second, consciousness of citizenship. Put the two together and one begins to derive social–local identity.

To examine how this variant of identity can be accommodated in the transition to sustainability, Cherni takes four perspectives, each of which is drawn from the case studies that follow. Security, insecurity, empathy and apathy are seen as the social processes through which identity is played out. Security forms the basis for leadership, entrepreneurship, coalition-building and opportunism of the kind revealed in Graz, on the one hand, and Vale do Ave on the other. In the Portuguese case, local initiatives of self-help were set in motion to improve the job capacity of young people, and European cohesion funds were sought to help reduce the pollution that was inhibiting new inward investment. Identity through insecurity is particularly noticeable in Peniche and Timbaki, where local fishermen and farmers found a way out of their income losses. In doing so, however, they selected non-sustainable routes, essentially because more sustainable options were not available. Institutional arrangements currently in place precluded such 'real' choices.

Empathy fosters devotion and cohesion. This was noticeable in Åtvida-berg where civil servants, teachers and local employers combined to tackle environmental deterioration, raise civic awareness, and create the demo-cratic dynamic to set the regulatory authorities in train through an element of European funding. The legacy of this semi-feudal community helped to form the basis of Internet work in a common endeavour to attract wealth and to be different from nearby Linköping. Yet Åtvidaberg wants to mimic Linköping in using high-tech forms and in creating more civic empower-ment for excluded youth through its own variant of LA21.

Cherni is anxious to make identity range from individual self-esteem and personal confidence-building, to network solidarities as they evolve at the local level. There is still much to be done in relation to apathy, alienation and a variable sense of self-esteem. In Mile Cross in Norwich, economic deterioration has led to increased unemployment and fewer opportunities to move into the modern electronic age. Female low-paid, part-time jobs help to fill the gaps, but place strains on family relations, especially where mothers are single. Apathy expresses itself in tolerating, but not accepting, vandalism, drug abuse, alcoholism and family disruption. The key is the evolution of the Norwich City Community Power pro-gramme, linked to its LA21 initiative, which has begun to respond creatively to young peoples' concerns via a series of new measures, including the provision of job training and community development programmes.

For the purposes of this book, and for future research, the following observations are offered:

- Identity relies heavily on how the self is perceived, how confidence is built or shattered and how cohesion and compatibility with groups and networks can be promoted. This is a difficult arena. It requires a high degree of detached capacity, a dose of intuitive understanding and a sensitivity to the barriers of personal likes and dislikes. Perhaps there is not sufficient attention in postgraduate training to providing a sound basis for methodological approaches.
- Identity is a vital basis for any marked transition to sustainability. It is arguable that such a transition cannot take place without the civic consciousness of networks and solidarities. Again, from a personal development vantage point, and also from methodological experience, such research modulations in how individuals evolve as consumers and citizens through a growing sense of social–local identity remain ill-developed.
- Identity may well allow tolerances of disfunction that interfere with any meaningful transition towards sustainability. This is also tricky, because tolerance may be a function of oppression, of a trained incapacity to be empowered, of educational and family breakdown, and generally of insecurity. So apathy need not be an organized response. It could be the product of powerlessness and official treatment that is demeaning and hurtful.
- Identity can be the salvation of democracy if it is nurtured into new participatory forms, and so long as the patterns of formal governance are supportive, accommodating and allow co-evolution of the two. Creative and well-monitored pilot schemes are needed that are designed for international comparison and review.

THE EUROPEAN DIMENSION

Europe is much bigger than the EU, but neither has a common identity. Only the market rules across the national boundaries, and the advance of monetary union in 12 of the 15 member states, formalize the loss of national economic sovereignty. But irrespective of entry, all member states will be required to cut public spending programmes, pension schemes, care and parenthood subsidies and other social security arrangements. The new focus will be on skill-training and selective investment in lagging regions, coupled with a series of public–private partnerships in investment and management. These are designed to incorporate the discipline of the private market to the social responsibility of the public sphere. This may be achieved through various forms of management agreements and performance indicators. Because the ultimate risk of the project failure rests with the private sector, that sector is very robust in ensuring its full safeguards. Therefore although they look attractive, public–private partnerships rarely consider sustainability principles. This is now a time to help redesign them.

Europe faces a serious dilemma. Overall, unemployment is rising among a series of vulnerable groups. These include ethnic minorities, disaffected young people and redundant out-of-skill workers. Such groups need training and a variety of opportunities to enter the formal workforce. For many, the requirement of formal economic training may not be what they seek. They may do better out of the informal economy. A recent study for the EC reveals that the size of the informal economy is very large, especially in the cohesion states. In Greece, it is estimated at 40 per cent of total earnings, Italy 30 per cent, and even in the UK and Scandinavia it could be between 10 and 20 per cent. Perhaps local–social identities among the insecure hold up through informal economies. We do not know of any systematic research to prove the point. The advent of monetary union may strengthen the role of informal income earning as members are forced to tighten the belts of their formal spend.

Guy Standing (1997, p215), a director of the International Labour Organization (ILO), sums up the dilemma:

> *There is a moral hazard characteristic of the EMU agenda. Govern-*
> *ments will be increasingly tempted to attribute their welfare cutting*
> *measures to the dictates of EMU, conveniently trying to shift public*
> *opinion from themselves to super-national 'treaty obligations'. That*
> *will be close to reality as well.*

In the same book, Jurgen Weiler (Standing, 1997, pp279–287) and Jurgen Habermas (pp262–264) point out that there can be no common European 'demos' or democratic entity of 'polis' that transcend national boundaries and provincial administrations. These might be based on changing city–hinterland regions (Graz–Felbach; Linköping–Åtvidaberg) new configurations of local identity (Mile Cross, Norwich and Hackney) and exciting variants of European political alliances.

Such reconfigurations of locality may have to be nurtured and stimulated by fresh approaches to democracy. This may take place in the sustainability transition through the following developments:

- new forms of civil society, aided by specific measures to create empowerment;
- a willingness in formal governance to co-evolve with informal governance;
- a recognition that the rights of the vulnerable may be matched by their own realization of their individual and collective responsibilities to upgrade everyone and not just themselves;
- a sense that social maintenance and ecological care will involve respectable and dignified modes of economic and social activity in years to come as productive employment dwindles, and as the age dependency gap widens;
- a realization that labour is less mobile when families form, jobs are more than survival mechanisms, and social–local identity binds people to their neighbourhoods and 'civil regions' (the polis of Habermas and Weiler). This may, in turn, mean that wage differentials, training schemes to assist migration and locally funded social-security benefits

may have to recognize the regional stability of labour markets, even in a period of multiple employment livelihoods and expanding local, informal economic activity.

THE LOCAL DIMENSION

At the core of this book is the tension between globalization and localization. Yet it is clear that while localization is an active process emerging in many ways, well-developed localism, as opposed to nationalism or Nimbyism (not in my backyard), is much harder to identify.

Similarly, any sign of an integrated transition to sustainability, with all three relationships supporting and reinforcing each other, is also rare. Most sustainability indicators that are tested by governments and local authorities show evidence of a continuing drift towards unsustainability. There is still a question of how far the 'transition' is a real one to date, or how it has advanced no further than putting the basic building blocks in place.

There are few political social-sector organizations of any sort, including non-governmental organizations (NGOs) and political parties, that have taken on sustainability as the central theme of their work. Organizations in the voluntary sector tend to be internationally focused (there is a developing network of '1992' organizations: NGOs seeking to promote Agenda 21 and the Rio outcomes) or locally focused: community organizations who have emerged from an LA21 process seeking a discrete identity. Very few operate at a national policy level, partly in recognition of the low priority given by governments to sustainability.

Those organizations that are working to link economic, social and environmental issues tend to approach sustainability from the social sector. Examples include the European Public Health Alliance or the Community Development Foundation in the UK (Church and Cade, 1997), or specific partnerships such as those emerging from city-regeneration projects. However, even though they may recognize the benefits of such integration, they are not using the language of sustainable development.

It is at the local level that much of the most innovative work on sustainability is taking place, making the transition a process that is largely unrecognized and undervalued, both in the media and by central government. There is also the question: is such local activity an 'irrelevant fringe' or a 'leading edge'? The tendency of some partisan commentators to overstate local activity has led to questions about whether the 'new localism' is creating myths rather than realities (see Marvin and Guy, 1997).

Yet the alliances and relationships that are developing out of such new forms of local action are building slowly in influence and power. While the emphasis on participative democracy has caused concern among those wedded to representative democracy, most European governments are now recognizing that some decisions and actions will prove more effective if the power to decide and act is made at the local level.

The tension between participative and representative structures and ways of working is one of the key limiting factors in the transition to sustainability. The new alliances that enable the development of social–local identities are overwhelmingly participative in nature and are often seen as undermining the more traditional representative structures, notably in local government. The transition is likely to accelerate when those on both sides recognize their own limitations and the benefits that can derive from a more effective coupling of the two ways of working.

CONCLUSION

The principal conclusions of this study are as follows:

1 Governance is no longer ordered or hierarchical. In the response to global change, active agents in local communities seek partnerships and coordinated programmes of action through various levels of government from local to multinational. The fluidity of governance offers opportunities and threats to various social groups, depending on their access to resources and support, and on their collective capacity to identify and accommodate change.

2 The European cultural picture is a muddle between globalizing benefits and vulnerabilities, and localizing opportunity and threat. The institutions of governance in the EC (the legal entity of the EU) are not designed for democracy, union of cultural aspirations nor for a common political cause. European integration stubs against the toe of regional differentiation and local identity, with no ready means of political expression or legal continuity to accommodate.

3 The transition to sustainability in Europe will be nurtured through:
   • new forms of civil society, notably via local empowerment;
   • a recognition that the rights of the vulnerable can be matched by self-help and assisted intervention programmes aimed at promoting social identity;
   • a willingness in formal governance to open up opportunities to connect to informal governance;
   • an acceptance that maintaining social well-being and ecological integrity will become respectable and dignified contributions to the social order as the scope for productive employment dwindles and the age-dependency gap widens.

4 Labour may become less mobile and adaptable when families form and when local identity binds people to their neighbourhoods and to 'civic regions'. This may mean that wage differentials, training options to prepare for out-migration and social security benefits will have to recognize the national stability of labour markets, even in a period of rising unemployment.

5 Sustainability, as a holistic and comprehensive driving force, was not recognized by any of the actors involved in the case studies. LA21, the local variant of the transition to sustainability, provides some background for this transition; but it is not proving to be an organizing

focus for change. More effective is the drive for improved local democracy, and for specific strategies for empowerment. Neither of these
drives is linked explicitly to LA21, but could be captured by effective
multiple-layering of governmental coordination, and by a better
integration of formal and informal democratic relationships.

6   Social–local identity plays out in many forms:
   - informal deals and illegal arrangements to by-pass regulations that
     are perceived to be unfair or disadvantageous;
   - collective survival in the face of growing ill health and poverty, with
     an increased sense of alienation from patterns of authority;
   - grasping external developmental and educational assistance to train
     the locally unemployed, and to improve marketability of local
     produce;
   - alliances of mutual support in the face of mixed ethnic composition
     which create solidarity within communal insecurities;
   - in impoverished regions and in places of great social flux, where
     social identities do exist (internally supported perceptions of frustr-
     ation and solidarity vie with a lack of comprehension of real needs
     on the part of external formal governance; there is often no language
     or mechanism for dialogue);
   - in agricultural regions, where the pattern is one of seeking environ-
     mental health and better income security, while not losing family
     values and neighbourly support (the dialogue across formal and
     informal governmental realms lacks connectivity and compre-
     hension; among the impoverished and the vulnerable a sense of
     fatalistic resignation is offset by supportive patterns of informal
     mutual aid).

7   The disadvantaged in all the case studies have their own dignity and
distinctiveness, but little social esteem. They deeply distrust authority,
either because it is threatening or dismissive, or because authority shows
hostility or ineffectual pity. There are few places where their concerns
are being recognized and dealt with in the LA21 processes. It is therefore
understandable why many have little faith in new initiatives, largely
because such initiatives do not respond to their real needs. LA21 may
be regarded as just another governmental ruse, even when it offers
empowerment.

8   Visionaries, entrepreneurs and those with positions of leadership can
and do find support across levels of government and across the
boundaries of the region and the nation state. By doing so, they promote
innovative initiatives with a clear commercial opportunity and form
social as well as economic alliances to achieve this.

9   Social identity becomes fragmented when immigrants come and go
and the local demographic mix becomes increasingly varied. The
response is to form micro-partnerships and self-help organizations. The
challenge for policy-makers is to identify these and build a more
collective social consciousness through social market support. LA21 is
not sufficiently locally geared to do this. Partnerships are ephemeral,
and the positive scope for multilayered governance is not being captured

by this local–social energy, which is desirable if the transition to sustainability is to succeed fully.

10   Sustainability has discourse, but no shared meaning in global–local relations. These relationships evolve from established worldviews of wealth creation, tolerated inequality, an incapacity to remedy growing social exclusion in a sustainable format, lack of good indicators of ecological well-being, social connectedness and reliable wealth generation. Multilayered governance is not being played out through sustainability channels. It is the multitude of social identities that permit global change to be accommodated at the local level. In economic and social terms, these identities are not given the credit they deserve.

These observations support the views expressed earlier in this chapter that Europe is in a special flux of integration and disintegration. There is no collective vision on how sustainability and democracy can combine to overcome the threats and build on opportunities and alliances. This will need a special form of new governance, as yet ill perceived by modernists.

REFERENCES

Church, C and Cade, A (1997) *An Environment for Everyone: Poverty, Exclusion and Environmental Action*, Community Development Foundation, London

Clarke, T (1999) 'Twilight of the corporation', *Ecologist*, vol 29(3), pp158–162

Coffey, C (1998) 'European Community funding and the sustainability transition' in T O'Riordan and H Voisey (eds) *The Transition to Sustainability: the Politics of Agenda 21 in Europe*, Earthscan Publications Ltd, London, pp130–150

Gowan, P and Anderson, P (eds) (1997) *The Question of Europe*, Verso Press, London

Habermas, J (1997) 'Reply to Schmidt' in P Gowan and P Anderson (eds) op cit, pp259–264

Levidow, L and Carr, S (ed) (2000) 'Precautionary regulations of genetically modified crops in the European Union', *Journal of Risk Research*, vol 3(3) pp187–286

Marvin, S and Guy, S (1997) 'Creating myths rather than sustainability: the transition failures of the new localism', *Local Environment*, vol 2(3), pp54–70

Norris, P (1999) *Critical Citizens: Global Support for Democratic Governance*, Oxford University Press, Oxford

O'Riordan, T (ed) (1997) *Ecotaxation*, Earthscan Publications Ltd, London

O'Riordan, T and Voisey, H (eds) (1998) *The Transition to Sustainability: the Politics of Agenda 21 in Europe*, Earthscan Publications Ltd, London

Puttnam, R, Phatt, S and Dalton, R (2000) *What is Troubling the Mature Democracies?* Princeton University Press, Princeton, New Jersey

Standing, G (1997) 'The new insecurities' in P Gowan and P Anderson (eds), op cit, pp203–219

Weiler, T H H (1997) 'Demos, telos, ethos and the Maastricht decision' in P Gowan and P Anderson (eds) op cit, pp265–294

2 GLOBALIZATION AND LOCALIZATION

Heather Voisey and Tim O'Riordan

INTRODUCTION

The intention of this chapter is to examine the notions or concepts of globalization and localization, and to explore them with reference to sustainable development. In this way, hopefully, it will clarify the utility of globalization and localization as concepts that are designed to throw fresh perceptions on change at the local level, set against the transition to sustainability. The following questions have guided this analysis:

- What do we mean when we talk about globalization?
- What do we mean when we talk about localization and locality?
- What does globalization say that is of use in terms of local sustainable development and the capacity to respond to sustainability at the local level?
- What does the literature on globalization say about the nature of sustainable development?

This chapter will look first at the theories of globalization and some of the counter evidence. Second, it will examine the literature on locality and how this can be conceptualized, as well as at the relationships between the global and the local. Finally, it will examine the implications of looking at the pathways to sustainability.

GLOBALIZATION

Globality, globalization, globalism – these are all ambiguous words that have come into common usage since the 1960s, but have only been part of the social science vocabulary since the early 1980s. Despite the relative newness of this language, it abounds in the literature on international relations, sociology and human geography and is creeping into the lexicon of social scientists studying the nature of global environmental change. However, the definition of these terms is often left unstated. Globalization through popular interpretations (journalistic and media representations) is a process of primarily economic, but also social and political, change that encompasses the planet, resulting in greater homogeneity, hybridization and interdependence – a 'global enmeshment' (Hurrell and Woods, 1995) of money, people, images, values and ideas that has entailed smoother and swifter flows across national boundaries. These processes are driven by technological advance, the growth of the informational sector, international cooperation, and processes of structural adjustment to a new global capitalist economic and political order headed by multinational corporations and international governmental institutions.

Associated with this concept are ideas of the promotion and domination of Western culture and capitalism to the exclusion of all other cultures and economic systems, a loss of social diversity and the disappearance of local distinctiveness and community in favour of global culture and society. These ideas carry with them feelings of loss of control by the individual over their lives, the inability of national governments to act in the best interests of its citizens, a fear of blandness and a society based on consumption rather than collective good. This is the rhetoric surrounding the concept of globalization, but the reality of the processes of change and their scope is somewhat different. What is occurring with the growing body of academic work on globalization is the emergence of literature that moves beyond the rhetoric of globality to an understanding of what this means, what the causes are and how it can be theorized: in short, a discourse.

Drawing mainly on Milton's discussion, within the social sciences the notion of 'discourse' has both general and specific meanings (Milton, 1996, p166). Generally, it 'refers to the process through which knowledge is constituted through communication'. At a specific level, however, there are two meanings. First, discourse can refer to 'a particular mode of communication; a field characterized by its own linguistic conventions, which both draws on and generates a distinctive way of understanding the world', and can compete with alternative understandings (Milton, 1996, p166). Second, discourse can be 'an area of communication defined purely by its subject matter' and as such is not associated with a way of communicating or interpreting the world, and does not compete but 'merge[s] and separate[s] as participants define and redefine their subject matter' (Milton, 1996, pp166–167).

This distinction is important as sustainable development and globalization are both discourses of the second type, but operate within the first type – namely, the interaction or economic, political and cultural world views. O'Riordan and Voisey (1998), for example, show how various interpretations of social change influence the characterization of sustainability. They point to political, ecological, economic, anthropological, legal and sociological angles on sustainability, emphasizing how the discourse varies both with disciplinary perspective and style of democracy. The relevant table is reproduced here with a second, comparative table for translating this material into discourses of globalization and localization (see Tables 2.1 and 2.2). Using the second specific definition of discourse for globalization indicates that this is an emerging area of study not

Table 2.1 *Patterns of discourse that apply to the transition to sustainability*

	Market	Regulatory	Equity	Revelatory
Myths of nature	Expandable	Precautionary	Breached	Negotiated
Social values	limits	limits	limits	limits
Policy orientations	Price signals	Rules of contracts	Equality of opportunity	Communication
Distributional arrangements	Markets	By agents of rule-makers	By democracy	By negotiation
Generating consent	Compensation	By agreed rules	Negotiation and compensation	By reasoned discussion
Intergenerationality	Future looks after itself	Future helped by present	Future planned by present	Future envisioned
Liability	Spread losses	By redistribution	Burden-sharing	By negotiation mechanisms

Source: O'Riordan and Voisey (1998, p42)

Table 2.2 *Patterns of discourse that apply to globalization and localization*

	Market	Regulatory	Equity	Revelatory
Globalization	Expandable limits	By agents of role makers	Mixed scanning for vulnerable	Evaluation of social responsibility
	Competitive advantage	By common agreement	Reliance or global watchdog activities	Corporate and governmental reputation
		Reliance on voluntarism and negotiated agreement	Solidarity agreement	Stakeholder ownership and involvement
Localization	Initiative	Precaution and pragmatism	Social–local identity	Deliberative and inclusionary procedures
	Opportunism through social markets	Links to global standards negotiated by local stakeholders	Local citizenship initiatives through social networks	Social commitments to participatory involvement through best-value procedures

constrained by existing social science disciplines. Taylor (1996) has suggested that a new social science beyond disciplinary boundaries can be created. Globalization has presented a challenge to social sciences which are embedded in the notion of a nation state (Taylor, 1996; Yearley, 1996; Robertson, 1992, especially Chapter 6).

The response has occurred in two stages. Initially, the aim was to reformulate models. Then, more radically, there was a move towards interdisciplinarity – with the development of global referents at the periphery of the social sciences (culture studies) – and transdisciplinarity, with new frameworks that attempt to transcend the existing disciplines (for example, urban studies which focus on global cities). There is a discourse of globalization, and a very influential rhetoric about the changes encompassed by it. But what globalization actually means is very difficult to pin down. There is more than one process, more than one globalizing world, and a multitude of possible explanations.

Theories of globalization

Theoretically, there are many precursors to the concept of globalization. Three of the main approaches are: world-systems theory, globalization as an outcome of modernity and globalization as a dual process which centres around culture.

World-systems theories

Globalization from the perspective of a world system is associated largely with the work of Immanuel Wallerstein. His world-systems theory is involved principally with the global capitalist economy and combines a sociological and historical look at its development and maintenance, arguing that it is created by a single 'division of labour' – more complex, extensive, detailed and cohesive than ever before. This body of work posits that the world system consists of three worlds: a centre or core, a semi-periphery and a periphery. There are many criticisms of this approach (see Bergesen, 1990), but the most pertinent is that it represents only a mono-causal explanation of globalization. Other theorists have emphasized it more tellingly as a multidimensional process. It can also be criticized as being an historical rather than a theoretical description of a 'unique historical process' (Milton, 1996, p145). The same criticism can be levelled at the international relations world-system model, which holds that there is a global political network, created by the increasing interdependency of sovereign states and the consequent proliferation of intergovernmental organizations. Although at one time this process was seen as leading towards a world state, this is now not an assumption that can be supported, even as a theoretical abstraction.

Modernization and globalization

> [I]n a general way, the concept of globalization is best understood as expressing fundamental aspects of time–space distanciation [namely,

the conditions under which time and space are organized]. Globalization concerns the intersection of presence and absence, the interlacing of social events and social relations 'at distance' with local contextualities. We should grasp the global spread of modernity in terms of an ongoing relation between distanciation and the chronic mutability of local circumstances and local engagements . . . globalization has to be understood as a dialectical phenomenon (Giddens, 1991, p22–23).

Globalization can thus be defined as the intensification of world-wide social relations which link distant localities in such a way that local happenings are shaped by events occurring many miles away and vice versa . . . Local transformation is as much a part of globalization as the lateral extension of social connections across time and space (Giddens, 1990, p64, quoted in Waters, 1996, p50).

Giddens (1990, p7) puts social relations at the centre of his analysis, which comprises four areas: the world capitalist economy, the nation-state system, the world military order and the international division of labour. These, he argues, relate to his four institutional dimensions of modernity within which the processes of globalization take place: capitalism, surveillance, military power and industrialism. Giddens (1990, pp55–56) sees capitalism and industrialism as two different dimensions. Capitalism relates owners to capital wage labour; industrialism applies to the link between people and the natural world, including the environment. In this analysis it is modern institutions, such as money, that are globalizing as they disembed mechanisms, lifting relations out of local contexts and enabling them to take place across the globe in a manner that was previously regarded as inconceivable.

Criticisms of this approach centre on the complexity of this multi-dimensionality, as well as its failure to provide any specific implications that arise from these globalizing processes, rendering it a 'descriptive, nominalistic definition approach to global-level phenomenon' (Yearley, 1996, p16). For Robertson (1992, p145), globalization is not just an outcome of the Western project of modernity as Giddens claims. Giddens is also criticized for not taking cultural matters seriously enough.

Culture and dual processes

Milton (1996, p215) has examined the theoretical approaches to globalization from the perspective of culture, defined as 'consisting of everything we know, think and feel about the world'. She distinguishes between those who refer to globalization as the way the world is seen or imagined, defined as cultural phenomenon, and those who refer to events going on in the world, which although dialectically related to culture are not part of it. The two approaches already discussed are the latter, whereas Robertson (1992, p8) treats globalization as occurring both outside and inside culture: 'Globalization as a concept refers both to the compression of the world and the intensification of consciousness of the world as a whole.'

In this sense globalization is a dual arrangement, not just events taking place in the world, but also through cultural transformations. This approach models the 'global field' or the 'global-human condition' as having four major components. Each represents how globalization has proceeded, as well as how it is possible to make sense of globality. The components are: humankind, selves, national societies and the world system of societies. The intention is to illustrate global complexity – that globalization can take many different forms as a result of diverse understandings, although Robertson (1992, p175) argues that in contemporary times it has taken just one form. Each of the corners on Figure 2.1 have been made more identifiable by a process of clarification between the forces of globalization and local identity response. As a consequence, the understanding of the many interpretations of globalization has improved. Simultaneously, each corner has also altered in the way they are constructed. Each is autonomous and yet constrained by the other three. However, Robertson does not attempt to define the mechanisms that have caused globalization; instead he sees his model as an appropriate starting point, an outline, that requires greater work on the relationships between the four components.

This model moves away from an historical explanation of events. It takes into account understandings as the prime factor in social relations, and illustrates multidimensionality. Globalization here is not simply a modernizing or Westernizing process that is relentless in its progress. While some people may be globalizing, others may be deglobalizing as a result of

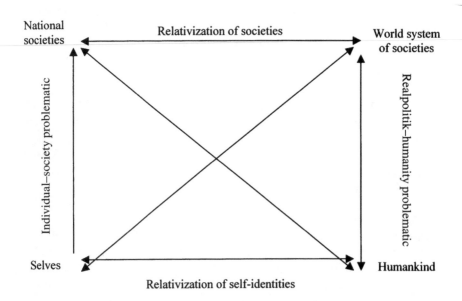

Source: Robertson (1992, p8)

Figure 2.1 *Interpretations of globalization as a set of relationships linking individual 'schools' to various spatial configurations of 'society' and, in turn, reorientating a sense of personal and collective identity*

diverse perceptions of the global. Deglobalization, that is, attempts to undo the compression of the world, is 'encapsulated within the discourse of globality' (Robertson, 1992, p10) as a result of an emphasis on the cultural.

Deglobalization is in opposition to 'globalism', a negative term for the intention and desire to make more global, otherwise described as 'one-worldism'. For Milton (1996), Robertson's model provides a framework in which to examine how environmentalism can be transformed into a cultural phenomenon, namely 'transcultural discourse'. This is a second-order communication that crosses cultural boundaries. However, it is still not clear what globalization is from this discussion and how it relates to experiences of 'globalizing processes' at the local level. It does indicate, though, that culture is a crucial dimension to any examination of global-ization and is integral to the discourse of sustainability.

A global culture?

A global culture has been characterized as an 'extrapolation from recent Western cultural experiences of "postmodernism"' (Smith, 1990, pp176–177). Smith argues that assertions of a global culture are premature because the meanings of images communicated through worldwide telecommun-ications networks, as mechanisms of a global culture, are still created by the historical experiences and social status of the populations receiving them. The globe does not possess the collective cultural identity required for common perception and understanding. In other words, national cultures do exist as derived from historic experiences, but 'a global culture is essentially memoryless' if perceived in national terms (Smith, 1990, p179). Arguments for the existence of a global culture seem to suggest that the structural changes of economic globalization will bring about the conditions, impetus and content of a global culture (Waters, 1995).

Smith believes such arguments fall foul of economic determinism and disregard the role of shared experiences and memories in creating identity and culture. He also demonstrates that the nationalistic project is still in evidence through cultural competition, as can be seen by the recent disintegration of Yugoslavia and the recreation of separate nations on ethnic lines. The idea of nationhood is strong for 'threatened' communities, by which he refers to communities who feel excluded, neglected or suppressed in the distribution of values and opportunities. Alternatively threatened communities may be suffering from a lack of social cohesion, particularly in the face of a take-over from another culture. Nationhood, therefore, holds within its meaning the commitment to the idea of a national society; it contains the 'aspirations for collective autonomy, fraternal unity, and distinctive identity' (Smith, 1990, pp181, 185). As a result, nationalism looks set to continue rather than to diminish.

Smith (1990) continues with this theme. He believes that we are entering a phase of 'cultural areas' which are not constructed, nor necessarily directed or intentional, but are the result of historical circumstances. Paradoxically, these may be a form of nationalism linked to the political goals of peace and economic prosperity for nations, creating 'pan-nationalisms' based around common cultural characteristics (political idealism, institutions, rights and moral principles). European cooperation can been seen as an expression of this. However, cultural areas, as a loose and casual collection of cultural elements, are not a challenge to the national cultures, nor do they equate to the pursuit of a global culture in the face of the stronger pursuit of competition between cultures.

For Robertson (1992, p112) one of the crucial issues in social sciences is developing an understanding of globality without reference to the idea of culture as nationally defined. He is not arguing that society based around the idea of a nation is disappearing; indeed, this idea is being 'revamped . . . as the multicultural society, while "old European" and other nationalisms have reappeared – but in new global circumstances'. Asserting that the idea of societalism – namely, the commitment to the idea of a national society – is a crucial aspect of contemporary global culture, he claims that a global culture does exist and indeed has a 'very long history' if it is seen as a discourse on global or world themes where humankind has identified itself within its empires, civilizations, communities and societies in response to an ever widening context (Robertson, 1992, p113). It is this external versus internal discourse that is at the core of global culture.

What the above discussion of global culture indicates is that, depending on your interpretation of culture and the global, it is possible to argue that global culture exists or it does not. Smith's approach is useful in illustrating that if we conceive of culture along the national lines of orthodox social science, then there is no global culture as we know it. Instead, there is at best a number of loose cultural areas. Robertson's wider definition, using the second order of discourse and the cultural phenomenon side of globalization, shows that it is possible to see some form of global culture as present today and in the past.

This general theme of polis (a collective cross-nation identity), and demos (a national identity that is secure enough to share meaningful connections in economy and culture across national borders) is central to the case studies that follow. Globalization is helping to widen the basis of the demos, but has yet to create an effective arrangement for a polis that shares common aspirations for sustainability and that transcends national borders. In Chapter 3, Svedin, O'Riordan and Jordan examine the conditions that may enable multicentred and many-layered patterns of governance to help fill this void.

The myth of globalization

Allen and Massey (1995, p3) have demonstrated that images of globalization are often compelling and suggestive, emphasizing certain aspects while neglecting or underplaying others; they are, in effect, distorted.

> [T]here appears to be a number of globalizations, a number of worlds, taking shape. There is the globalization of telecommunications, the

> *globalization of finance, the globalization of culture . . . the globalization of environmental concerns, and that of the struggles of indigenous peoples. Moreover, the networks of connections that each lays down do not map one on to the other. Some parts of the world are densely highlighted in some accounts, but not in others.*

The 'story' of economic globalization focuses on the global market where borders are crossed and distances travelled with minimal effort by firms, currencies and commodities. However, it is not really a borderless economy; instead, it is a more level playing field. The significant borders are those created by major economic interests rather than countries (Allen, 1995, p110). Global firms are the supposed driving force of globalization, but the definition of what it means to be truly global – having a full production presence in all the relevant major markets – is met by few firms, for example, those operating in the banking and finance area. Such a global experience of economic integration is common only to a few places, and a few people, mostly in the Western world. Significantly, the free movement of labour, surely a characteristic of a truly globalized economy, has not progressed as well as that of capital and currencies, indicating that substantial barriers remain.

The rhetoric of political globalization is that of the continuing erosion of the nation state's powers and abilities to control or regulate an increasingly volatile and uncertain global world in the face of many changes – for instance, environmental risks or the rise of transnational organizations on the world stage. These organizations involve actors other than governments who usually operate at an international level and cut across the territorial interests of nation states (such as Greenpeace). However, many of the issues that such groups mobilize around involve limited states and people, or many states but not in a uniform manner, so such organizations may not be truly global in scope. The central distortion here is the tendency to speak about environmental, economic and social processes as if they are undeniably worldwide in scope and uniform in impact.

Cultural globalization refers to the homogenization and hybridization of worldwide culture (Allen, 1995, p113). The basis for this is supposedly the new technologies of communication. These are said to unsettle and loosen more traditional cultural ties, influences and established lifestyle codes, thereby exposing localities to different consumer styles, with the message that to consume is to be part of one (Western) world. Demand is produced by the global marketing of cultural styles and symbols and is met by global standardization of products. But such a homogenizing view of a global culture is false in two main ways. First, it is presented in a monolithic manner: we do not all understand and value consumer products or American entertainment in the same way (Allen, 1995, p117). Second, rather than eroding local differences, global consumerism has to work through them, exploring local differences in order to market them on a wider scale. Additionally, a global culture based on the consumption of Western styles and symbols is one that has to be bought into, which for a substantial part of the world's population is not possible. Such a view also underexplores the influence of migration on culture and the creation of multicultural societies.

Summary of globalization

What can we gain from the above discussion of the nature of globalization?

- It is a contested concept around which much debate occurs, creating a discourse – defined as an area of discussion, rather than a mode of thought.
- Globalization challenges the orthodox embedded statism of the social sciences and creates expansions into new interdisciplinary and trans-disciplinary areas.
- Globalization is differential, affecting places, people, societies, cultures, economies and markets in different ways through space and time.
- Globalization has many dimensions, not all of which are appreciated in any 'story'. These stories do, however, have a strong impact on perceptions of the process. Whether they are positive or negative, they are part of the globalization discourse and are thus manifestations of globalization and a 'global culture'.
- Globalization is linked to debates about the nature and existence of the nation state, economically, politically and culturally.
- Culture is one of the central elements of the theoretical discourse and goes some way to shedding light on globalization as an awareness of the global when making sense of the 'local' or immediate world.
- There is a fracture between the empirical and the theoretical sides of the debate on globalization. Indeed, the literature on globalization does not appear to provide a good basis for empirical analysis of societal change since there is no one model that it is possible to use.

APPROACHING THE LOCAL

Local sustainability is not just about sustainability undertaken at the sub-national rather than national or international scale. The experience of sustainability and other changes (such as local investments by multinational firms or new communications technology) and the choices that are made in adapting to change are influenced and mediated by the social processes that exist within that locality, and impact upon real people at this level. Before we can begin to discuss the interplay of the local and the global, and sustainable development at the local level, it is necessary to set out what is meant by locality. This is by no means an easy task!

Locality is one of the two concepts (the other is community) that have been used by social scientists to explain differences between places at different times (Day and Murdoch, 1993). 'Community' as a concept has been used in sociological literature for around 200 years to refer to place and the importance that it has in people's experience. However, community has been strongly criticized for the normative and value-laden way studies have approached it (Bell and Newby, 1971; Day and Murdoch, 1993). In much of the literature on sustainable development, community is seen as the panacea of the sustainability transition (Holdgate, 1996). However, Evans (1994, p106) argues that the sustainability transition requires a deeper understanding of existing multiple local–social networks, rather than a harking back to the unobtainable and naive 'chimera of community'. This would enable policy-makers to gain a better idea of the social, economic, cultural and political needs of these local networks so that they become 'stable and self-regulating' in the long term.

Conceptualizing locality

For social scientists 'locality' has faced similar problems to community as a concept (Day and Murdoch, 1993, p86). The debate about the nature of locality has come to centre on whether any given locality has agency or causal force, and where its boundaries are. In addition, there have been methodological and conceptual problems with much locality-based research, where economic processes are perceived as the driving local force, and where political and cultural changes follow (Day and Murdoch, 1993). Margaret Stacey (Stacey 1969, pp138–39) argues for locality as a network of institutions: 'the locality is a context in which one can explore for hypotheses about the interrelations of institutions'. When looking at institutional adaptation to environmental change, it is clear that there are many definitions or approaches to the concept of an institution. A wide stance on the definition of an institution, following Jordan and O'Riordan (1996), should be taken. This would cover formal and informal institutions, ranging from social mores and cultural patterns of behaviour, to organizations and rules as set out in law.

Stacey's perception of locality can be very useful in looking at the sustainability transition as mediated through local institutions. She introduced the concept of a local–social system to describe the ideal network of institutions against which we can measure real case studies. Institutions in this context can also be described as 'communities of interest'. Only a small number of the various possible institutions will occur in one specific place for any one person. But it is possible to show that for a given locality, its inhabitants are engaged in social relationships that form a local–social system; this network provides the basis of social–local identity.

The institutional concept of locality is expanded by the understanding that a local–social system would reside within larger society and therefore would have vertical links to that society. As an approach, it is useful in that it allows us to address how social relations are embedded in place, it moves away from favouring one type of institution over another, and it makes no assumptions about homogeneity and internal coherence. This is so because there are large differences between social actors and institutions with regard to what sustainability means. Furthermore, it allows us to see how institutional networks can extend internally and externally so that wider social, economic, political and environmental forces are not ignored. Their effects are generally mediated through local bases such as family, work and voluntary groups, so the local focus is relevant. We can see with Stacey's approach:

> ... *how the institutions in which people are enmeshed structure, and are themselves structured by, the experience of 'locality' ... and also how these institutions are implicated in wider networks of relationships. It is through their participation in certain key institutions that actors are able to effect or resist change ... we must be prepared to give due weight to the part played by locally integrated institutional networks in securing particular economic, social and political outcomes in given places at given times* (Day and Murdoch, 1993, p93).

The point of this discussion is that it is necessary to look at how change affects local–social actors and how this change is affected by the locality within which it is experienced. To do this, an institutional approach avoids both the normative or purely descriptive conceptions of locality, allowing us to look at the factors driving social and economic change, while taking into account cultural factors, such as a sense of belonging or how change is understood. As demonstrated by Massey (1994), it also allows us to move towards an integration of the concepts of globality and locality. This is important because it moves away from the intangibility of community towards something more real, observable and achievable. It therefore continues to situate such identities within 'place', allowing for an incredible diversity of social process.

Summary of locality

What does the above discussion mean in terms of looking at the locality?

- Community and locality are essentially contested concepts that are difficult to define in practice.
- Individuals cannot be looked at in isolation to their locality, or the local–social system within which they are actors, since both influence their experience of change.
- An institutional network approach uses a wide definition of institutions, allowing us to look at differing perceptions of change and vulnerability to that change, and to ascertain the economic, social, cultural and political resources that are available to people within the locality. It also allows us to focus on adaptive processes or their potential.

There are relative winners and losers in any change, and the sustainable transition is no different. It is at the local level, in a specific time and place, where conflict between needs is most obvious and keenly felt. Using an institutional network approach, it is possible to conceptualize this interaction on a number of levels: as policy change and response; as behavioural and cultural change; as political bargaining and the exercise of power; as resource distribution. In effect, it allows for interdisciplinarity to occur by looking at how institutions adapt and interact and, as such, is a very dynamic concept.

GLOBALITY, GLOCALITY AND LOCALITY

If we wish to understand the local character of our lives, the changing nature of the places in which we live, we have to grasp both the wider, global context of which we are part and what it is that makes us distinctively local . . . [W]e are part of more than one world. We live local versions of the world and in so doing we have to locate ourselves within the wider global context (Allen and Massey, 1995).

This quote sets out explicitly how the global and the local are linked. It is at the local level that change is experienced, but that can only be understood with reference to what is happening elsewhere in the world. Giddens (1990; 1991) has also pointed out the reflexive relationship between the local and the global. For Ismail Serageldin (in de Borchgrave, 1996, pp160–161) the emphasis is on the local, which occurs throughout the world as people face greater insecurity about their futures than ever before. As a result, people feel the need to embed themselves within the familiar, the safe past that they had, the place that they call home: 'Localities, if you will; something they can relate to; tightening the circle in which they feel secure'. This could be seen as localism, the promotion of the local over any other level of social interaction. Or it can be seen as the relation of global processes to the 'local' context as a way of gaining understanding about them. Theorists have viewed the phenomenon of localization as part of wider globalizing processes. Local transformation, for Giddens, is not counter-globalization but a consequence of the global spread of institutions of national self-determination and democratization; this therefore illustrates the process of globalization.

Definitions of the terms local, locality, localism and localization, all refer to place and the distinctiveness of that place. This may seem to run counter to globalization in reaffirming boundaries. Although political boundaries or territories may be becoming more permeable, cultural boundaries are being strengthened as localities of place are defined in relation to other localities across the globe. Therefore, the spatial dimension cannot be ignored by discourses of globalization. It is possible to see a locality as a dynamic arrangement of institutional networks and social and cultural constructs. These combinations will be different for every individual but there will be some areas of commonality – such as language, landscape and religion.

Social relations make places, make local worlds . . . The social relations that constitute a place – a place that almost by definition is unique – are not all confined to that place . . . This complex geography of social

> *relations is dynamic, constantly developing as social relations ebb and flow and new relations are constructed. And it is the combination over time of local and wider social relations that gives places their distinctiveness* (Meegan, 1995, p55).

There are attempts to bring together analyses of global and local processes, particularly in the area of human geography, although the emphasis is often on local economic responses. Local-level response to globalization is a process of adaptation that can run counter to the objectives of sustainable development. Peck and Tickell (1994) show that competition between localities over the slice of global economic activity through the establishment of science parks and inward investment agencies is, in the long term, not beneficial to the locality. These are beggar-thy-neighbour strategies that do little to effect real change at the local level, and as such do not further the long-term pursuit of sustainable development in meeting either environmental or social goals. It is in work like this that the term 'glocalization' has been coined to describe how the global and local levels interact in the current intense period of capitalist restructuring. They are viewed as a single process but are made up of two often contradictory forces which affects how space is perceived in economic and social interaction (see also Swyngedow, 1992).

For Meegan (1995) the representation of place is often structured around opposition to others, but here more than economic factors are taken into account – for example, competition with another city for economic resources or for cultural identity, or a marginalized position in Europe, or a fight for political control with national or regional government. Liverpool is the example used to illustrate that local worlds can be produced within global worlds. A place is not homogenous but is characterized by gender, race, ethnicity, religion, class, housing type, etc. Such social and spatial segregation can produce a 'localism' in which sharp distinctions are drawn between insiders and outsiders, shaping responses to local issues. Countering the claims of increasing cultural homogeneity, the local music scene in the city shows that instead there is a process of cultural exchange, indicating that it is impossible to separate the local from the global.

Massey (1994, p151) argues that what is required is a progressive sense of place that takes into account its multiple identities, not a single sense of place as a manifestation of 'reactionary nationalisms, competitive localisms or introverted obsessions with "heritage"'. She sees a place as being the construct of a 'particular constellation of social relations, meeting and weaving together at a particular locus' (1994, pp154–156):

> *Instead, then, of thinking of places as areas with boundaries around, they can be imagined as articulated moments in networks or social relations and understandings, but where a large proportion of those relations, experiences and understandings are constructed on a far larger scale that what we happen to define for that moment as the place itself, whether that be a street, or a region or even a continent. And this in turn allows a sense of place which is extroverted, which includes*

> *a consciousness of its links with the wider worlds, which integrates in a positive way the global and the local . . . Globalization of social relations is yet another source of (the reproduction of) geographical uneven development, and thus of the uniqueness of place.*

The local cannot be described or understood without reference to the global, or rather the wider context of the local. Places are formed out of particular sets of social relations that interlock and interact at particular points in space and time. Indeed, globalization can create a locality.

The environment and sustainable development

Discourses on the global environment reflect the theories of globalization set out above in the way they analyse the causes and solutions to environmental degradation. As Milton (1996) points out, the concepts of the world-system model can be seen in the work of many environmental commentators. They perceive environmental problems as the result of economic and development polices, pursued by nation states, and often talk of a centre and periphery, a 'North' and a 'South'. This view has informed many critiques of this system, which argue for continued development that would enable Southern countries to emerge from environmental and economic problems. It is also argued that modernity, and the institutions of modernity and their overweening desire for progress, have routinely caused environmental degradation on a global scale. Modern technology produces degradation anywhere, and in fact is intensified by the transportation of products to the markets of the world. Seeing globalization as a consequence of modernity has meant that it is far harder to prevent environmental degradation. This is because tracing the causes is difficult, with pollutors often far from the site of pollution or environmental degradation. Responsibility is difficult to apportion and methods of prevention are difficult to apply.

Culture is the 'principle mechanism' through which human–environment interaction can occur (Milton, 1996, p215). An analysis that puts culture at the centre, as Robertson's model attempts, enables us to look at how addressing contemporary environmental problems is synonymous with an awareness of the global level, in terms of a global ecosystem or a global human community. Milton breaks down global environmental change discourses into two types: globalizing and deglobalizing. For proponents of the first view, globalization is the best way to protect the environment for human use by adopting common standards, goals and resources that are managed on a global scale. Opponents to this view see globalization, particularly as manifested in the global economy, as the biggest cause of environment degradation. Instead, we should deconstruct global institutions and local communities should have self-determination and control over their own resources.

These two views have implications for sustainable development in terms of democracy and cultural diversity. Sustainable development falls into both camps as demonstrated by the phrase, 'think global, act local'. It requires a global awareness of the interconnectedness of processes, places and people as well as their relationship to each other. This will change attitudes and behaviour at a local level; as such it is a globalizing phenomena. It is about both global cooperation to prevent further environmental degradation, and local communities making decisions about how they are going to implement sustainability principles. As briefly discussed in the locality section, 'community' is a concept with a lot of idealistic baggage. But both views allude to it: globalists see democracy as community participation in decision-making; anti-globalists see democracy as self-determination by the community. Ignoring questions about the existence of 'community', there are problems with globalist and anti-globalist approaches.

The goals of sustainable development have been defined by international agencies in meetings such as the United Nations Conference on Environment and Development (UNCED). However, local people can participate only in the implementation. As indicated by the locality–localization discussion, LA21 could be a forum where more than participation occurs. Rather, interpretation and transformation of these goals into objectives and actions that are meaningful to people at a local level can take place, but local self-determination is not mandated explicitly. The anti-globalist perspective would seem to encourage this. However, self-determination could mean decisions to carry on environmentally degrading behaviour, or to act in ways outside of the goals of sustainable development. How can such locally decided unsustainability be reconciled? There is an assumption in the global environmental discourse that people, grouped into local communities (because of the idealistic way these are perceived), will not act contrary to sustainable development. This is the myth of a 'primitive ecological wisdom', and is the reason why environmentalists in both camps support the maintenance of cultural diversity, but only within the context of sustainable development or behaviour that does not degrade the environment (Milton, 1996). What is exposed here by a focus on discourses and culture is that there are contradictions in how sustainable development is viewed. For these contradictions to be resolved, there is a need to appreciate how people understand the environment. It is also important to move away from the ideals of community to a more realistic appreciation of what locality is, how power operates and how it deals with its relationship to the global and globalizing concepts.

Any examination of sustainable development at the local level is likely to demonstrate that there can be no standardization of the transition to sustainability. It is unique to that locality and is defined as a place or a local institutional network. Thus we expect to find that the principles of sustainability are interpreted and adapted to local circumstances, just as are other processes of globalization. Taking culture into account therefore by highlighting people's understandings of globalizing processes and the actions that these produce should provide a key to analysing local sustainability.

CONCLUSION

This chapter highlights a number of points and issues for discussion:

- Both globalization and locality are contested.
- Globalization and localization are not competing processes; instead, local identity is a manifestation of globalization or greater interconnectedness.
- Globalization has a number of characteristics that are neither negative nor positive. It is not about the destruction of the locality in favour of greater homogeneity. Rather, it is about the greater interconnection and relativism between localities, economies, polities and cultures. Localization is an adaptation to these processes, a reaffirmation of what is local in the face of other localities. Therefore, it is not a struggle to counter globalization, but the restatement of identity within multiple identities.
- Globalism and localism are negative terms referring to attitudes which dominate at the expense of all else; they are exclusionist.
- The conceptualization of globalization so far does not have much utility in addressing sustainable development at the local level unless culture is put at the centre. However, there is still room for progress in looking at how this can occur.
- How can Europe be characterized as a result of the discussion in this chapter? It is a manifestation of globalization, illustrating increasing interconnectedness along economic, political and cultural dimensions to varying extents. It can also be seen as a pan-nationalism. It may also be a locality defining itself in relation to other localities, such as Asia or America, and not just in an economic sense.
- Globalization may only be of relevance at the local level in terms of some specific effects, such as employment, rather than the whole of the globalization debate. It is at this level that policy responses to change can be seen. It is suggested that only at a local level does globalization have policy relevance, since it is only here that a particular effect is perceived. Nevertheless, the actual complexity of globalization may not be realized, only one facet or dimension of it.

REFERENCES

Allen, J (1995) 'Global worlds' in J Allen and D Massey (eds) *Geographical Worlds*, Oxford University Press, Oxford, pp121–143

Allen, J and Massey, A (eds) (1995) *Geographical Worlds*, Oxford University Press, Oxford

Bell, C and Newby, H (1971) *Community Studies*, George Allen and Unwin, London

Bergesen, A (1990) 'Turning world-systems theory on its head' in M Featherstone (ed) *Global Culture: Nationalism, Globalization and Modernity*, Sage Publications, London.

Evans, B (1994) 'Planning, sustainability and the chimera of community', *Town and Country Planning*, vol 63(4), pp106–108

Day, G and Murdoch, J (1993) 'Locality and community, coming to terms with place', *The Sociological Review*, vol 7, pp82–111

de Borchgrave, A (1996) 'Interview: Globalization – the bigger picture; an interview with Dr Ismail Serageldin', *The Washington Quarterly*, vol 19(3), pp159–178

Giddens, A (1990) *The Consequences of Modernity*, Polity Press, Cambridge

Giddens, A (1991) *Modernity and Self-Identity: Self and Society in the Late Modern Age*, Polity Press, Cambridge

Holdgate, M (1996) *From Care to Action – Making a Sustainable World*, Earthscan Publications Ltd, London

Hurrell, A and Woods, N (1995) 'Globalization and inequality', *Millennium Journal of International Studies*, vol 24(3), pp447–470

Massey, D (1994) *Space, Place and Gender*, Polity Press, Cambridge

Meegan, R (1995) 'Local worlds' in J Allen and D Massey (eds) *Geographical Worlds*, Oxford University Press, Oxford

Milton, K (1996) 'Environmentalism and cultural theory: exploring the role of anthropology', in *Environmental Discourse*, Routledge, London

Peck, J and Tickell, A (1994) 'Jungle law breaks out: neoliberalism and global–local disorder', *Area*, vol 26(4), pp317-326

O'Riordan, T and Jordan, A (1996) 'Social institutions and climate change' in T O'Riordan and J Jäger (eds) *Politics of Climate Change: a European Perspective*, Routledge, London, pp65–104

O'Riordan, T and Voisey, H (eds) (1998) *The Transition to Sustainability: the Politics of Local Agenda 21 in Europe*, Earthscan Publications Ltd, London

Robertson, R (1992) *Globalization: Social Theory and Global Culture*, London, Sage Publications

Smith, A D (1990) 'Towards a global culture?' in Featherstone, M (ed) *Global Culture: Nationalism, Globalization and Modernity*, Sage Publications, London.

Stacey, M (1969) 'The myth of community studies', *British Journal of Sociology*, vol 20, pp134–147

Swyngedow, E A (1992) 'The Mammon quest. Glocalization, interspatial competition and monetary order: the construction of new spatial scales' in Dunford, M and Kafkalas, G (eds) *Cities and Regions in the New Europe: the Global–Local Interplay and Spatial Development Strategies*, Belhaven, London pp39–67

Taylor, P J (1996) 'On the nation-state, the global and social science', *Environment and Planning*, vol 28(11), pp1917–1928

Wallerstein, I (1990) 'Culture as the ideological battle ground' in Featherstone, M (ed) *Global Culture: Nationalism, Globalization and Modernity*, Sage Publications, London

Waters, M (1995) *Globalization*, Routledge, London

Yearley, S (1996) *Sociology, Environmentalism, Globalization*, London, Sage Publications

3 MULTILEVEL GOVERNANCE FOR THE SUSTAINABILITY TRANSITION

Uno Svedin, Tim O'Riordan and Andrew Jordan

FROM GOVERNMENT TO MULTILEVEL GOVERNANCE

The transition to sustainability in Europe will have to take place through a complicated and ever-shifting set of governing structures. These structures underwent a slow but nonetheless radical transformation in the latter part of the last century, as government was increasingly replaced by governance. According to Stoker (1998, p17), the word 'government' refers to activities undertaken primarily or wholly by states bodies, particularly those 'which operate at the level of the nation state to maintain public order and facilitate collective action'. Typically these latter functions were performed by the state within its own territory via different parts of the public sector. The term 'governance', on the other hand, refers to the emergence of new styles of governing in which the boundaries between public and private sector, national and international, have become blurred. For Stoker, then, 'the essence of governance is its focus on governing mechanisms which do not rest on recourse to the authority and sanctions of government'. Under a system of governance, more services are supplied by the market, with the state retaining control over core functions such as law and order, regulation and civil defence. Because of policies pursued by many industrialized states such as privatization, new public management and cutting the size of the civil service, the operations of the central state have in many countries become gradually more reduced, with more and more services provided by government agencies and the private sectors. In consequence, governance also involves a search for new means of steering and controlling activities through more indirect mechanisms such as financial control and incentives.

The shift from government to governance is also bound up with the trend towards more internationalized patterns of policy-making, in which important decisions are increasingly being made across a range of different administrative tiers or levels (Rosenau, 1997; Svedin, 1997). These stretch from the supranational down through the sub-national to the local. The term 'multilevel' governance is popularly used to describe the increasingly dense set of interconnections between actors who operate at these different levels of governance, sometimes channelled through states, but very often bypassing them. Again, there is no commonly agreed definition of this term and interpretations seem to be numerous and varied (see Hix, 1998). According to Gary Marks and his colleagues, multilevel governance in Europe has the following essential characteristics (Hooghe and Marks, 1996, pp23–24):

- The state no longer monopolizes policy-making at the European level. Decision-making is shared by actors at different levels, including supranational bodies such as the EC and the European Court.
- Increasingly, collective decision-making among states involves a significant loss of control for individual states as they are forced to accept decisions adopted by the majority.
- Levels of governance are interconnected rather than nested: national and sub-national actors (both public and private) act directly at all levels, by-passing the normal channels of interstate negotiation. For example, many local authorities in Europe have their own offices in Brussels so that they can lobby directly at the European level.

On the basis of these trends, Marks et al reach strikingly similar conclusions to Rhodes in relation to the contemporary challenges confronting state leaders:

> . . . [s]tates are an integral and powerful part of the EU, but they no longer provide the sole interface between supranational and sub-national arenas, and they share, rather than monopolize, control over many activities that take place in their respective territories (Marks, Hooghe and Blank, 1996, p347).

Rhodes (1996, p652) accepts that the term 'governance' is popular but imprecise. Within that constraint he argues that it represents 'a new way of governing' (Rhodes, 1997, p15). Instead of direct government control, he identifies a series of interorganizational and self-managing policy networks that complement markets and regulatory structures. The key to Rhodes's analysis is the shift from central state-led government to a system of governance based upon poly-centric linkages between the public and private sectors. This, he argues, is helping to produce a more differentiated or 'hollowed out' state as more and more governmental functions are shifted either down to alternative, market-based delivery systems, or up to supranational actors such as the EU. Public–private partnerships in the design and construction of major infrastructure projects are but part of the modern manifestation of all this. So, too, are the interesting relationships of regulatory agencies, public organizations and private enterprise that implement policy at any level of action.

Kooiman (1993, p4) summarizes this set of relationships as follows:

These interactions are based on the recognition of interdependencies. No single actor, public or private, has all knowledge and information required to solve complex, dynamic and diversified problems; no actor has sufficient overview to make the application of particular instruments effective; no single actor has sufficient action potential to dominate unilaterally in a particular governing model.

Rhodes (1996, p660) helpfully summarizes four features of governance:

- interdependence between organizations: governance is broader than government, covering non-state actors with shifting boundaries between public, private and voluntary sectors in a series of networks;
- continuing interactions between and within these networks, caused by the need to exchange resources and negotiate shared purposes;
- game-like interactions, rooted in familiarity, trust and shared commitments to legitimacy;
- a significant degree of autonomy from the state, which seeks to steer the networks to achieve its policy goals, but cannot fully control them.

This chapter accepts that governance is a series of evolving relationships across space and interests. Another feature is the tendency for more decentralized arrangements to self-organize, that is, to develop their own sense of autonomy and self-interest. This in turn makes the centre's traditional job of coordinating policy within and across different sectors and levels of activity – now demanded by the sustainability agenda – ever more difficult. The rise of voluntary, or negotiated, agreements in environmental management is but one manifestation of this. The state sets the aims to be achieved, but important aspects of the implementation process are let to non-state actors. Another is the inevitable tendency for sustainability issues to span a range of different government departments and agencies. The resulting mismatch between institutional form and the inherently interconnected nature of sustainability problems generates 'policy messes' (Rhodes, 1985). These occur in situations when policy problems demand a coordinated response involving several agencies and levels of government activity, but for a variety of political and bureaucratic reasons do not receive it. Another example of the new governance-setting is the increasingly quasi-corporatist pattern of consultative and advisory bodies, commissions of investigation, and lay-professional membership in safety and public-health bodies found in European states. What we are witnessing here is the emergence of a more policy-centred policy process within changed organizational structures.

The new frame also rests on the implicit premise that there is some kind of shared responsibility to make this creative and participatory pattern of decision-making work and to be responsive to new demands. These demands, in turn, are being encouraged by pluralistic pressures arising from the social, economic and environmental conditions of sustainability. For all its ambiguities and contradictions, sustainability as a norm is creating a sense of a common objectives among a varied set of actors by caring for threatened natural resources, for vulnerable and potentially disrupted populations, and for reliable wealth creation that encourages entrepreneurs to flourish while still looking after the good of the planet.

Along with all this comes a fresh sense of civic participation. In a world that is both globalizing and fragmenting into more and more governmental units, people are adapting in order to cope. According to Rosenau (1992, p291):

> *Given a world where governance is increasingly operative without government, where lines of authority are increasingly more informal than formal, where legitimacy is increasingly marked by ambiguity, citizens are increasingly capable of holding their own by knowing what, where and how to engage in collective action.*

This is the basis of Chapter 4. Empowerment comes, in part, through identity and self-esteem. Patterns of multilevel governance can provide a promoting context to such an aim, but the outcome is not necessarily automatic. It is important to heed Rhodes's (1996) warning that without proper systems of democratic control and oversight, governance risks being less, not more, accountable than government if more and more decisions are taken outside the traditional governmental system.

Micro–Macro Layering

When we try to understand local sustainability issues in the context of a more multilevelled system of governance, we have to address as a central issue the relationship between the macro- and the micro-levels. This has to do with the distribution of functions over a range of governmental levels, of the causal relationships that exist among the phenomena appearing at various levels, and the political dynamics connected to policy integration and international cooperation. This could be called intergovernmental 'layering'. We need to reflect upon the roles of the specific layers and their relationships.

The 'layering' topics are not covered by the micro–macro relations along ladders of phenomena at various scales within the sphere of nature alone, or through corresponding relations within the socio-economic cultural sphere. There is a need to connect these spheres of vertically structured different 'maps', which reflect different natural resource availability and social realities including patterns of actor networks.

An example from the land use–land cover domain helps to clarify the issues raised here (see Figure 3.1, and the report by Pritchard, 1998). On the right vertical side we find the various phenomena that could be related to different levels in the natural world from a farm field via a sub-region to an ecological watershed area (in this case, at the top). At the left-hand vertical side are the social phenomena at corresponding levels. One has to be very careful about the word 'corresponding' since there is no given relationship between the two vertical 'layers'. The relationship between them is sometimes referred to as 'the fit', which is a key 'layering' issue when we are discussing sustainability problems.

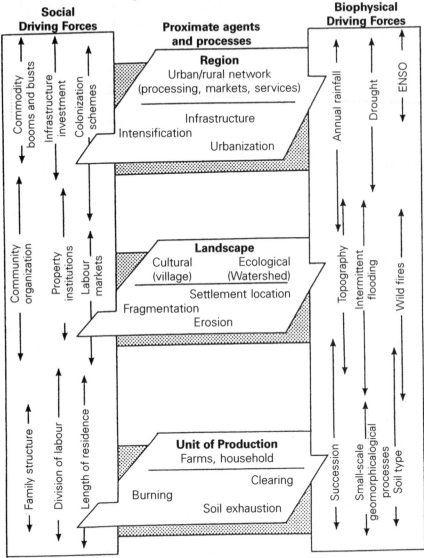

Note: Multiple scales of driving forces and proximate agents of change. One example of multigovernance is the river catchment. Its role is to integrate influences of various kinds, at different times and over various spatial scales. The natural connectedness of the catchment means that management regimes based on operations on separate layers will not work. Instead, there is a need to create inclusive policy structures that integrate policy analysis, decision-taking and implementation.

Source: Pritchard et al (1998, p12)

Figure 3.1 *Governing at different scales for catchment management*

The issue of 'fit' may be exemplified by the ecological phenomena occurring on an island in the sea. For many natural phenomena the systems boundary in moving from the sea to the island dry land is quite clear. Most species of flora or fauna belong to the one or the other realm. A fish is normally not found walking in the forest and a flower is seldom found at the bottom of the sea. Some species, however, move across the border (across the systems boundary), which for many is an unsurpassable barrier.

If however, we disregard some of these border-transcending life forms, the seashore between the water and the island soil is a reasonably useful delineation of systems. For some aspects in the socio-economical realm, this border may also serve as a systems boundary for management institutions. Perhaps the island is an administrative region with certain specific institutional arrangements associated with it. However, the administrative border may not be drawn at the waterline but at a distance out at sea (for instance, national sovereignty borders and economic zones).

So the fit between the natural and the socio-economic worlds of phenomena may be more or less congenial depending upon circumstances. Sometimes watershed-management institutional boundaries correspond to the physical watershed supplying a river with all of its water – sometimes not. The degree to which the 'fit' is a good one also varies depending upon the factual level between the micro and the macro. The global planetary climate system may fit the worldwide political–administrative realm of the United Nations (UN). But then there is the issue of what is meant by UN responsibility in relation to climate change and the connection to other domains of political influence – for example, the nation states or aggregates of such entities as the EU. Potential discrepancies between formal responsibilities and the factual capacities to act are important to consider.

The basic observation (as seen from 'below', from the micro, and 'above' the ladder of governing scales) is that small local systems appear to be embedded in somewhat larger systems, which in turn are embedded in even still larger ones. This holds especially true when we look at local ecosystems (such as a lake) located in a watershed region, again connected to spatially still larger-scale water management regions, such as cross-border river basin systems. If we disregard the exact nature of the causal relationships between these 'Chinese boxes' in 'Chinese boxes' in 'Chinese boxes' and do not examine too hard what really constitutes 'a system', the image of a hierarchically ordering scale-ladder of systems appears. The larger frame sets the boundary conditions for whatever can appear at the lower level.

Newtonian natural science has put great emphasis on 'compartmentalizing' and 'localizing' phenomena, trying to explain complex systems by explaining their parts and essentially defining all system performances as the outcome of the sum of the performances of the consisting sub-systems. This approach has been tremendously successful as far as 'machines' in the more physical sense are concerned. Technology has accumulated this approach for the better part of its rise to stardom in human society. Machines are, in fact, the most ideal natural science systems; they consist of well-defined, single-task parts that add up to a complex system. The beauty of engineering work is to correctly define the tasks, construct the parts optimally with regards to the tasks and to keep the interactions between the parts simple.

This approach has also, to some extent, influenced thinking about the form and structure of human society. The hierarchical, functional form of any modern society seems to be influenced by a form of thinking that corresponds to the worldview of Newton. There are usually hidden underlying assumptions behind this paradigm that has helped to create a sense of solid foundation. One of them relates to the local characters of causal influences. Locality means that entities in any system can only be influenced by causes that are effective in the nearby spatial domain. In other terms, this usually means that 'local' causes have direct local effects, and that 'distant' causes have indirect effects only – for example, by providing the effects through the sequence of intermediary systems entities. There is no 'direct' link between spatially distant systems.

Today's gradual breakdown of hierarchies is most visible in the socio-economic cultural realm. We may talk about a sequence of administrative–political frames corresponding to ever-increasing spatial scales, such as a municipality, a region and a nation. Although there may be some hier-archical traits in such sequences, there are many feedback loops. A national parliament may set the rules for the municipalities, but the actors at the municipality level may have a strong influence through various political mechanisms on the rule-setting processes in the parliament. If we include a 'new' level as the EU level for countries that voluntarily have agreed to be part of such a structure, it is even more evident that the arrows of influence go both ways: both upwards and downwards among the institutional layers.

If you have a 'local' concern as a starting point, this erosion of hierarchy is important. The local level seems politically so strongly and hierarchically embedded in the decision-framing from a sequence of higher-level activities that the freedom to act seems restricted. It may even be argued from such a perspective that a sustainable development future is not possible to design and implement at the local level, as all important influences that frame the outcomes – be it the national economic policy or the EU support funds for agricultural purposes – seem to come from 'outside' (top-down). On the other hand, any implementation of a move towards sustainability must be based on vigorous and wise actions at the local level.

The entire issue about 'layering' now shifts from a stereotyped hierarchic ordering of functions, from top to bottom, to an issue of mutually reinforcing phenomena in feedback loops over sequences of scaling layers. The 'layer-ing' issue turns out to be the issue of understanding the causal relations in the total system. Here we have to address issues of what the dominant lines of influences may be. For certain phenomena these may well be top-down in character. The strong role of the nation state in countries such as France and Sweden are examples of this. The constitutional limitations of a unit directional line of political influence in more federalistic countries such as Austria and Germany modifies such images. The degree to which certain types of collective responsibilities are incorporated within the societal design in different countries may also influence the perspective, as a comparison between the UK and Sweden shows, where the different conceptions of the state's role is the key to understanding the variations of 'layering' connections. There is a great importance in understanding the 'local' political culture, which provide these governance preconditions.

It is not only the different styles of sequencing of political–administrative layers in a comparative European perspective that are interesting. Equally important are the changing organizational dynamics of the factors involved. The influence from the implicit direct coupling between the EU-level and sub-regions within a nation state illustrates the mechanism where the nation-state level is undermined. The deliberate joint venture by several neighbouring municipalities to arrange a watershed management scheme collectively 'from below' may severely compete with sub-national, regional, institutional top-down types of solutions for the same type of problems.

One key mechanism is the earlier mentioned feedbacks between layers. Another is the influence at the 'same hierarchical level' of different nodes in a network, creating a situation of mutual adaptation. Such intersystem couplings may be more or less local in character, the simpler schemes emerging when one node directly influences the neighbours. However, non-local feedbacks have to be considered, especially in a globalized world of instant and ubiquitous financial markets.

THE INSTITUTIONAL PARADOXES OF SUSTAINABILITY

In dealing with these tendencies, within the context of sustainability, different paradoxical insights are brought into light. The local level of political administration seems to be locked within a web of stronger and stronger influences from above, creating strong impressions of conditions about what can be done at the local level. The addition of 'new' governing levels, such as the EU, may indicate even more remoteness to influence and power. The decisions taken in more and more multinational corporate boardrooms, at more and more remote and 'higher' hierarchical levels of decision, follow in the same direction. A Volvo sub-contractor in a small Swedish village is now dependent on decisions made by Ford in the US and not any longer by decisions made by the 'nationally minded' Volvo headquarters in Gothenburg. Yet, at the same time the hierarchical eroding forces are also there: new technologies in the information sector provide the capacity to be more local; new networking arrangements and new alliances of political corporation add to the impression of a quickly changing governance.

Some of the factors of change that lie behind this transformation include:

- technology change – for example, in terms of entirely new communication solutions but also in terms of other types of high-tech innovations in entirely different fields;

- organizational change – for example, in terms of new networks and strategies based on approaches that use networks rather than hierarchical arrangements;
- new modes of generating knowledge.

Equally important are the changes in perception about such factors among a wide variety of actors. This highlights the importance of the 'trust' factor in the political dynamics towards sustainability. These issues arise in the Swedish analysis of Linköping and Åtvidaberg (see Chapter 6), as well as in the Norwich case of Mile Cross (see Chapter 10). In both instances, social–local identity is limited by criss-crossing governmental arrangements that are insufficiently connected to create suitable conditions for sustainability. Local municipalities must attempt to overcome administrative hindrances by formulating and implementing policies that are based not only on local conditions, but also reflect the objectives of municipalities and regional governments. Such changed views may help to create 'leap-frogging' approaches for those who have the capacity to use the dynamics of the new situations. This is very much the case in Feldbach (see Chapter 7) and may well be emerging in Vale do Ave (see Chapter 8).

FROM LAYERS WITHIN NATIONS TO LAYERS IN THE EU

Traditionally, there have been three levels of government and public administration in most European countries. The relative importance of these different levels has, however, varied considerably between countries and over time. The first level is the central national level. All member states of the EU are now considered democratic, although a number of them have experienced non-democratic forms of government during the 20th century, some as late as the 1970s. Each member state has a parliament, some have a president, and others are monarchies. The strength of the central government is dependent upon a number of factors among which tradition, the election system and the country's constitution are the most important. The second level is the regional level. The importance of this level differs between countries. There are considerable differences between, for example, the power of the German Länder and the power of the new devolved country governments of the UK. The third level is the local scale. Again, a country's constitution and tradition combine to create varying degrees of autonomy for local government in the different member states of the EU. The *Kommun,* or municipalities, of Sweden have, for example, the right to collect income tax from their inhabitants and to determine how funds are utilized within a reasonably loose framework laid down by the central government. Municipalities in the UK, on the other hand, lost much of their autonomy during the 1970s and 1980s, and despite the political rhetoric of New Labour, still have to gain much of this back.

With the development of the EU, however, a fourth layer of governance has been added. Individual nation states have given up part of their sovereignty to a new actor – the EC. The rationale for this process is at the core of the paradox of political power. In order to gain political power, political power must be relinquished. The globalization of the political and economic systems has led to the erosion of the power of national governments in favour of a more multilevel pattern of institutional arrangements. In order to regain some of that power, national governments have attempted to pool some of their political resources in the institutions of the European Communities, and through these institutions, regain some of the political power that they have lost.

While the creation of the EU has provided national governments with a new political platform, it has also initiated a new layer of governance that has provided sub-central authorities with channels of influence that enable them to by-pass central government. Local authorities in France, Italy and Spain can work together to develop regional interests. Swedish municipalities cooperate with local authorities in Latvia and Estonia and help them to prepare for EU membership. Projects of this kind are often part-financed by the EU, which encourages cooperation between sub-central governmental agencies.

During recent years, sub-central governments in Europe have developed closer relations with the EU and its commission. These networks of actors have increased in importance to create the processes of 'layering' and 'delayering'. Three types of networks can be identified. These are lobbying and exchange networks, policy networks and intergovernmental relations networks.

Pressure groups, organizations, businesses or sub-central government form lobbying and exchange networks. Their aim is usually to lobby EU institutions or to facilitate the exchange of information among network participants. Four categories of networks can be determined: namely, peak, spatial, thematic and sectoral:

- Peak groups include pan-European umbrella networks, such as the Council for European Regions and Municipalities (CEMR), which aim to coordinate local and regional governmental influence in Europe.
- Spatial networks are networks between regions with specific spatial or geographical characteristics. These networks attempt to advance regional interests and may be initiated by the EU. The INTERREG initiative, aimed at improving relations between richer and poorer parts of Europe, is an example of this kind of network.
- Thematic networks are created to lobby EU political institutions and may be formed in response to a specific EU policy programme.
- Sectoral networks are initiated by regions with comparable economic attributes and aim to support economic growth in similar economic sectors, or to alleviate the effects of changing economic conditions through EU aid.

In recognition of these historical transformations, Marks and his colleagues (1996, pp343–346) identify two contending theories of governance in the EU. One is that *state-centric* government through nations pools sovereignty in international organizations, as well as devolves power downwards to regional and local authorities. Marks et al contend that the overall direction of policy is that of a national government's political needs. Typically, state-centric government relies upon unanimous voting for key policy issues in the EU. This ensures that no member state needs to be committed beyond what it is willing to tolerate. The core claim of the state-centric model is that 'policy-making in the EU is determined primarily by state executives constrained by political interests nested within autonomous state arenas that connect sub-national groups to European affairs' (Marks et al, 1996, p345).

The second theory framework offered by Marks et al (1996, pp346–350) is, as we discussed above, *multilevel governance*. Here, the state is not autonomous: decision-making is shared explicitly by actors, and not monopolized by state executives. Super-national EU institutions such as the EC and the European Court of Justice have power in their collective right. Decision-making typically becomes more multilevel when decisions are taken by qualified majority voting in the EC Council of Ministers. Crucially, this inevitably involves loss of autonomy by national executives. Therefore multilevel governance is interconnected, not nested, and integration takes place through a huge variety of organizational and policy structures. As a result, state level ministers agree to share power and to delegate authority to multilevel structures, thus shielding themselves from the political fall out of unpopular EU-wide policies (such as the CAP and the CFP that figure so largely in the case studies that follow).

SUBSIDIARITY AND MULTILEVEL GOVERNANCE IN THE EU

If governance in the EU is, as we and others contend, becoming more multilevel, then an obvious question which arises is: what is the best level to address a particular set of issues or policy problems – the supranational, the national or the local? This may seem an entirely abstract, theoretical matter, but it has hugely important implications in terms of addressing the sustainability agenda, and in terms of the basic democratic accountability of any resulting actions. Clearly, some environmental issues such as climate change are better addressed at the supranational level; however, mechanisms need to be found that make appropriate trade-offs with economic and social concerns at successively lower levels, while ensuring an appropriate level of democratic accountability. The further one moves problem-solving up and away from the local, the more elongated the channels of democratic representation become.

The EU has been trying to resolve complicated governance issues such as these since its inception in the 1950s, but it was not really until the 1990s that the need for a more systematic political response became apparent. The focus for this debate is the concept of subsidiarity. Although it entered popular discourse in the immediate aftermath of the Maastricht Treaty negotiations in 1991, subsidiarity has always been a well-established Euro-federalist principle. It is conventionally understood to mean that decisions in a political system should be taken at the lowest level consistent with effective action. The *Oxford English Dictionary* defines it as 'the principle that a central authority should have a subsidiary function, performing only those tasks which cannot be performed effectively at a more immediate or local level'. Subsidiarity therefore provides a strong presumption in favour of *decentralization*. However, in the EU, subsidiarity has taken on a meaning which is sufficiently open-ended to satisfy both advocates and opponents of decentralization (Teasdale, 1993). Thus, the British saw subsidiarity as a means of reserving power for national government against the EU.

In German eyes subsidiarity, defined as action at the lowest effective level, coupled with the creation of a Committee of the Regions, promised to safeguard its federal system of government (involving the federal state and the regional Länder) from excessive European intervention. Arguably, Article 3b of the Treaty on European Union (TEU) tries to reconcile these two very different visions of a future Europe: one based around a strong network of independent nation states, the other involving a constitutionally enshrined allocation of powers across multiple levels of government – in a word, federalism. However, the links between subsidiarity and democratic accountability were clearly in the minds of negotiators long before the Danish voted 'no' to the Maastricht Treaty in a national referendum. The opening article (A) of the TEU talks of 'creating an ever closer union among the people of Europe, in which *decisions are taken as closely as possible to the citizen in accordance with the principle of subsidiarity*' (our emphasis). As the depth of public opposition to deeper integration became clearer in the aftermath of Maastricht, the EC sought to emphasize that '[t]he aim of the subsidiarity principle is to see to it that decisions are taken as close as possible to the citizen' (CEC, 1993, p1). Significantly, the 1999 Amsterdam Treaty requires decisions to be taken '*as openly* and as closely as possible to the citizen' (our emphasis).

The events of the early 1990s provided an ideal opportunity for the sort of searching constitutional discussion of the overall assignment of tasks between and within different administrative levels in the EU that political elites had long shied from. But for various reasons it was spurned. Instead, subsidiarity has emerged from the post-Maastricht debate as a technocratic process of review and reform termed 'better law-making' rather than as a tool for reallocating existing responsibilities (Jordan, 1999a,b; Jeppesen and Jordan, 2000). Politicians have, in effect, stepped back from instigating a potentially open-ended debate about the democratic implications of bringing EU policy-making 'closer' to the citizen.

The episode usefully reveals the tensions between advocates of the two models of European governance introduced above: state-centric and multilevel. The former is consistent with a nationalistic perspective which searches for a state-centrist position. The latter fits a more federalist position arguing for the integrity of sub-national governmental structures that enjoy a high degree of autonomy. It may eventually be that the more federalist line prevails. But, as we have seen, the early indications are that states are struggling successfully to retain their dominant role. For the purposes of this book, the debate over subsidiarity reflects the struggle between polis and demos, and the huge suspicions that lie between economic and political notions over the future shape of European governance. The trend is towards a looser form of governance, but the desire to control from the centre, whatever that means, remains as powerful as ever. The results are important inconsistencies in policy-making, with every sign that local-level vulnerabilities will increase in the tracking of sustainability.

These trends result in harsh pressures on local authorities in all parts of Europe. Earlier, the national government or parliament could be approached with regard to the design of regional or national economic policies. Today, other levels of power above the national have added complexity to the situation and the seats of 'real power' have become remote. Decisions are strongly influenced by central banks in other countries and by remote economic actors such as transnationals and investment companies that invest pension funds in whatever country is deemed most suitable. The multinational character of big business, increasingly remote from local settings, lies behind the 'branch-plant phenomenon' whereby commercial decisions taken at company headquarters may have life and death consequences for an entire local community.

One example from the Nordic scene is drawn from the electricity domain. In the earlier parts of the century Åtvidaberg had its own hydro-power company. In the last decade, this company (Forskraft AB) was sold to the nationally operating power company Vattenfall AB. This company is expanding to cover the whole of northern Europe. Global-reach companies come down to the doorstep of the individual who is supposed to make electricity purchase choices locally in terms of a world energy market.

These processes are not exclusively disadvantageous for local communities. While governmental networks have become, in many cases, more obscure and remote, the shift from more hierarchically sequenced 'vertical' paths of decision-making has also opened up new possibilities for local authorities. New forms of relations have been created that allow patterns of power to leap across traditional, strictly hierarchical, structures. Within this context, a London suburb or a Swedish rural municipality may obtain a grant for developing a community initiative directly from the EU, without too much interference from intervening levels of government. Business opportunities for private companies in small municipalities can be opened up due to direct contacts with world markets and support from the EU's programmes for small- and medium-sized industries, for rural development or for old industrial centres. A company in the semi-rural area of Åtvidaberg in Sweden can specialize in fibreglass masts for leisure sailing boats, and companies in Norwich can be at the forefront of the global biotechnology industry. These and many others can conduct business directly with their customers thousands of miles away. These developments enable some local communities to preserve a satisfactory taxation base and provide service for their inhabitants. We can find new types of drivers not only for economic local prosperity but also for sustainability. For example, the eco-city of Graz or the high-tech city of Linköping are using EU, national and local funds, along with private-sector participants, to promote clean technology for the new round of economic enterprise.

GREEN POLITICAL THEORY AND MULTILEVEL GOVERNANCE

Subsidiarity therefore raises the question of what is the most appropriate level of action in a multilevel system. However, the principle itself provides no clear answers. Economists give primacy to efficiency arguments in deciding how to allocate tasks between and within different administrative levels. Economic theories of federalism strongly suggest that the EU should act only when there are significant economies of scale to be gained by addressing policy problems at the supranational level, and when there are significant 'cross-border' (spillover) implications (Peterson, 1994, p130). Following the principle of fiscal equivalence, the government unit responsible for a particular task should therefore include within its jurisdiction everybody likely to be affected by its decisions. Only then can the full costs of actions be properly internalized. However, the problem with such an approach is that in reality policy competences to determine sustainability policies are already shared messily between levels, making it difficult to identify and assign costs and benefits to acting at particular levels. Arguably, it is difficult to compare meaningfully the economies of scale obtained by taking decisions at higher levels, with the deep-seated desire to bring decision-making as close as possible to the citizen.

What can green political theory bring to the debate? Does it provide a means of balancing the democratic and economic elements of subsidiarity? The most well-known typology of green political values ranges from deep green through to very light green (see Figure 3.2). Typically, light greens have great faith in the ability of humans to *manage* nature and live in harmony through the application of science and technology. They believe that sustainable development requires only a judicious mix of regulations and market-based instruments such as green taxes to correct market failures and to ensure that the environment is fully considered in decision-making. Deep greens – or ecocentrists – on the other hand, see science and technology very much as part of the problem rather than the solution. They tend to view humans as one small part of nature rather than a superior resource 'manager'. Accordingly, humans need to find ways to live with nature, rather than 'over' it.

In contrast to legal approaches, green political theory is not afraid to engage with the more normative aspects of subsidiarity. Deep greens in particular openly celebrate local diversity (Dryzek, 1987, p217):

- Small-scale communities are seen to be more reliant on their local environment and therefore more responsive to local disruption.

Table 3.1 *Environmental worldviews and levels of governance*

	Light Green		Deep Greens	
	Cornucopian	Accommodation	Communalist	Deep Ecologist
Green label	Resource exploitative	Resource conservationist	Resource preservationist	Extreme preservationist
Type of Economy	Anti-green: unfettered markets	Green: markets guided by market instruments	Deep green: markets regulated by macro-standards	Very deep green: markets heavily regulated to reduce 'resource take'
Management strategy	Maximization of GNP: human-environmental resources infinite substitutable	Modified economic growth: preservation of 'critical' environmental resources	Zero-economic growth	Smaller national economy: localized production (bio-regionalism)
Ethical position	Instrumental (man over nature)	Extension of moral considerability: inter- and intra- generational equity	Further extension of moral considerability to non-human entities (bio-ethics)	Ethical equality (man in nature)
Level of decision-making	Unspecified: depends on problem	Unspecified: depends on problem	Regional/local	Local
Sustainability label	Very weak sustainability	Weak sustainability	Strong sustainability	Very strong sustainability

Note: Various ways of comprehending governance according to ideology. The groups on the left tend to prefer decentralized market structures, with increasing degrees of state intervention. The groups on the right look for less hierarchical forms of governance, with more polycentric modes of division making. In essence, the two wings adopt very different positions in their vision of multilevel governance in a future Europe.

- Decision paths are therefore shorter, making it easier to respond to new challenges when they arise.
- Local action actively promotes the social responsibility and participation which is deemed necessary to achieve sustainable development.

According to deep-green ecocentrists 'decentralization' is a means of redressing the distrust people feel about national and supranational politics. Ecocentrists would argue, moreover, that local participation addresses the widespread feelings of powerlessness and fatalism held by people in the face of an increasingly globalized world (see also Dobson, 1990). These sentiments are captured in the phrases 'think global and act local', and 'small is beautiful'. Lighter greens, on the other hand, are much more agnostic with regard to the question of task assignment: they are happy to leave the matter to experts who will use technical, legal or scientific criteria – just the sort of project upon which the EU is currently engaged.

Does green political theory specify what is the most appropriate level at which to address environmental problems? The key dilemma here is between devolved democracy (which fits the main tenets of green thought but risks dissolving into conflict between localities, Nimbyism or a deregulatory 'race to the bottom') and state control (which is often the only realistic political level at which the competing demands of local, regional and international actors can properly be mediated). Having interrogated a range of positions and perspectives including socialism, Marxism, individualism and ecocentrism, Robyn Eckersley (1992, p182) concludes that a judicious mixture of international and local-level initiatives offers the best solution. Small, she argues, may not be beautiful if power is devolved to local communities that choose, or are forced, to adopt a development path which degrades the environment.

The EU has ample experience of this. It is worth remembering that one of the great strengths of EU environmental policy to date has been its ability to pull up the environmental standards of the so-called 'cohesion' member states to the level enjoyed in northern Europe. Moreover, completely localized systems of control do not necessarily address the externality problem: supraregional decision-making is still required to solve international problems (Eckersley, 1992, p174). For Eckersley (pp182–183), the best solution therefore includes:

- breaking down the economic and political power of states by revitalizing parliamentary democracy at the state-level;
- creating a 'multilevelled decision-making structure by breaking down state sovereignty and shifting power upwards to 'international democratic decision-making bodies' and downwards to local bodies (Eckersley, 1992, pp185, 183).

Some would argue that this vision is not far from where the EU currently stands.

The obvious difficulty with green political theory is that it does not really get us any closer to answering the practical question of how to allocate specific tasks across different levels other than that 'global' problems should be addressed globally and vice versa. Indeed, there is a case for concluding that the multilevel arrangement of the EU is already partly, if not wholly, compatible with Eckersley's prescriptions. Therefore, while remaining unclear on the crucial questions relating to task assignment, green theory does develop an interpretation of subsidiarity which is diametrically opposed to that enshrined in Article 3b.

CONCLUSION

The adding of the EU-level above earlier local, sub-regional and national levels does not necessarily reinforce an old hierarchical layering of power. It may easily, through the added new combinations, erode 'the old system'. There are clear examples that this is happening right now. In addition, other eroding factors – for example, due to new technologies, new networking patterns of alliances, new mechanisms in the global economy – help to reinforce such tendencies. The question of who gains and who loses control thus cannot be answered in a simple fashion. It seems as if active actors, even at the most local levels, can move more easily and more dramatically in this new ambiguous setting than passive actors. Thus the globalization processes may deliver the paradoxical effects on local circumstances both to enhance and diminish vulnerabilities.

The way in which local communities – both in a formal institutional sense and in a broader informal sense – operate and how the cultural framing of democracy processes develop is thus of basic importance. The key to a locally-based sustainability, which also has to be understood in the same 'layering' terms, will thus be less dependent on a general recipe and instead will be seen as the outflow of a pattern of many interplaying factors. Many of these will depend upon the way in which local situations are handled. An interplay between a sufficiently forceful visionary capacity, its consolidation in everyday politics, and its acceptance in the population are all important factors in the case studies that follow.

These processes also quickly change in their connotations. What one day may be seen as a policy of mismatch versus real needs may soon turn out to be quite reasonable – and the reverse. Thus the time factor and timing aspects have to be more strongly taken into account when considering how to deal with the combinations of constantly changing factors. The aspect of path dependence in the movements towards a more sustainable development therefore grows in importance. The pressure on old rigid political systems to improve their capacities for flexible responses is also part of the reality to create a more sustainable future. The quickly changing landscape of new layering patterns and the erosion of old ones is part of this challenge.

REFERENCES

CEC (1993) *Bulletin of the European Communities*, vol 27, no 11
Dobson, A (1990) *Green Political Thought*, Harper Collins, London

Dryzek , J (1987) *Rational Ecology*, Basil Blackwell, Oxford

Eckersley, R (1992) *Environmentalism and Political Theory*, UCL Press, London

Hix, S (1998) 'The study of the EU II: the 'New Governance' agenda and its rival', *Journal of European Public Policy*, vol 5(1), pp38–65

Hooghe, L and Marks, G (1996) 'Contending models of governance in the European Union' in A Cafruny, and C Lankowski, (eds) *Europe's Ambiguous Unity*, Lynne Rienner, Boulder, CO, pp161–175

Jordan, A (1999a) *The Politics of Multi-level Environmental Governance: Subsidiarity and EU Environment Policy*, CSERGE, University of East Anglia, Norwich.

Jordan, A J (1999b) *Subsidiarity and Environmental Policy: Which Level of Government Should Do What in the European Union?* CSERGE Working Paper, GEC 99-13, CSERGE UEA: Norwich

Jordan, A J and Jeppesen, T (2000) 'EU environmental policy: adapting to the challenge of subsidiarity', *European Environment* (forthcoming)

Kooiman, T (1993) 'Social political governance: an introduction' in T Kooiman (ed) *Modern Governance*, Sage Publications, London, pp5–20

Marks, G, Hooghe, L and Blank, K (1996) 'European integration from the 1980s: state-centric versus multi-level governance', *Journal of Common Market Studies*, vol 34(3), pp341–378

O'Riordan T (1999) 'Climate change' in T O'Riordan (ed) *Environmental Science for Environmental Management*, Longman, Harlow, pp161–211

Peterson, J (1994) 'Subsidiarity: a definition to suit any vision?' *Parliamentary Affairs*, vol 47, pp116–132

Pritchard, L, Colding, J, Berkes, F, Svedin, U and Folke, C (1998) *The Problem of Fit Between Ecosystems and Institutions*, IHDP Working Paper No 2, International Human Dimensions Programme, Stockholm

Rhodes, R A W (1985) *The National World of Local Government*, Allen and Unwin, London

Rhodes, R A W (1996) 'The new governance: governing without government', *Political Studies*, vol 44(4), pp652–667

Rhodes, R A W (1997) *Understanding Governance*, Open University Press, Milton Keynes

Rosenau, J N (1992) 'Citizenship in a changing global order' in J N Rosenau and E-O Czempiel (eds) *Governance Without Government: Ordered Change in World Politics*, Cambridge University Press, Cambridge, pp291–287

Rosenau J N (1997) 'Global environmental governance: delicate balances, subtle nuances, and multiple challenges' in M Rolén, H Sjöberg and U Svedin (eds) *International Governance of Environmental Issues*, Kluwer Academic Publishers, Dordrecht, The Netherlands, pp19–56

Stoker, G (1998) 'Governance as theory', *International Social Science Journal*, vol 155, pp17–28

Svedin U (1997) 'International environmental governance – a round up of a discussion' in M Rolén, H Sjöberg and U Svedin (eds) *International Governance of Environmental Issues*, Kluwer Academic Publishers, Dordrecht, The Netherlands, pp173–176

Teasdale, A (1993) 'Subsidiarity in post-Maastricht Europe', *Political Quarterly*, vol 32(1), pp47–67

4 SOCIAL–LOCAL IDENTITIES

Judith Cherni

INTRODUCTION

As global capital markets restructure, national and local markets liberalize, and more stringent environmental controls and withdrawal of European funding prevail; as a result, the 'environmental' dimension to European policy is beginning to shift towards 'sustainability'. This process is beginning to take on a new urgency as European unification progresses and the exercise of power by the state changes. The impacts of those changes on urban and rural localities, however, have become ever more controversial. Castells (1997) believes that these transformations represent only one side of major trends that shape contemporary times and characterize the internal dynamics of Europe at the end of the 20th century. The other side, he claims, is represented by *identity*. Alongside the restructuring of capitalism, there is also a surge of collective expression and affirmation of citizenship (Castells, 1998). Potent terms have been employed to define identity and contemporary society:

> *Identities are so important, and ultimately so powerful in this ever-changing power structure because they build interests, values and projects around experience, and refuse to dissolve by establishing specific connection between nature, history, geography and culture. Identities anchor power in some areas of the social structure, and build from there their resistance or their offensives* (Castells, 1997, p360).

Castells takes the view that identity is strengthened by the flux of economic, social and political change. He goes further. He thinks that the bonding characteristics of local social networks, designed to be activated for survival against adversity, may act as inbuilt bulwarks against otherwise oppressive change at local levels. All the case studies that follow suggest that such a process may indeed be taking place. But not all local people benefit. There are the vulnerable and the apathetic, and they may not so readily or so happily respond. This outcome is also evident in the case studies, so the appropriate theory is given attention in this chapter.

Together with the fact that identity has recently become a central recurrent subject in the literature, defining unambiguously the notion of identity as a social concept is still elusive. It is hardly surprising that different interpretations have abounded. There is a strong lack of consensus on how individuals and groups build their own identities, and which social structure bestows power to particular patterns of identities. Contemporary identity has been approached as part of reflexive action that takes place in a world of new social controversies and different politics. Furthermore, it is said that the role of the individual is being interpreted as a new historical self, with new identity, and that industrialization risks are tightly connected to new cultural identities. This view is attributed to the various adherents of Ulrick Beck (1992, 1996).

This chapter postulates that the development of an identity, particularly in places where globally influenced economic structural change is taking place, is a complicated convergence of socio-political and psychological processes. To realize the role of social identity, a workable conceptualization is needed.

Definitions of identity in contemporary society have generally originated in various disciplines. Despite their contribution, these definitions are based, unavoidably, on fragmented and narrow examinations. Yet, a multidisciplinary approach is most appropriate if the subject is to be addressed as a complex one. Therefore, a more comprehensive view of identity will be obtained when connecting social, psychological, political and spatial dimensions. This chapter draws on discourse from social psychology, sociology, political science and geography. It applies a critical view to various approaches taken within these disciplines.

It is argued that a social identity embodies an individual's societal circumstances and a sense of locality, while also reflecting a deep politically conscious self with multiple visions. Interpreting an identity as granted by cultural, spatial or individual characteristics is too narrow. Social processes and structural change that take place at different spatial levels, and which affect individuals unequally, confer social identity a unique dynamism and vitality. It is also argued that this identity is neither spatially nor socially uniform, and that there are clear distinctions within it. Social identities are unique expressions of both structural conditions that express change and continuity on the one hand, and the desire to preserve a minimum of stability and independence in an era of declining protectionism, multi-national corporatism and dominant economic determinism, on the other. This chapter thus develops an alternative view of social identity, and social–local identities in particular, that envelops its vigorous and distinct political nature.

Two main issues are addressed in this chapter. First, the text draws on debates from the four mentioned disciplines grouping their contentions under three main subjects – society and self, identity and social change, and identity between the global and the local. Second, it develops the concept of social–local identity during a time of social change, sustainability transition and Europeanization. The term represents a fertile entry point for any analysis of the responses to globalization and localization as it enables a conceptual and practical synthesis of socio-psychological and political, spatial and environmental conditions. The chapter subsequently introduces the stratified character of social identity. The conclusions of the case studies that follow are that the current political and economic interplay among the power of global forces, the intervention of the nation state, and the response of local communities very often threatens the livelihoods for many local people, while enhancing the opportunities for financial advancement and empowerment for others.

SOCIETY AND THE SELF

Psychology and sociology are the two disciplines most often associated with the study of identity. Psychologists tend to think in terms of individuals and inner processes. For them, identity seems to be something that exists within the individual's personality through various cognitive processes.

Richard Eiser (1995, p161) argues that people travel through reservoirs of belief and value patterns to obtain a sense of security and certainty when faced with new dangers, or unanticipated changes in their working or social lives. The degree to which individuals do this successfully is a function of experience, social support networks and self-esteem. Needless to say, all of these are connected.

In contrast, sociologists tend to think of individuals in terms of society and its institutions, conceptualizing identity as a set of definitions and roles (Baumeister, 1986). In social-psychological terms, the working of *social identity* means that actions are determined primarily by the implications of group membership (Kelly and Breinlinger, 1996). In other situations, *personal identity* is more salient and behaviour seems to be governed primarily by personal concerns. In this chapter, identity is approached from the social rather than the individual personal perspective. Identity therefore establishes *what* and *where* the person is in social terms.

> *When one has identity, he is situated – that is, cast in the shape of a social object – by the acknowledgement of his participation or membership in social relations. One's identity is established when others* place *him as a social object by assigning him the same words of identity that he appropriates for himself or* announces. *It is in the coincidence of placements and announcements that identity becomes a meaning of the self* (Stone, 1962, p93, cited in Turner, 1987, p121) (emphasis in original).

On the other hand, from an interactionalist tradition, social psychologists Wiley and Alexander (1987) have stressed that the social person is shaped by interaction and that social structure determines the possibilities of action. For Stryker (1987), structural features are understood in terms of people's involvement in particular social networks. These in turn embed them in particular identities.

For social psychologists, an adequate view of identity runs along a continuum from the personal to the social. Definitions that involve the entity of the self seem to be most useful. Without a concept of self, individual behaviour is either simply role-determined or shaped by some resolution of forces between a given social role and the inheritances of biology. Self is the concept that eludes mechanistic determinism and is the vehicle for conceptualizing a balance between structural determinacy and individual creativity. Yardley (1987, p120) points out that 'the idea of self conveys the image of autonomy in engagement with society'.

The self connotes two essential parts, the member's *identity* – awareness of membership, the sense of belonging to a group – while *ideology* refers to the member's worldview about the group's position in society (Gurin and Townsend, 1986, in Kelly and Breinlinger, 1996). The latter involves a sense of collective discontent or acceptance of the group's relative power or material resources, an appraisal of the legitimacy of the social structure by which the group is advantaged or disadvantaged, and the belief that collective action is required to realize the group's interest. Social identity is thus conceived in terms of the social self, a dynamic combination of identity and a conscious body of ideas. In this sense, the self and the social are linked through centrality of group identity in the self-concept; perceived similarities in the personal characteristics of group members, and an awareness of a common fate in the way in which group members are treated in society.

Kelly and Breinliger (1996) made a useful distinction between macro- and micro-social perceptions of group identity and the individual. They emphasize that social and economic mobility is possible at an individual level, while also claiming that the only way to change conditions more generally is through group action. Thus, the potential for individual mobility need not eliminate a sense of group, or political consciousness – that is, a social identity and loyalty. By way of synthesis, the self comprises both a sense of being (and hence indicates identity and ideology) as well as a sense of doing (performing actions consonant with supportive patterns of beliefs). Therefore the central concept developed in this chapter is that of social identity, and that of social–local identity in particular.

The issue of self-esteem is an important part of identity and the self. It is the power of self that is the crucial first step in imagining the possibility of resistance or another reality. Pulido (1996) pointedly argues that people, regardless of how oppressed they might be, do not inevitably have a common identity. A shared identity must be cultivated and refined through interaction and struggle with other groups. It is impossible not to have any personal identity, but for those who receive daily the message that they are despised and worth nothing, the internalization of these perceptions can lead to a negative personal sense of low self-esteem contributing to oppression and self-destruction. Resistance, let alone a movement, stresses Pulido, will never occur if the oppressed lack either a collective or an affirmative identity. But 'an affirmative identity will not necessarily lead to mobilisation' (Pulido, 1996, p47). Szasz (1994) wittily commented, when referring to community landfills, that being a dump, being dumped on or being forced to live with others' waste products undoubtedly reduces self-esteem. Stigma – the threatened loss of social status, the symbolic soiling of the community and its image – is a powerful motivator for political mobilization. In addition, Szasz argues that the presence of a landfill with others' waste treatment facility signifies the social stigma that the community, and by implication its residents, are at the bottom of society's class and status hierarchy.

Self-esteem is an important component of political empowerment. This particular topic is given attention in Chapter 10 in Mile Cross in Norwich. But it also appears in the responses to fishing catch reductions in Peniche (Chapter 8) and in the local uplift to economic and social revival in Feldbach (Chapter 7).

In summary, Kelly and Breinliger (1996), drawing conclusions about causality of identity, stress that it is difficult, if not impossible, to define identity because all the factors may be outcomes of identification and participation, as well as determinants. Indeed, they are probably both. Nevertheless, the attempt to generate one theoretical, and critical, framework that derives knowledge from relevant disciplines – social psychology, sociology, political science and geography – and from case studies is worthwhile. It provides a foundation for: understanding people's responses in the light of structural change; for thinking about the social and ecological effects derived from the EU political configuration; and for considering who benefits and who doesn't in the context of political and economic current restructuration and prospective environmental sustainability. These points were given a full airing in Chapter 1, and will be further developed in Chapter 11.

Social identity, as a central trend in the transition to ecological sustainability, consists of a sense both of being and doing. Both of these components are necessary to sustain self-esteem and promote essential coping responses to external change, either good (opportunities) or bad (destructive). The split in any 'self' between identity – denoting membership, belonging and ideology – indicating the group position derived from historical and spatial social processes, is highly instrumental in revealing the fundamental continuum between society as a whole and each individual's social identity. A more complex notion of identity, however, is necessary to approach contemporary transformations. This is because, in addition to social-psychological motives, other dimensions interact to constitute a social identity (see Table 4.1). In the following sections, inseparable components of social identity are discussed as they emerge from the other disciplines.

IDENTITY AND SOCIAL CHANGE

In the political and sociological literature, important attempts have been made to connect identity to social processes in contemporary society. Identity has been interpreted in terms of an emerging modern selfhood which centres around a new awareness that we are now significant actors

Table 4.1 *Main discourses around identity*

Social-Psychology	Sociology	Political Science	Geography
Otherness (Stone)	**Cultural identity** (Collier and Thomas; Milton; Belay; Smith)	**New social movements** (Inglehart; Castells)	**Community and locality** (Dalby and Mackenzie; Barnes and Sheppard)
Interaction (Wiley and Alexander; Stryker; Turner)	**Post-modern individualization** (Weigert; Giddens; Beck)	**Liberation ecology** (Pulido; Peet and Watts; Martinez-Alier)	**Local place and conflict** (Massey; Young)
Self and society (Kelly and Breinliger; Gurin and Townsend)	**Global identity** (Mc Luhan and Fiore; Robertson)		

in the physical environment and local society (Weigert, 1997). Identity is thus explained as an experiential and psychological reality. On the one hand, it is an immediate and intimate sense of personal existence – I know myself, therefore I am. On the other, identities are seen as social constructs in which others know me, therefore I am. The theoretical sources that underlie this claim postulate that this new historical self is emerging, formed by a mode of interaction with different groups that generate different selves, and that it creates awareness of the self in action: 're-sighting the human situation within an earthly commons or biosphere underwrites a new self'' (Weigert, 1997, p161).

An increasingly popular view is that identity formation is taking place consonant with the break from modernity by freeing itself from a classical industrial society (see Giddens, 1997; Beck, 1998). This process creates the insecurities of the contemporary spirit and brings about new forms of post modernity, namely the 'risk society' and 'reflexive modernity'. This perspective maintains that 'industrial society exits the stage of world history on the tip-toes of normality, via the back stairs of side effects, and not in the manner predicted in books with a political revolution or democratic elections' (Beck, 1998, p11).

Relating different cultural identity and risks, Beck claims that new social movements come into existence as a consequence of the collective con-sciousness of unavoidable risks that may bestow additional vulnerability on innocent groups. People respond through new social relationships, and communities may be created through the various forms and social experiences of the protest ignited by administrative and industrial encroach-ment on personal lives. In this sense, the new social movements are expressions of the new risk situations perceived. They also result from the search for social and personal identities and commitments in detradition-alized culture. Part of this identity could be interpreted as new forms of cultural and social identity; these 'often have politically provocative effects'

(Beck, 1984, p98). Construction of contemporary identity is marked by one central axis of social conflict: individual social perceptions of risk and the political dynamics of the risk society. Individualization, which is one of its central philosophical tenets, opposes the categories of large-group societies (of classes, states and social strata), and the workplace loses its significance as the locus of conflict and identity formation.

Identity formation is emphasized within the context of new social movements. These are defined by Scott (1990, pp6–7) as:

> . . . a collective actor constituted by individuals who understand themselves to have common interests and, for at least some significant part of their social existence, a common identity. Social movements are distinguished from other collective actors, such as political parties or pressure groups, in that they have mass mobilization, or the threat of mobilization, as their prime source of social sanction and hence of power.

New social movements are more aligned with expansion of rights and quality-of-life issues or post-materialist values that are contingent upon people fashioning new collective identities that allow them to work together, such as feminism, environmentalism and gay rights. Rooted in civil society, actors are dispersed and emphasize democracy. According to Inglehart (1990), among others (for example, Rawcliffe, 1998), new social movements develop around particular themes of concern and reflect the politicization of domains previously considered apolitical, or primarily personal.

There also exist 'identity politics' as a sub-category of new social movements. These represent a level of activism that seeks to affirm various forms of otherness, the expansion of rights and the characterization of social difference (Young, 1990). Identity politics has resulted in a proliferation of identities. Such a plurality gives rise to groups and individuals becoming aware of their differences, attaching significance to certain separating qualities and contesting the relevance of other designations. Identity politics are associated with post-modern scholarship and politics. Individuals may simultaneously identify as consumers, citizens, feminists, workers and human-rights activists, differing markedly from the previous construct that conceived of the individual whether as a worker, a black or a woman. While this development reflects reality, it does present a whole new set of political questions and challenges. This has led to the charge that new social movements have been categorized as obstacles to creating socially con-structive change by the way they have relativized all forms of oppression and domination, and displaced what were once central struggles for social justice – usually race and class. In post-modern politics, the struggle is against the established order outside 'normal' channels, but there remains no grandiose plan for a better society. Furthermore, new social movements are rarely drawn from the socio-economically disadvantaged or from repressed minorities.

In the case studies that follow, one example of a new social movement is the conscious attempt by the city of Norwich to empower the most disadvantaged in order to give then a more effective and respected role in determining the shape of their own communities. In the Swedish case studies, however, where there is no specific attempt at creating empowerment, the alienated and the vulnerable remain differentially without social–local identity, ironically in the wake of a drive towards sustainability.

Identity, in terms of quality of life issues, and the extension of individual rights together with a burgeoning identity politics, particularly in rich countries, relate mainly to a post-1968 shift to 'post-materialist' cultural values (Inglehart, 1990). This thesis states that there has been a cultural shift towards 'subjective' post-materialist values as economic distribution conflicts cease to be acute and societies are more sensitive to ethnic, ecological, gender and other preoccupations. Environmentalism, feminism and other new social movements, it is argued, illustrate the new social controversies and political styles that are transforming the politics of advanced industrial societies. Post-material values, such as environmental quality it is claimed, replace traditional ones such as the nuclear family. Organizational transformation acquires the highest significance, while the process of changing political styles becomes as important as the content of policy itself. These factors shape identity in a different way.

Interpretation of social identity in the above terms focuses on the relationship of the individual to society from a viewpoint that separates, rather than connects, the self and others. Here, identity is primarily a reflexive action that is constrained to identify with and accept a group that has shared systems of symbols and meanings as well as norms and rules of conduct. A view of identity in these terms is not, however, sufficient because it avoids integrating the continuum between identity and the conscious body of ideas as the core of the social self and the principal foundation of social identity. This explanation further omits adequate reference to powerful societal forces, such as internationalization of basic activities which, in various spatial and temporal dimensions, may decisively affect the position of the self and group consciousness.

The common and misleading understanding of environmentalism as a social movement concerned only with questions of ecological integrity, identity and non-material quality of life – for example, the well-being of the planet's ecosystem and biosphere – is categorically challenged on the basis of the struggles of the poor. In the developing world, there is a solid collective identity mobilized against dangerous effluents of capitalist industrial wealth and there is increasing evidence for a strong interest in the environment by poor states. Peet and Watts (1996) contend that where environmental space is being used to the benefit of the rich, as for example in the Amazonian forests, there are, in fact, even more reasons to become an environmentalist, particularly in poor countries or regions. The social identity of the poor, the powerless and the alienated thus incorporate elements of both old and new social movements.

The construction of 'new' social identities must not be limited exclusively to selected populations. In reality, contemporary social identity also develops in populations other than those that have reached generalized high living standards, or attained high levels of self-awareness and have reflexive attitudes. There are sufficient material and survival reasons to develop social identity in pursuit of quality-of-life issues in any non-affluent European country (see Martinez-Alier, 1997). This point is relevant in Val do Ave (Chapter 8) and Timbaki (Chapter 9), where the most economically vulnerable (children and women) suffer from environmental degradation and ill health in a disproportionately targeted manner, yet have no collective identity to resist.

Clearly, understanding the role of social identity in this period of social transformations is imperative, but all struggles cannot be reduced to identity conflicts. While the search and need for an enabling and appropriate identity is a subject in itself, it is also intimately linked to larger issues of positionality, power and the effort to overcome poverty. For this reason, and because of the multifarious ways in which social reality is constructed, it is impossible to categorize subalterns' identity as belonging to either old or new social movements (Pulido, 1996). Subalterns' response provides a model of how two concrete aspects of life – materiality and identity – combine to create people's social reality. Pulido stresses that we must never lose sight of large-scale structural patterns; neither can we assume to know the needs and concerns of the subalterns. The poor do care about much more than advancing their material position. But we cannot fall into the trap of ascribing a unitary resistance identity through opposition by subaltern groups, even though such groups may present themselves in a highly unified way. In reality, identities are rarely so cut and dried. Instead, they are marked by contradictions and continual change. The assumption, for example, that all of Timbaki's citizens should and do support the European environmental legislation ignores the possibility that it may be contrary to some Timabakians' economic and political interests.

IDENTITY BETWEEN THE GLOBAL AND THE LOCAL

Cultural identities

So far it has been argued that any individual's sense of identity is complex and that individuals' engagement with multiple identities is addressed through cultural identification. Cultural identity lends support to the view that any defined identity, such as national identity, contains within it several other cultural parameters of identity construction and negotiations. 'Society within the nation-state', explains Belay (1996, p323), 'pushes and pulls individuals toward a variety of identities such as ethnicity, gender, race, class and the like'. Collier and Thomas (1988) define cultural identity as identification with, and perceived acceptance into, a group that has shared systems of symbols and meanings as well as norms of conduct.

Milton (1996, p66) advances the view that social identity is drawn on culture which exists in people's minds and is expressed through what they say and do. It is thus formulated from perceptions and interpretation and is the mechanism through which human beings interact with their environment. Cultural identity consists of a full range of emotions, assumptions, values, facts, ideas, norms, theories and so on through which people make sense of their experiences. The balance between different identities, and the particular characteristics drawn upon in any one encounter or in any one period, will constantly shift.

A multiplicity of identities is illustrated by Belay (1996), but see also Taylor (1989). Using widely employed parameters to define identities, Belay has grouped them into six categories of *cultural identity*:

- sociological identities, such as those related to gender, age, religious adherence and network sub-cultures such as gay/lesbian;
- occupational identities, evident in institutions such as schools, associations and the workplace;
- geo-basic identities, corresponding to the various cultures that have evolved in different geographical regions of the world;
- national identities, where the nation state is perhaps the most powerful parameter of cultural identification;
- co-cultural identities, exhibiting identification with cultural communities that represent different geo-basic groups, but belonging to the same nation;
- ethnic identities, constructed on the basis of one or more cultural elements, physical contiguity, language or dialect, blood or kinship relationship.

The case studies that follow exhibit all of these interpretations of cultural identity. Sociological identities are evident in Val do Ave and Timbaki; occupational identities are evident in Feldbach and Linköping; geo-basic identities are examined in Peniche; national identities exist in almost all instances (possibly not Aigaleo and Hackney); co-cultural identities and ethnic identities are manifest in Aigaleo and Hackney. Throughout these case studies, it is the various ways in which these identities give meaning to people's lives and social support networks (often through informal economic exchanges) that provide the basis for accommodating the transition to sustainability.

Cultural identity has brought into focus the significance of cultural factors in conceptualizing the evolving tensions and transformations both within and between nations. Nationalism provides perhaps the most compelling identity 'drive' in the modern world as it consists of typically shared cultural, territorial or ancestral, legal and economic features (see Smith, 1991). Nevertheless, in a period of significant economic and political transformation in Europe, including objectives to advance sustainability, it is likely that individuals' identities can be also strongly aligned with a whole complex of other signifiers, such as place, race, gender, socio-economic position, environmental sustainability and ethnic grouping. Undeniably, the nation state has had a crucial influence in deconstructing as well as constructing contemporary identities. In the light of globalization and European unification, interpretations of the current power of the nation state have endorsed contrasting views – for example, that the power of the state is neutral, disintegrated, regaining legitimacy or hiding its influential power behind apparent incapacity.

Castells (1997, p271) emphasized that due to mentioned changes in global and supra-national domains, the state is now increasingly less able to respond simultaneously to the vast array of demands and challenges that a civil society's plurality of identities makes upon our nation states. Local and regional political institutions have seemingly more authority to approach local problems. This 'delegation' results from two convergent trends. One is the territorial differentiation of state institutions through which regional and national minority identities find their easiest expression as, for example, in the new Scottish Assembly or regional assemblies in Spain. The other is the response by national governments to the strategic challenges posed by the globalization of wealth, such as stock markets and central banks, communication and power. These responses often allow lower levels of governance to shoulder responsibility for linking up with society by managing everyday issues, in this way rebuilding legitimacy through decentralization. This is evident in the case of Sweden, Austria and the UK in the case studies that follow. Local and regional governments can be viewed as the manifestation of decentralized state power, the closest point of contact between the state and civil society. The expression of cultural identities, which are hegemonic within a given local territory, is sparsely included in the ruling elites in the nation state (Castells, 1997).

Global processes and social identity

Robertson (1992) identified a trend towards common human identity as an important cultural component of globalization. Whereas 'the community' has over time acquired different connotations such as a village, a nation, a kin group or a category identified by gender or sexuality, increasingly, in recent decades, 'the community' has been defined as a whole humanity. Many specific events – for example, sense of global insecurity, the creation of international organisms such as Amnesty International and the UN, and the development of a global communications network – have helped strengthen a sense of common human identity. McLuhan and Fiore (1968) introduced the notion of 'global village' as a metaphor for a world connected by an intricate web of information and communication networks. It post-ulates a dynamic that makes the entire globe, and the human family, a single consciousness.

Belays (1996) argues that globalization merely ushers the intensification of interactional processes that are less centred around the nation state, thereby introducing a new expression of territoriality and temporality to cultural identification. Globalization, as interpreted by O'Riordan (1997, p17), is defined essentially in terms of what is perceived not to be con-trollable by central governments who think of themselves as accountable. It is this sense of loss of control over forces that could be devastating to the well-being of 'ordinary' people that gives rise to so much misgiving over the apparently dangerous forces of globalization: '[g]lobalization creates a desire for locality in the form of a democratic entity that gives meaning to global action with local effects'. It refers to patterns of change that cannot be altered by national governments, let alone by local governments.

Failure of proactive social movements and new political parties to counter economic exploitation, cultural domination and political oppression has apparently played a role in constructing social–local identities. This situation, argues Castells (1997), leaves people with no choice other than to surrender or to react on the basis of the most immediate source of self-recognition and autonomous organization, namely their locality. Under such conditions, civil societies shrink and fragment and identities deconstruct. A search for meaning takes place in the reconstruction of defensive identities around communal and territorial principles, such as anti-nuclear waste dumping campaigns, and of wider project identities, such as the protection of near-extinct species or the promotion of equal opportunities. Territorial or local identity is therefore often a defensive identity, an identity of retrenchment in face of the unpredictability of the unknown and uncontrollable. In the 1970s and 1980s, people found themselves defenceless against a global whirlwind of change and they stuck to themselves: whatever they had, and whatever they were, became their identity. So emerged the paradox of increasingly local politics in a world structured by enlarging global processes.

Identity in relation to locality and place

Castells (1997, p60) has pointed out that people resist the process of individualization and social automization highlighted by post-modernists, preferring to cluster in community organizations that, over time, generate a feeling of belonging and, ultimately, a communal, cultural identity. A process of social mobilization is necessary for this to happen as '[s]ocial movement is a collective actor, constituted by individuals who understand themselves to have common interests and, for at least some significant part of their social existence, a common identity' (Barnes and Sheppard, 1992, p12). Dalby and Mackenzie (1997) point out that, focusing on the immediate environment and social achievement rather than on opposition, political struggle may be an important part of the process of constructing a shared identity. Social identity is both contested and reformulated in local arguments about how a community should respond to a development initiated, organized and financed by corporate agencies based outside the locality. This trend is evident in the Portuguese case studies, and to a lesser degree in the Greek and Swedish examples.

Focusing on places and localities, in each community the social alliances and their political expression are specific. Social–local identity is always formed by the juxtaposition and copresence of particular sets of social interrelations and local networks, and by the effects which those configurations produce. Moreover, and significantly, a proportion of the social interrelations in one specific place will go beyond the area being referred to in any particular context as place. However, in principle, it has always been difficult to distinguish the inside of a place from the outside (Massey, 1994, p169). Indeed, it is precisely in part the presence of the outside – the wider capitalist system, market liberalization, European unification, globalization within – which helps to construct the specificity of the local place. The ten European case studies are understood as more than local bounded areas: each locality is a set of spaces of interaction. In such spaces, people's differing identities may not only react to change but also promote it, or criticize or formulate other changes.

This is most obviously the case in Peniche and Felbach. In Peniche, the community of traders and restaurateurs clustered to support the 'illegal' trade in locally caught fish. In Feldbach, the visionary local council devised ways to create a collective opportunity for economic revival, through which new social–local identities could be formed.

Local places do not have a single, pre-given, identity because they are constructed out of the intersection and the articulation of multiple social relations. They are frequently riven by internal tensions and conflicts (Massey, 1994, p137). Local environments per se do not induce a specific pattern of behaviour nor, for this matter, a distinctive identity. Globalization, sustainable growth and political unification do not produce a single identity. Neither in the temporal or territorial sense is identity singular and fully reactive, since individual creativity and conscious collective ideologies are essential parts of it. The various social groups in a place will be differently located in relation to the overall complexity of social relations, and their reading of those relations and what they make of them will also be distinct.

Massey (1994, p151) argues that we need to think about 'what might be an adequately progressive sense of place, one which will fit in with the current global–local times and the feelings and relations they give rise to, and which would be useful in what are, after all, political struggles often inevitably based on place'. Massey's view of continual change implicit in place is also implicit in the similar dynamism and complexity that is found in the phenomenon of social–local identity. This is shaped not only by people's position, space and structural change, but also by a sense of identification and group ideas.

Where globalization and European unification have struck, affected groups might assume not only multiple cultural identities that are over-lapping and/or competing. Different political perspectives also affect how the disparity between global and local processes is interpreted at the grassroots level, how social groups attempt to overcome increased economic vulnerability, cultural alienation and hopeless powerlessness, and why citizens may stand either against or in favour of institutionalized changes, protection of the environment, green business and economic regeneration. Residents, differently positioned in society and with different political inclinations, may well share the same locality. Table 4.2 summarizes the key dimensions, contemporary context and stratification of social identity.

Table 4.2 *Social identity and social transformations*

Social Identity	
Key dimensions	Self and society Political power; political status; political activism Economic position; sustainable development Ideological background Network interaction Spatial definitions
Contemporary contexts	Social change; globalization; local; nation state; sustainability legislation; risk
Stratifications of social identity	Security Insecurity Empathy Apathy

SOCIAL–LOCAL IDENTITY

From the analysis so far, it would be misleading to talk of a singular social–local identity. Although a person may experience multiple identifications, social–local identity applies to residents who: see themselves as part of local, but also of extra-local, groups; who share similar personal characteristics such as economic position, power, and ethnicity; are conscious of the treatment that society metes out to its members; who see a common fate; and have similar political visions. They act and react according to their beliefs, conditions, possibilities and visions, and in this way we can see how, in practice, the conceptual being and doing are connected. In other words, we are talking not only of prolific manifestations of dynamic societal and personal processes, but also of living identities who denote those who benefit from top-down change, such as sustainable development, and those who do not.

It is possible to draw vital distinctions within social–local identities as a key to unveiling their status in relation to more generalized conditions (Table 4.3). Such characterization gives a useful entry point to a form of global–local politics aimed at advancing democratic objectives and implementing sustainability.

Social–local identity through security

Local residents of economically accommodated and affluent groups respond positively to structural changes or may actively encourage them. This is particularly so in the case studies of Graz and Linköping. The local identity of these residents is with the group who strives for individual security. Small- and medium-sized entrepreneurs, industrialists, land and property owners, financiers and their institutions, businessmen and small investors

Table 4.3 *Typology of social–local identities in the transition to sustainability*

Analytical dimensions	Types of social–local identity			
	Through security	Through insecurity	Through empathy	Through apathy
Group income	Middle/high class	Low-middle income	Intellectuals middle/any income	Any income, middle/low
The self	Sense of individual challenge	Sense of collective injustice Vulnerable	Sense of altruism and critique	Sense of individualism
Political power	Partially empowered Privileged	Disempowered Alienated	Relatively empowered	Resigned to be powerless
Political status	Elite	Ordinary people	Intellectuals Ordinary people	Ordinary people Changeable loyalty
Political activism	Participation Development	Losers in formal democracy	Campaign/ disseminate	Inactive
		Resistance Struggle	Lobby Give opinion Passive supporter	Going with the flow Occasional support
Social position	Entrepreneur, Proprietor, Financier	Waged, Unwaged Farmer	Integrated Protected Experiment	Integrated but at the margins
Sustainable growth	Accommodated	Disadvantaged marginal		Seek opportunities
	Mediate partnerships Adopt risk	Survival coping strategies	Cooperate, promote, protest or assent	
		Hope/accept/ oppose/resent Threat		
Self and society	Competition Union Indifference Temporary and convenience solidarity	Degrees of cohesion Indifference High internal group solidarities	Cohesion Discrepancy Common objective	Isolated Seek cultural solidarites
Spatial definition	Regional National International Territorial	Local Occupational Ethnic Territorial	Multinational Language Territorial or non-local	Local Culturally connected Territorial
Outcome	Risk Transformation Opportunity, advantage Gain	Impoverishment, instability Failure in formal economy Success in informal economy Lose	Success/failure Reputation Bear witness Indirect winner Indirect loser	Almost always middle-range winner Survivor

have a clear interest in their own region or locality. This group is conscious that society offers them opportunities for personal progress and has a strong sense of challenge, survival and enterprise. It adheres to green consumerism and assists smart-greening of capitalism. This is represented in the Ecoprofit initiative in Gratz, Austria, which emphasizes an effort of cooperation with municipality, local university and economic enterprises towards sustainable production programmes. Members often exhibit united local and regional fronts. Lobbying for common interests can exert additional pressure on government, for example, to withdraw excess tariffs or to stop local dumping of toxic material. Such has been the case of Vale do Ave, Portugal, with its highly water-polluting textile and clothing plants that are also labour intensive. This, however, has been achieved mostly through the flourishing informal economy that thrives on social–local identity.

Individuals may be actively involved in local environmental politics; large sections may also remain inactive, or exercise passive support. In general, they constitute the political and economic local elite: '[l]ocal notables are intermediates between local societies and the national state: they are, at the same time, political brokers and local bosses. Local and regional social alliances are frequently ad hoc arrangements, organized around local leadership'(Castells, 1997, p271). However, this population must take risks due to its political position in the national and international arena. These people actually constitute a necessary group for implementing national and international measures for sustainable growth. Thus, the concept of sustainability can be a key unifying factor in forming local common identity when the population's economic and environmental position is one of relative security. This combination is particularly evident in the case of Feldbach (see Chapter 7).

Social–local identity through insecurity

Global and supra-national structural changes have all had profound impacts on citizens who live under, on or just above subsistence conditions in the transition to sustainability. They are likely to be exposed to long-term environmental hazards from new economic developments, de-industrialization, or from deliberate annihilation of economic sectors due to reorganization of European economic objectives. The group's identity develops out of consciousness that is characterized by a general sense of collective injustice and discontent over its members' exclusion from political power and material resources. Such is the case of the fishing sector in Peniche in Portugal where legislation to reduce regular catch adversely affected their source of income.

The case studies have shown that individuals' occupations range from working the land, fishing, employed, running small businesses, to manual work and even unemployment. This population struggles to make ends meet and is more likely to have suffered rather than benefited from structural changes. Intensive agriculture, for example, has been the main survival strategy for Timbaki's farmers. Nevertheless, from the mid-1980s, liberalization of the market and substantial reduction of the EC's agricultural and industrial subsidies, together with increasing public rejection of excessive use of fertilizers and pesticides, have severely weakened the farmers' economic and social position. On this same issue, there have also been some improvements in the lives of the local insecure population. For example, in Crete, the agro-industrial cooperative of Timbaki along with approximately 100 local producers makes organic olive oil which, in contrast to conventional olive oil, has a high selling price.

Solidarity seems to be intrinsic to the group. But rather than assuming that their identity is always a preconstituted identity, this is also formed and shaped in time by their opposition to a proposed facility, dump, industrial plant, or other development or policy that is perceived as a threat (Dalby and Mackenzie, 1997), or by sharing supportive programmes. Mobilization is not, however, an automatic outcome of social identity, since insecure people, regardless of how oppressed they may be, do not inevitably have a common local identity. Self-esteem is a crucial factor in overcoming conditions of alienation. This is the intended aim of the Norwich community empowerment scheme (see Chapter 10). In Peniche, structural adjustments to integrate environmental sustainability policies in the fishing sector have resulted not only in high unemployment but also in severe devastation of the fishing community, leading to a serious disfunctional community. In the Norwich case, the youngsters of this deprived estate were conscious of their isolation and aggravated by the manner in which they were treated by authority. Yet, they felt secure in their social–local identity as is outlined in Chapter 10. General inactivism can be attributed to lack of organization, financial means and communication rather than an absence of a common cause. Certain populations may be too weak, too engaged with survival strategies or too frightened to express discontent, oppose undesirable developments or to advocate beneficial changes.

Social–local identity through empathy

Individuals will feel ill at ease with many features of restructuration, whether directly or indirectly opposed to it or capable of avoiding its threats. Individuals who belong to the group of identity through empathy boast full personal dedication to social causes, participate moderately or remain passive supporters. O'Riordan (1997, p17) emphasizes that this kind of relationship in turn enables individual local activists to feel connected to invisible networks of like-minded but unobservable behaviour that, in aggregate, will make a difference on the planetary stage. As in the case of identity through insecurity, the identity that emerges out of empathy with the surroundings and victims is a more cohesive identity than that which is grounded in security.

Active and inactive empathizers may range from the relatively affluent to those on the margins, for example, eco-warriors, the underemployed, professionals and students. In the case studies, the goal of sustainable development has been one main ideological organizing principle for this group. Political power is neither denied nor granted to them as a group; the group acquires power as a result of successful campaigning. Residents hold the political conviction that collective action can more directly change the condition of those who suffer and improve the treatment of the environment.

In such cases, individuals come to define themselves through their activism (Kelly and Breinliger, 1996). While it is not uncommon that internal conflicts will prevail within a movement, people will develop deep cohesion and devotion in their political struggles. On the less active front, signing petitions, joining protests or boycotting suspicious products have constituted most of what individuals engage in with the purpose of protecting their environment. Identity through empathy does not revolve around considerations of perceived effectiveness, but reflects a feeling of moral duty or responsibility to stand up and be counted, and to register a protest about injustice even if one cannot hope to bring about change. In Linköping, for example, where residents are not particularly involved in politics, a move has been registered towards expressing opinion, participating in demonstrations and boycotting in relation to environmental issues. In Graz, officials, entrepreuneurs and environmental groups have combined in the cause of promoting an eco-city, based ostensibly on uncritical interpretations of the transition to sustainability.

Social–local identity through apathy

Apathy is a misleading word. It is used here to cover a widespread sense of holistic resignation, a recognition of disempowerment and a feeling of helplessness and loneliness in the fact of apparently non-caring external forces. Apathy does not mean a lack of awareness or a misfit in social non-connectedness. It is a culturally induced outcome that is consciously understood.

In this chapter, identity through apathy applies to those who develop a strong sense of individualism necessary to cope with changing conditions. Although they could exercise power, they prefer to remain unknown, unaccountable. If it is convenient, they may change loyalties to different political parties as long as benefits are foreseen. Since its economic position is usually accommodated but only at the margins of the formal economy, it might look for advantage in rising opportunities. Apathy envisions the short term, and usually does not engage in political activism.

The misleading sense of the word refers to the actual power of such identity. By avoiding ideological solidarity and showing indifference to global or local changes – and by avoiding cohesive networking, yet identifying with cultural changes, such as technology and fashion – this identity is, in reality, supportive of changes, whatever those imply.

In Timbaki, a case of *partial* identity through apathy was found. The farming families recognized their dilemma of growing impoverishment and ill health caused by the transition of the salad market to other parts of

Europe and their increasing exposure to agrochemicals. Their resignation was shaped by the case of capacity in local government to assist them, and the high degree of policy disorganization in the Greek government

In Åtvidaberg, local people recognized the economic drag of a degraded environment and economy. With the help of EU structural funds and active networks of regional entrepreneurs, the formerly apathetic were activated into the cause of making the transition to sustainability and wealth-creating exercise.

CONCLUSION

This chapter has presented a conceptual discussion of the notion of an identity in the transition to sustainability within recent sociological, psychological, political and geographical discourses, as well as an analysis of how social identity may emerge and operate in relation to the European case studies. The chapter has also dealt with an emerging set of social–local identities in relation to global economic forces of change and locally responsive sustainable growth strategies. The arguments of the chapter have surrounded the development of one main term, that is, social–local identity. These three words were joined together since they best approximate the complex, political and dynamic idea of identity in this important period of change.

The conceptualization of social identity acknowledges that whether an event is interpreted as socially and environmentally threatening, such as the local manifestation of controversial sustainable development policies, that interpretation depends to a large extent on a sense of identity grounded in social positions in relation to an individual's material life, empowerment and visions of society. Identity in these terms entails an attribution of problems encountered which is external rather than internal, placing the burden of responsibility for change with ideology, economic structures, political institutions and group mobilization, not only with personal characteristics and choices.

Three main themes have emerged. The first deals with the need to acknowledge the socio-psychological link between the individual, on the one hand, and changing contemporary society on the other. In setting that link, globalization and localization may enhance or destroy self-esteem. The idea of the social self is fundamental as it expresses an important interconnectedness between a thinking 'being' and fully active, semi- or non-active 'doing'. These are integral parts of an identity.

Related to this is the second theme which focuses on the need to recognize the multidimensional and multifaceted nature of social–local identity. Rather than conceiving individuals' identity as transparent and simple, individuals will experience a number of forms of identity, notably in the interplay of the global and the local. It has been shown that social–local identity is, in reality, stratified because it emanates from exposure to vital circumstances associated with political and economic processes that take place in and beyond the boundaries of locality. This, in turn, may shape a number of local identities that emerge and develop through security, insecurity, empathy and apathy.

The final theme deals with the geographical and environmental dimensions of social–local identity. Here, it is important to recognize how different perspectives of locality, globality and community influence how local–social identities have emerged in a rapidly changing Europe. The discussion has highlighted how local places, such as Peniche and Graz, offer more than the locale for social and cultural interaction in the political and economic survival. Local places have also been shaped out of these interactions, presenting threats as well as opportunities for local–social identities to exploit, or to let pass.

The foregoing analysis leads to three conclusions. First, social–local identities are, potentially, powerful forces for accommodating global–local change. Change can go in many directions, benefiting some and failing others. The argument that local identities are born in part out of self-defence, and the fact that social identities only sometimes translate into collective mobilization, does not detract from their contradictory characteristics and inherent collective potential either to challenge, legitimize or oppose existing power relations.

Second, the complexities among global, national, regional and local levels of association help to condition people's daily life and their struggles for survival, power and justice. The final set of local responses is not one of geographical scale, in fact, the local, national and the global are intimately linked. To understand internal local divisions and social outlooks, we need to transcend local spatial scales to focus on wider social processes such as those of European unification, market liberalization and the transition to sustainability. Thus, social–local identities might also encourage trends towards more general widespread liberation and democratization.

Finally, social–local identity is not a single uniform trend that can operate against the constraints of globalization. A discernible fragmentation in these identities, as outlined in Table 4.3, illustrates this point. Global restructuring is crucial to shaping the characters of contemporary society. But the attributes of social–local identities have deeper roots. Persisting unsustainable and undemocratic practices have pervaded society, entrenched in the foundations of social inequality. This subject calls for further examination, in particular for societies that have been deeply transformed by recent European unification and market liberalization. It is arguable how far such changes have either exacerbated and/or improved social and environmental conditions in local communities. But the four facets of social–local identities distinguished here indicate that this transition is creating patterns of direct and indirect gain and loss for particular groups throughout Europe, much of which remain hidden from view.

REFERENCES

Baumeister, R F (1986) *Identity: Cultural Change and the Struggle for Self*, Oxford University Press, New York and Oxford

Beck, U (1992) *Risk Society: Towards a New Modernity*, Sage Publications, London

Belay, G (1996) 'The (re)construction of negotiation of cultural identities in the age of globalization' in H B Mokros (ed) *Interaction and Identity Transaction*, New Brunswick and London, pp56–72

Castells, M (1997) *The Power of Identity*, Blackwell, Oxford and Massachusetts

Castells, M (1998) *The End of the Millennium*, Blackwell, Oxford and Massachusetts

Collier, M J and Thomas, M (1988) 'Cultural identity: an interpretative perspective' in Y Kim and W B Gudykunst (eds) *Theories in Intercultural Communication*, Sage, Newbury Park, CA

Dalby, S and Mackenzie, F (1997) 'Reconceptualising local community environment, identity and threat', *Area*, vol 29 (2), pp99–108

Giddens, A (1997) *Modernity and Self-Identity: Self and Society in Late Modern Age*, Polity Press, Cambridge

Inglehart, R (1990) *Culture Shift in Advanced Industrial Societies*, Princeton University Press, Princeton

Kelly, C and Breinliger, S (1996) *The Social Psychology of Collective Action: Identity, Injustice and Gender*, Taylor and Francis, London

Martõnez-Alier, J (1997) 'Environmental justice (local and global)', *CNS*, vol 8 (1), pp91–107

Massey, D (1994) *Space, Place and Gender*, Cambridge, Polity Press, London

McLuhan, M and Fiore, Q (1968) *War and Peace in the Global Village*, McGraw-Hill, New York

Milton, K (1996) *Environmentalism and Cultural Theory: Exploring the Role of Anthropology in Environmental Discourse*, Routledge, London and New York

O'Riordan, T (ed) (1997) *Ecotaxation*, Earthscan Publications Ltd, London

Peet, R and Watts, M (1996) *Liberation Ecologies: Environment, Development, and Social Movements*, Routledge, London and New York

Poguntke, T (1993) 'Goodbye to movement politics?', *Environmental Politics*, vol 2 (3), pp379–404

Pulido, L (1996) *Environmentalism and Economic Justice: Two Chicano Struggles in the Southwest*, The University of Arizona Press, Tuscon

Robertson, R (1992) *Globalization: Social Theory and Global Culture*, Sage, London

Scott, A (1990) *Ideology and the New Social Movements*, Unwin and Hyman, London

Smith, A D (1991) *National Identity*, Penguin Books, London

Stryker, S (1987) 'Identity theory : developments and extensions' in K Yardley and T Honess (eds) *Self and Identity: Psychosocial Perspectives*, John Wiley and Sons, New York, pp111–131

Szasz, A (1994) *EcoPopulism: Toxic Waste and the Movement for Environmental Justice*, University of Minnesota Press, Minneapolis and London

Taylor, C (1989) *Sources of the Self: the Making of Modern Identity*, Harvard University Press, Cambridge, MA

Turner, R H (1987) 'Articulating self and social structure' in K Yardley and T Honess (eds) *Self and Identity: Psychosocial Perspectives*, John Wiley and Sons, New York, pp79–99

Weigert, A J (1997) *Self, Interaction and Natural Environment: Refocusing Our Eyesight*, State University of New York Press, New York

Wiley, M G and Alexander Jr, N C (1987) 'From situated activity to self-attribution: the impact of social structural schemata' in K Yardley and T Honess (eds) *Self and Identity: Psychosocial Perspectives*, John Wiley and Sons, New York, pp220–234

Yardley, K and Honess, T (eds) (1996) *Self and Identity: Psychosocial Perspectives*, John Wiley and Sons, New York

Young, I M (1990) *Justice and the Politics of Difference*, Princeton University Press, Princeton, New Jersey

5 METHODS OF INQUIRY

Maria Kousis and Geoffrey Gooch

This chapter will highlight the importance of the case study approach in examining the effects of globalization and localization on the European sustainability transition. It will outline the essential components of the data collection, as well as the data analysis process. Specifically, it will discuss the use of multiple sources of evidence, the creation of case study databases and how to pursue a chain of events. For the selected case studies across five nations, sources of evidence include documentation, newspaper articles, archival records, surveys, indepth and focused interviews, as well as observations.

INTRODUCTION

The case study methodology used in the studies that empirically illustrate the conclusions of this book has a long tradition in the social sciences. One of the earliest known examples is the work of Aristotle, who examined the city states of ancient Greece in order to create a typology of forms of government. Aristotle used the results of his inductive study of over 200 city states to distinguish between rule by one, a few or the people. He also made the important distinction between forms of government that for-warded the good of the ruler or rulers, and of the populace in general. While much has happened in the social sciences during the 2300 or so years since Aristotle conducted his studies, case study research methodology has continued to thrive and still provides important insights into many different areas of society in the late 20th century.

The methodology used in our studies provides an example of how case study methodology can demonstrate the significance of comparative cultural studies of inquiry, and how the methods used can provide both support for tentative theories while at the same time generating new and unforeseen research questions. The case studies have been conducted in Greece, Portugal, Austria, the UK and in Sweden. The studies conducted in these countries provide examples of ways in which the member states of the EU are tackling the move to sustainability, and demonstrate the diversity of the solutions that are being tried. The methodology has been explorative and adaptive. At the same time, the studies have been guided by a common set of questions, formulated by the participating research groups after a period of discussion at the beginning of the project.

As Yin (1994) has pointed out, case study methodology is useful when the questions being asked are 'how' or 'why', and when the issue being examined is contemporary and in a real life context. In the case of the move to sustainability, the phenomenon is definitely contemporary. It is only relatively recently that the member states of the EU have begun to implement strategies aimed at changing future goals. The transition to sustainability is also something experienced in a real life context. For the farmers of Crete, the fishermen of Portugal, the inhabitants of inner London or the populace of a rural Swedish community, implementing policies that aim to achieve a sustainable society means far more than the rhetoric of politicians or academics. These policies involve radical changes in life styles and consumption patterns. For the relatively wealthy inhabitants of northern Europe, this may involve life-style reorientation; for the less wealthy farmers and fisherman of the Mediterranean regions this may involve major changes in standards of living.

Our study has also been comparative. Despite the fact that methods and case study areas have differed considerably between the five countries involved in the project, each group has sought to find answers to a similar set of questions. The ways that new issues have been discovered during the life of the project has been an important aspect of the work. Exploration has gone hand in hand with illustration. Comparisons can be made at many different geographical and administrative levels. Central governmental legislation has, of course, been an important aspect of the project, but not the main focus. Instead, we have chosen to examine initiatives, problems and possible solutions at the local level. This is because we have felt that the move to sustainability, while not losing sight of global implications, must be grounded in local identity. It is at the local level that the majority of the citizens of the EU feel many environmental and economic problems most intensely. Furthermore, the move to sustainability cannot be achieved by only taking into consideration environmental issues. The environment at large is often perceived as abstract and difficult to envisage. The issues that affect people in their everyday life are often easier to come to terms with. By concentrating on the local level, we have attempted to provide insights into the processes that both most affect the citizens of Europe, and those that they can themselves influence on a day-to-day basis.

The processes presented in the preceding and following chapters have been explored through a variety of coordinated methodologies. The project has, however, had another ambition besides providing empirical illumination for the processes taking place. It has also aimed at creating and developing innovative methodologies. We have attempted to investigate how people and localities perceive, behave and cope with global–local change. The research has therefore been based on case study methodology using a variety of methods in which we have accepted that there will be a degree of non-comparability. A selection of different areas from the participating countries has been examined which look at a combination of ecological, social, economic, cultural and political factors. The details of our methods will be described in the next sections of this chapter.

THE INFLUENCE OF NATIONAL CONTEXT ON RESEARCH APPROACHES

This project involved five European countries, each with considerably different political systems, economies, institutional arrangements and numbers and kinds of interest groups. The countries also differ significantly in size. The largest is the UK, with a population of about 57.9 million. The smallest is Austria with about 7.8 million inhabitants. Greece has approximately 10.3 million, Sweden 8.6 million and Portugal 9.8 million inhabitants. The countries have also been members of the EU for different periods of time. The UK became a member in 1973, Greece in 1981, Portugal in 1986 and Sweden and Austria in 1995. It is therefore important to examine the ways that these aspects might have influenced the construction of the research strategies. The first aspect that will be examined is political culture.

Political culture

While this is not an easy term to define, political culture has been important for our approach. It has played a major role in influencing the research methods chosen by the groups, and has also been an area of study in its own right. Political culture involves the accepted 'rules of the game' of politics. For example, the open right of access to official documents enjoyed by Swedish citizens is almost unknown in most other European countries. Other examples include different voting systems and their effects of politics. The British voting system, which is based on majority voting, often produces strong governments while the proportional voting systems used by other European countries tends to produce weaker governments that may depend more on coalitions. The consensus political style of the Scandinavian countries also contrasts sharply with the more contentious politics of much of the rest of Europe. These differences not only influence the ways that policy decisions can be taken and implemented, they also influence the ways in which the research agendas have been planned and the areas of study available to the researchers. Our case studies have investigated the specific ways in which decisions are taken, the possibilities for citizens to influence those decisions, and the degree of openness of the systems being studied. Since one of our interests has been to study public empowerment – that is, the means by which people can gain control of the processes that affect their lives – the ways in which political culture can aid or hinder participation has been seen as an important variable.

The constitutional and political systems of the participating countries demonstrate a wide variety of alternative ways of organizing participatory democracy. The UK has an old, yet unwritten constitution. It is a constitutional and hereditary democracy with a bicameral parliamentary system. The Upper House or House of Lords is in the process of being transformed into a second chamber with a mix of elected and appointed members, some of whom, doubtless, will be hereditary peers. At the time of writing, the final configuration of membership was not known, though the process of determining the eventual mix is bound to be contentious. Furthermore, as yet undecided is precisely what the role of the new Upper Chamber will be vis à vis the Lower House of Commons. It is likely to be similar to the arrangements of today, namely an influential debating chamber, but with no power of veto over the commons. Sweden is a constitutional monarchy but the king has extremely limited political power. The parliament is unicameral and has 349 members. These are directly elected by proportional representation. Austria is a federal republic with nine provinces. The Austrian Federal Assembly is bicameral, with 183 members in the national council and 64 members in the federal council. The federal president is head of state. Portugal is a republic with a president as head of state. The assembly of the republic is unicameral and has 230 members. The Greek constitution is from 1975 and the head of state is the president. Parliament is unicameral and consists of 300 members elected through a modified proportional voting system.

Political culture has also influenced the research strategies of the groups in this project. An open political system provides more opportunities for researchers to gain access to decision- and policy-makers. The cooperation of politicians and civil servants is obviously a precondition of successfully conducting an examination of key actors. Gaining access to official documents from municipalities and central and regional government will also be easier and less time consuming in a more open political climate. This does not mean that access to other forms of documentation, such as that from private companies, will be easier. Even the organization and recruitment of interviewees to focus group interviews may be more difficult in countries in which there is widespread scepticism towards all forms of politics – including policy analyses conducted by university academics.

In this project, the recruitment of people for the focus groups was more problematic and acute in, for example, Greece and the UK than in Sweden. Disenchantment with politics may also lead to problems when researchers need to conduct mass surveys. Research groups that can use mail questionnaires and achieve high response rates are at an advantage when compared with groups in countries where respondents need to be contacted personally, and where response rates are generally low. Swedish mail surveys, for example, can expect to achieve response rates of over 70 per cent, while teams in other countries can only hope to manage 40 per cent, even when using methods involving direct contact with respondents.

Institutional arrangements

If the key actors and target groups represent the actors' perspective in our studies, the examinations of institutional arrangements represent the structural perspective. Without going into the debate about the relative importance of structure and actor, and the predominant explanatory value of the one or the other, it should be noted that institutional arrangements were considered important in our studies and were therefore one of our major subjects of study. Institutions and policy processes can be studied from both an 'insider' and 'outsider' point of view. The 'insider' is directly involved in the processes which take place and has a vested interest in the outcome of the study. The 'outsider' studies the processes from a different vantage point, and attempts not to become involved in the processes. In our project some groups and researchers have taken the 'insider' perspective and become actively involved in the processes taking place, while others have preferred to study the transition from the outside. The position taken depends both on the preferences of individual researchers and on the practical possibilities for involvement. Institutional arrangements have been studied through examinations of official and other documents and through interviews with key actors. Citizen perceptions of these institutions have been studied through personal interviews, focus groups, surveys and observation. Societal views of institutions have been examined through content analyses of the press.

Two other important methodological aspects of the study should be noted. The first is that the geographical focus of the case studies is limited. Each of the five EU countries participating in the project selected two case studies. Geographical focus was therefore restricted both within the EU and within the national boundaries of the participating countries. No claims are made on the generality of the results. They must be seen as indicative and illuminative.

The second important aspect is the time frame of the studies. The case studies were each conducted in relatively short periods and therefore represent a specific period in time. Considering the subject of the study – the transition to sustainable development – longitudinal studies would have been able to provide other kinds of information that were not obtained here. EU research projects are, however, conducted in relatively short time spaces of two or three years and do not usually provide the possibility of conducting such longitudinal studies. The results should therefore be seen as geographical and temporal manifestations of the transition to sustainable development in the EU at the end of the 20th century.

MEASURING THE CONCEPTS

Sustainability

The concept of sustainability is at the heart of the work undertaken in this research project. The concept itself is discussed in other parts of this book, and in earlier works of a number of the authors represented here, for example in O'Riordan and Voisey (1998). This section will therefore only provide an overview of the ways in which the concept has been empirically studied. The methodology that has been used to examine the concept is a combination of personal interviews, focus group interviews, observation and content analyses. Different groups have used different combinations of methods, but the central issues investigated have been similar. The main questions have been the perceptions and visions of the key actors and target groups. Each group has attempted to examine the ways that problems and the causes of those problems are perceived. They have also studied the institutional arrangements that can either prevent or aid the transition to sustainability. Each group has also investigated the ways in which key actors and target groups envisage ways out of the dilemmas that they feel they are in. This includes attempts made to mobilize themselves and others, and the ways that they cope with difficulties. Our work does not include details on environmental indicators or emission levels, but the ways in which these details are perceived is important, since this influences future behaviour. Belief in the information provided by environmental experts, or scepticism in that information, influences the choices that individuals and groups make between alternative paths.

The research teams have taken a number of different approaches. Most have not asked key actors or members of target groups directly about sustainability, but have instead chosen to formulate questions that have been used as indicators. By asking about visions of the future, about belief in various solutions to present difficulties, and about perceptions of the causes of environmental problems, the groups have been able to bring in ideas about sustainability. In some cases people have simply been asked to talk about the kinds of problems that they feel are most acute. In other cases they have been asked directly about specific environmental problems. Researchers also may have simply listened. Besides these kinds of questions, the groups have asked about economic issues and have tried to pinpoint the kind of worries that people have. They have asked about perceived solutions to economic problems. Finally, the groups have examined participatory aspects of sustainability. The teams have sought to elucidate feelings of helplessness or empowerment – either through direct questions or open discussions – and also to find out more about the ways in which people and communities might become more involved in the transition to sustainable development. The work of the individual groups has built to different degrees on theories of environmental perception. Some have incorporated models of different forms of environmentalism into their work; others have taken a more exploratory approach.

Democracy and empowerment

The transition to sustainability should, according to documents such as LA21, be aimed at environmental and economic equity, and should be based on citizen participation and democracy. In order for these changes to take place, people must be empowered and able to influence policy formulation and implementation. It has been one of the aims of this project to examine the ways in which these goals are being achieved, the factors hindering the achievement of these goals, and the ways in which people can take responsibility for the processes involved. In order to do this, our research agendas have had to consider the ways in which democracy and empowerment can be measured.

The democracy of the 20th century has created professional politicians and party structures, and it is through these and through interest groups and organizations that citizens have been expected to participate in politics. The importance of these formalized structures and institutions has been acknowledged in the research agendas of the groups in this project. Politicians and other representatives of political parties have been interviewed, and perceptions of representative democracy have been examined. Representations of politicians in the mass media have been studied and citizens have been asked about their views on influencing politicians and political parties. How, then, have we been able to measure democracy? One of the first ways is obviously the formal right of citizens. What are their possibilities? How easy is it formally for them to raise issues on the political agenda, and how can they formally influence politicians? Besides this, the research has attempted to investigate public perceptions. What kind of influence do people feel they have? How do they perceive formal politics? These questions have been answered through interviews, focus-group interviews, and observation.

The concept of empowerment involves more than manoeuvring within formal political structures. During the 1960s and 1970s, new forms of political activity began to develop. As pointed out in Chapter 1, while formal politics has experienced a decline in the number of people who vote in elections, and in membership of political parties and those who are prepared to be nominated to positions in party structures, other forms of political participation have continued to gain force. A 'new' form of politics has developed that is based on direct actions, and non-hierarchical structures have been erected to compete with, and complement, traditional forms of politics. These forms of participation have also been studied in the project through survey questionnaires, interviews and content analyses of newspapers.

Locality and collective identity

Locality can be seen as reflecting four different dimensions:

- formal and informal social institutions and social networks;
- participation of social actors in these institutions;
- institutions as vehicles for securing political, economic and social outcomes;
- winners and losers in the sustainability transition at the following levels: policy change and response; behavioural and cultural change; political bargaining and exercise of power; distribution of power and resources.

All national research teams identified the major formal and informal institutions in each of their case studies and subsequently selected samples of key actors and target groups in order to collect data on their perceptions of their community's path towards sustainability. Locality is also visible in the participation of such actors in these institutions, as well as the roles that these institutions play in securing socio-political outcomes. In Sweden and Greece, such data are derived not only from interviews but from content analysis of the local press. Members of target groups and key actors, either individually or collectively, have also expressed their views about the costs and benefits in the sustainability transition by pointing out essential issues concerning policy, resource distribution, social change and power. These perceptions, along with other types of action or policy-oriented evidence, have been considered as part of a variety of collective identities. Given this type of analysed data, it is not possible to trace changes in collective identities over time.

RESEARCH QUESTIONS

Two questions have been predominant in guiding the work conducted in this project:

- Under what circumstances are global–local relationships perceived?
- How far and under what circumstances can civil or collective identity frame the strategies of local people and institutions in the face of global–local change?

Each national research group has attempted to answer these questions through a combination of methods. The perception of global–local relationships has been investigated using fieldwork, focus-group interviews, personal interviews, key-actor interviews and content analyses. The ways in which civic or collective identity frame strategies has been examined through content analyses, focus groups, participant observation and personal interviews. Tables 5.1 and 5.2 summarize the processes involved.

Units of analysis

The main unit of analysis is the community as a whole. The smallest unit, the individual, may express his or her views or may represent, as key actor, the views of the represented agency, group or organization. Intermediary units include a variety of groups, from business and political forums, to social, family, residential or interest groups. The data collected derive from a wide variety of sources. Use is made of secondary data such as available reports, studies, the census and archives. Primary data has been collected through surveys, content analysis of media reports, indepth interviews, circular semi-structured interviews, as well as focus-group interviews.

Table 5.1 *Phases of research by target groups and key actors*

	Research Phases	
Phase	*Power Structures*	*Civil Society*
1 Identify the main purpose of the project	Review of literature; collection of pertinent secondary data; delineation of concepts	Review of literature; collection of pertinent secondary data; delineation of concepts
2 Select case study localities and communities within these localities	Identify and select levels of power structures	Identify and select target groups within the community
3 Develop an understanding of the community	Develop understanding of different power networks in and outside of the community	Develop an understanding of social networks of target groups within the communal structure
4 Identify principal key actors and target groups	Selection of, and contact initiation with, key actors	Selection of, and contact initiation with, target groups
5 Investigate target groups' and key actors' interests, characteristics and circumstances	Identify key nodes within power networks, keys actors' perceptions visions and preferred solutions	Examine perceptions of insecurity, vulnerability and empowerment
6 Identify patterns and contexts of interaction between key actors and target groups	Identify key actors' formulation and implementation of policies, forms of communication and attempts to mobilize civil society	Identify target groups' mobilization and attempts to influence policy formulation and implementation
7 Define options for policy reformulation	Propose forms of institutional redesign, opportunities and alternatives	Propose forms of mobilization, empowerment and policy alternatives

The adopted approaches are more characteristic of 'participation in information giving', as provided through surveys, and 'participation by consultation', characteristic of qualitative interviews.

Sampling strategies

The selection of probabilistic and non-probabilistic sampling strategies was the result of factors such as the national or regional culture, the infrastructure obstacles, the training of the researchers, as well as time and money constraints. Non-probabilistic strategies were used more given the aim of producing tactically chosen samples, and less because they were not feasible. The non-probabilistic techniques used by the teams are combinations of purposive, snowball and quota sampling (for a description see Palys, 1997). These were selected on the basis of what was more efficient in terms of reaching the target groups and the key actors. Thus, the national teams chose different sampling procedures for each of the two case studies conducted in each country. In general, purposive and quota sampling procedures were followed for examining key actors, while snowball and quota sampling techniques were used in studying target groups. Probabilistic techniques were used in the Swedish survey and the Greek content analysis.

The sources of evidence and data collection principles

Although data collection methods were not standardized across the five pairs of case studies, the national teams showed a tendency to use similar sources of evidence to collect their data. From the six types available in case study analysis (Yin, 1994), four sources have been widely used in this project: documentation, archival records, interviews and observation. The ethnicity, collective identity and basic demographics profile of the community were studied using documentation data, such as minutes of meetings, formal studies or evaluations, or newspaper mentions or articles. Information from archival records, such as organizational records, maps and charts, lists of names or activities, already available survey or census data and personal records, provided additional material on the community's demographic and ethnicity profile. Interview data in the form of open-ended, indepth, circular, semi-structured, structured, personal, key-actor and focus-group information generated evidence on the power structure and collective identity of the community. Finally, direct or participant observation provided data related to the identities and ethnicity dimension of the communities.

The research approach has combined elements of quantitative and qualitative methods. Even though there was considerable variation among the different teams in terms of research traditions and specializations, all national teams made great efforts to use as similar methods as possible and to bring together as many sources of evidence as time and financial resources allowed. Such an overall strategy normally leads to a stronger

Table 5.2 *Types of data and units of analysis*

Types of Data	Policies; laws, archives; reports; census data; issues, strategies; actions	Focus groups; group meetings; participant-observation data	Content analysis; mentions in printed media	Key-actor interviews (semi/structured, indepth, circular interviews)	Personal interviews (surveys, structured/indepth, circular interviews)
Units of Analysis	Total system	Intermediate units			Individuals
The community as a whole (physical and social environment)	Social change in economy, society, environment and politics	Group perceptions of community	Community portrayal	Perceptions of community	Perceptions of community
Production groups political groups or organizations	Social organization: policies and practices	Group perceptions of political economy	Political economy portrayal	By inference	By inference
Interest groups/ organizations (eg trade, NGOs, women's groups, cultural groups)	Group perceptions of structure, change and orientation	Group perceptions of structure, change and orientation	Interest group portrayal	Perceptions of, structure, change and orientation	Perceptions of structure, change and orientation

Families, residential groups	Structure, change and orientation	Group perceptions of structure, change and orientation	Other group portrayal: by inference	Perceptions of structure, change and orientation	Perceptions of structure, change and orientation
Individuals as representatives	By inference	Group member perceptions	Key-actor portrayal	Perceptions of structure, change and orientation	Perceptions of structure, change and orientation
Individuals	By inference	Group member perceptions	By inference	Perceptions of structure, change and orientation	Behaviour, perceptions, attitudes

Source: Adapted from Lipset, Trow and Coleman (1956, p422) in Yin (1994).

data pool through triangulation (convergence of results), complementarity (showing different facets of same phenomenon), development (each method informs the next), initiation (emergence of contradictions and fresh perspectives) and expansion (adding scope and breadth to the study) (Creswell, 1994).

In general, the teams applied methodological as well as data triangulation, but not investigator or theory triangulation (Yin, 1994). In examining 'the circumstances under which global–local relationships are perceived', the following quantitative and qualitative methods were used: fieldwork, focus-group interviews, personal interviews, key-actor interviews and content analysis. Studying 'how far and under what circumstances collective identity can frame the strategies of local people and institutions in the face of global–local change' led to the use of content analysis, focus groups, participant observation, and personal interviews. Multiple sources of evidence have been used by most teams to examine specific items of each of the above research questions in each case study, such as collective perceptions of various aspects of global–local change with regard to the following:

- economic issues;
- crime;
- environmental degradation;
- structural change;
- political crises;
- psychological and social problems;
- poverty;
- future expectations.

Multiple sources of evidence were also used not for the sake of convergence on a single fact, but in order to address different facts of the community's economic, political, cultural and environmental features, for example, scientific reports of environmental degradation.

Box 5.1 *Creating case study databases*

According to Yin (1994), a case study database may be organized in the following ways:

- case study notes (from interviews, observations or document analysis: handwritten, typed, on audiotapes or PC diskettes, diary or index cards, etc);
- case study documents (bulky; compile annotated bibliography; establish a primary file and a secondary file to make documents retrievable later on, for example, interviews, code sheets, etc);
- tabular materials collected from the site or created by the team (from surveys or other quantitative analysis; counts of different phenomena; observational accounts; archival data);
- narratives: investigator composes open-ended answers to the questions in the case study protocol as an attempt to integrate the available evidence (from multiple sources) and to converge upon the facts of the matter or their tentative interpretation; these can be used to compose the actual case study report.

Intuitive Methodologies

Intuitive methodologies are not new and are followed consciously and subconsciously by most social science researchers in open-ended interviews and focus groups. The basis for this approach is grounded theory, as developed originally by Glaser and Strauss (1967). The principle here is that theory can be informed by qualitative approaches to examining underlying meanings to outlooks and behaviour. The act of pursuing the pattern of motivations and outlooks becomes a process of theory-building and hypothesis creation, rather than the conventional mode of theory-testing and hypothesis falsification. Intuitive approaches do not begin without a theoretical basis: they simply allow theories to be more open ended regarding how they may be used and amalgamated, with the capacity for more feasible and exploratory approaches to theory design.

According to Charmaz (1995, p28):

> *You start with individual cases, incidents or experiences, and develop progressively more abstract categories to synthesize, to explain and to understand your data to identity patterned relations within it.*

Strauss and Corbin (1990) and, more particularly, Miles and Huberman (1994, p5) both call for theoretical sensitivity on the part of the researcher. Miles and Huberman call for research to be seen as more of a craft than a slavish adherence to methodological rules. 'No study', claim Miles and Huberman (1994, p5), 'conforms exactly to a standard methodology. Each one calls for the researcher to bend the methodologies for the peculiarities of the setting'.

The advantage of this approach is that it allows for greater attention to be given to the political culture settings of interviews and focus-group research. For example, in Portugal and in Greece, interviews with fishermen and farmers were often associated with social networks of families, friends and colleagues. Many interviews took place in clubs, bars, cafés and docksides, as well as in kitchens and living rooms. Two interviewers were normally present, one probing and responding, the other recording. Conversations were allowed to flow according to the strength of the issue in question and the coherence of the argument offered. The use of a quasi focus-group format allowed the groups to offer opinion and judgement as they would undertake in their own social networks. This was deliberately incorporated because of the emphasis placed in this research on the bonding relationships between personal self-esteem and social connectedness, as refined in local–social identity.

Through this procedure, for example, it became possible to build up a picture of when individuals and groups trusted or looked for support in patterns of local–social identity. Portuguese inshore fishermen bonded over the use of their *quinhão*, the proportion of the catch that is shared by the crew. This is essentially a form of payment. But in a case when fish catches are at a premium, the *quinhão* has real value. How the individual crew members receive their allocation, and what actually happens to the fish, are obviously confidential and quasi-illegal matters.

The Portuguese research team employed two local people, the father of one of whom is the current president of a parish within the municipality of Peniche, the other a local historian with profound contacts with local people. These individuals already had the trust of the fishing families, who used their network of support to ensure that goodwill towards the researchers extended across the whole community. By using local people, the Portuguese researchers were able to be slightly more removed from the interviews. This meant that disputes over some of the data used on answers were resolved – for example, levels of earnings, the amount and distribution of the *quinhão*, and the degree of income from the informal economy entering fishing families homes – and answers were obtained with credible degrees of accuracy through the combination of trust and intuition.

In the Mile Cross case study, access to the various networks depicted in Figure 10.1 came through supportive local officials who were closely in touch with a range of local leaders. A researcher in the area had also spent a year getting 'under the skin' of a number of groups that were only informally organized. This individual therefore had contacts with the less empowered, as well as with city officials. Because the researcher had a privately sponsored studentship with official city council blessing, he had access to a variety of meetings and informal discussions that were critical for providing context. The drawback to this collegiate relationship is the honest reporting of evidence, also given by local people to the researchers, of dissatisfaction with the community empowerment programme and colleague officials. The handling of this information, crucial to the test of trust among all parties, proved to be a very delicate matter indeed.

Gaining access to individuals whose role is critical for evaluating networks and outlooks is a matter of continued negotiation based on goodwill, integrity and diplomacy. Researchers often have no other recourse than to sense the mood and the patterns of relationships among the actors, and to respond on informed whim. If this is done sensitively and with care, then this involves intuitive research at its most helpful. Because the 'researched' need the attention and enjoyment of the researchers, so the relationship gains its own legitimacy through a process of mutual support and appreciation.

Layder (1993, p40) places much emphasis on the significance of history and social memory. All groups are, to some extent, the prisoners of their past, their social and familial influences and their expectations. This means that processes of social interaction carry risk meanings that can best be understood when there is genuine trust and openness between the researcher and the researched.

The focus group is not simply a meeting of people. It is a theatre for discourse, for exploratory understanding and for revelation, namely the greater awareness of representing others' interests and being relevant. Much of the success of this outcome depends obviously on the composition of the group and the skills of the facilitator. In cases of empathetic identity, the facilitator should be sensitive to group norms. Where identity is rooted in insecurity or apathy, then a more proactive facilitative role is required. These approaches were pursued in the case studies that follow.

CONCLUSION

The mix of formal and intuitive approaches to the methodologies used in this study highlight the relationship between 'factual' data, derived from reports, documents and minutes of meetings, and the 'judgemental' evidence of individuals and social networks who play out social–local identities. The result was a healthy re-evaluation of the 'factual' evidence, found in every case study, and much more insight into how groups actually form views and build up their distinctiveness. Settings for any activity are features of wider patterns of demarcation and subordination, as outlined in the previous two chapters.

A word of warning is needed, however. The disempowered and the alienated are simply very difficult to approach and to incorporate within such studies. Gatekeepers try to control what is said and whom to see. The disempowered are even less likely to be found if gatekeepers are active, but normally are not readily identifiable even when the gatekeepers are subdued.

There is no easy solution to this. The method adopted in this work was to concentrate on building trust and creating patterns of information providers, who became participants to the research programme. Through them, a wider array of interested parties could be contacted, including local officials and politicians, many of whom in Greece, Portugal and Austria were networked into the local culture in a myriad of ways. These people, in turn, sought out the more disempowered and attempted to bring them in on the scheme. All of this takes huge amounts of time, much of which appears to be unproductive in its early days. A commitment on this scale can pay off handsomely if perseverance and determination are qualities that are appreciated among the respondents.

REFERENCES

Creswell, J C (1994) *Research Design: Qualitative and Quantitative Approaches*, Sage Publications, London

Glaser, B and Struss, A (1967) *The Discovery of Grounded Theory*, Aldine Publishers, Chicago

Layder, D (1993) *New Strategies in Social Research*, Polity Press, Cambridge

Mason, J (1997) *Qualitative Research*, Sage Publications, London

Miles, M B and Huberman, A T (1994) *Qualitative Data Analysis*, second edition, Sage Publications, London

Morgan, D L (1997) *Focus Group as Qualitative Research*, second edition, Sage Publications, London

O'Riordan, T and Voisey, H (1998) *The Transition to Sustainability: The Politics of Agenda 21 in Europe*, Earthscan Publications Ltd, London

Palys, T S (1997) *Research Designs: Quantitative and Qualitative Perspectives*, Harcourt Brace & Co, London

Ragin, C C (ed) (1991) *Issues and Alternatives in Comparative Social Research*, E J Brill, New York

Strauss, A and Corsin, J (1990) *Basics of Qualitative Research*, Sage Publications, London

Yin, R K (1994) *Case Study Research: Design and Methods*, second edition, Sage Publications, London

PART 2: THE CASE STUDIES

6 Decay and Revitalization in Two Swedish Communities

Uno Svedin, Anders Hjort af Ornäs, Ulrick Lohm and Geoffrey Gooch

Introduction

Sweden is characterized by a number of traits. As a country, it is:

- a quite wealthy nation despite economic setbacks of various kinds in the last decade;
- characterized by its Scandinavian general and political culture; included in this is its democratic institutions and styles of operation, which have been established over considerable time and without periods of civil war or dictatorships;
- characterized by engineering skills and ways of doing things that have deep roots going back hundreds of years, including mining competence and metallurgical skills which have created a high-tech, well-educated workforce with a strong work ethic;
- known for its strong self-esteem and pride in its environmental ethos, as well as its avant-garde policy posture vis à vis the rest of the world.

The two case studies in this chapter were chosen in such a way that, despite closeness in geographical terms, they provide insights in differences of approaches, visions and potential future paths, both in general as well as in particular, with regard to sustainability issues. These offer the perspective of *Gemeinschaft* versus *Gesellschaft*, two words which, in an incomplete translation from their German origin into English, roughly corresponds to an emphasis on social and cultural aspects of 'living together' versus ideas of society as a more formal, administrative and even juridicial construct.

THE SWEDISH PERSPECTIVE

The discussion about sustainability in Sweden has been characterized by:

- an emphasis on local management perspectives in terms of the LA21;
- a broadening of the earlier narrow 'environmental' repetoire to wider realms of issues connected with socio-economic development;
- a parallel attention at the national level on commitments in the international fora concerning climate change, biodiversity or forest issues, and at the same time on local implementation measures;
- an emphasis on new actors, NGOs and business as partners in the sustainaibility transition.

Three general areas of topical concern are of prime interest for this study:

1   The relation between the local and the global: in Sweden this is seen in terms of expressions of globalization impacts at local community levels. Local development is also highly dependent on national policies. In fact, the Swedish long-term history could seen to express a sort of centralized decentralization. One present-day manifestation is a strong emphasis on LA21. The degree to which local varieties of responses within the window of national signals express themselves is of great interest. This centralized decentralization does not only hold for the sequence of state national prescription at ministerial levels, down to the municipality board level, but also applies in terms of national sectoral agencies, their formation of policies and their transfer down to their local outposts which deal with roads, energy and water-quality control. It even holds true for vertically organized NGOs.

2   Stability versus instability: given an analysis of the interconnection between levels of government, it is interesting to address the issue about stability and instability. This theme applies to creative adaptability and the possibilities of shaping local conditions. The connection between local vulnerability and a lack of local democracy and participation has still to be worked out in Sweden. This field of investigation is highly related to studies of local perceptions of situations, of perceived causal connections related to environmental challenges and of perceived future options for individuals and communities.

3   'Technical' versus 'societal' approach: this issue has much to say about 'paths' to sustainability but also about perceived goals. It also pertains to images of what could be more or less easily altered in society – technical solutions or human institutions and behaviour. The factual choices of local strategies thus illuminate many issues under the surface. The issue also provides an interesting input to the issue of actor control and power. Which local groups can find expressions of social reform through means which are optimal for just these groups and not for others? Why are certain views about transforming society not represented?

Swedish environmental laws are currently undergoing a transformation and a new environmental code was adopted in 1998.[1] The code merges many old acts and introduces several dimensions, such as an increased emphasis on information and enhanced possibilities for citizens to be involved in environmental decisions. Simultaneously, the harmonization of Swedish environmental laws with the environmental directives of the EU are also bringing changes, such as the use of environmental quality criteria.[2] Local authorities have substantial responsibilities under the law, including the creation and surveillance of emission permits from industry, and the adoption of a municipal plan that regulates the use of land and resources.[3]

All three topic areas can be approached fruitfully through the processes associated with sustainability, which to a great extent in Sweden has been marketed under the label of LA21. In Sweden, LA21 is considered politically and morally, if not legally, binding; in 1992 the Swedish government formulated *A Swedish Action Plan for the 21st Century*. Ten sectors were identified as critical at the national level, although ecological aspects were at the fore. Increasingly, the importance of citizens' initiatives at the local level was emphasized. Chapter 28 of LA21 was taken as a direct incitement to local authorities to develop their own Agenda 21.

Sweden has 288 municipalities and a strong tradition of local government with its own taxation rights and responsibilities. By 1995, following this overall pattern, about 50 per cent of the municipalities had employed a specific LA21 coordinator, and by 1998, all 288 had begun formulating their LA21 directives. In approximately two-thirds of the municipalities, LA21 has been organized as a direct responsibility of the municipality boards. Despite this emphasis on a bottom-up approach, however, it has been difficult to achieve satisfactory levels of citizen participation, and only 3 per cent on average of the Swedish population is at present engaged in LA21 (SOU, 1997).

In support of this local activity in most Swedish communal territories, various forms of central funding is being channelled downwards with regard to 'framing' the issues. A special national-level state 'delegation' has been in operation over the last few years. A fairly substantial document (including sub-documents) has been developed by this delegation and has been given wide circulation in Sweden at many levels for offical comments and suggestions for further action. This process has been quite elaborate and has involved both public as well as private actors at various levels. This includes a very wide participation at the municipal level.

A broad, sustainable development programme amounting to more than five billion Swedish crowns (US$700 million) for three years has been devised to support a variety of projects. This programme has been led by a group of five cabinet ministers, which signifies the importance the present government attaches to 'sustainability issues'.

The first round of municipal projects has now received funding. These projects relate to technical as well as to 'social' types of projects. Examples of the first kind concern new forms of waste handling but also municipal energy production. Examples of the second kind concern support to school projects and to different NGO activites of a mobilizing kind. In general, the support has been given to municipalities that have been able to provide an interesting overall framework in which the projects express a local 'philosophy', concern and actor participation.[4]

The interplay between the local mobilization in terms of designing a process of identifying LA21 efforts and the allocation of directed funding goes far beyond project financing. Indeed, the content of decisions has 'signal' functions as well.

The two case study areas

The choice of the two Swedish case study regions has had as its basis the tension between similarities and differences. By choosing two areas which are situated close by – the centres are not more than 35 kilometres apart – the general geographical setting is similar, but not equal. Åtvidaberg is situated in a combined forest and small farm district, which as far back as the 17th century was characterized by mining. Linköping has always been close to the wide open spaces of wealthy agricultural lands; from medieval times onwards it has been an administrative, clerical and educational centre.

Despite closeness in terms of distance, these communities have had different positions in national life and their economical well-being has had different bases. Linköping is fairly large and Åtvidaberg is fairly small. Linköping is, in terms of its national administrative structure, a regional centre with a county governor, bishop and university. Åtvidaberg has none of these regional centre characteristics. However, it is a little too easy to deduce from this that Åtvidaberg is more 'peripheral' than Linköping in all senses, despite the obvious reliance of many inhabitants in Åtvidaberg on the wider job market in Linköping (which is reached through commuting arrangements). The balance of dependence and autonomy in the Åtvidaberg case has to be viewed against other aspects in local history.

By selecting Linköping and Åtvidaberg as a pair in the project, issues of congruence, conflict and external impact were addressed, such as the impact from Swedish national development historically, apart from global economic development. The intention was for the Åtvidaberg study to provide insight into community response to outside pressure, whether through an application of a Swedish model or under the influence of a unique Linköping–Åtvidaberg arrangement.

The choice of Åtvidaberg as a case study was not made arbitrarily; the place has an important role in early industrial development but failed to reach the extrapolated targets that would have meant a community of around three times today's size. The peak was reached by the mid-1970s when the dominating industry no longer could stand up against global information technology (IT) development. This was a fine mechanics, precomputer calculators company – the Facit concern.

This 'high-tech' industry profile is a common trait of both Linköping and Åtvidaberg. However, their respective styles in promoting this direction of interest and their forms of network to support it in a wider world context differ. Thus, the choice of the two connected and still somewhat independent areas is built on affinities and differences.

Åtvidaberg – ways towards diversification[5]

The town of Åtvidaberg has a heritage of copper mining dating back to the 14th century. For 200 years, from the early 18th to the early 20th century, the town evolved around the Adelswärd baronage's copper industry. Today, the municipality has about 12,000 inhabitants, of which 7500 live in the centre district. The population of Åtvidaberg was stable from the early 1960s to 1990, but throughout the 1990s, there has been a decline in the total population by about 50 citizens annually. Compared with the rest of Sweden, there is a deficit in the age cohort of 20–45 and Åtvidaberg displays a surplus in inhabitants who are older than 55.

The natural environment is characterized by many lakes and forests and the existing farms are often smaller than in the neighbour municipality, Linköping. Farming is also less intensive, mixing between forestry and cattle-breeding. The most important environmental problem concerns the legacy of the mining industry, which poses a threat to the drinking and fishing waters in the commune due to leakage of heavy metals from old mine tailings.

Copper production lost profitability towards the end of the 19th century. In its place, more modern industries emerged. In 1906, Baron Theodor Adelswärd formed Åtvidaberg Industries Ltd and pioneered the European production of office furniture and equipment. Moving from desks and other wood products to typewriters and calculators, the company developed into a worldwide business with 8000 staff and agents in 130 countries. During the 1960s, 80 per cent of the technical office equipment products went on exports. The company was renamed Facit AB in 1966 and dominated the private labour market until its bankruptcy in 1990.

Unemployment in Åtvidaberg is 7.7 per cent of the population aged 16–64 (March 1999), basically on par with the national average. Half of those are enlisted in public works programmes. Notably, unemployment among youth aged 18–24 is not only higher than among adults, but is higher than in the rest of Sweden. The primary reason appears to be that only 15 per cent of Åtvidaberg's youth go into post-high school eduction, compared with a national average of 25 per cent (33 per cent in Linköping). A relatively large share of the working force is active in the private sector, primarily in industrial production, and employment in agriculture, forestry or fishing is 4.3 per cent, twice the Swedish average. A substantial number of people, more than 1800, commute to work in other municipalities.

The elections of 1998 saw the Social Democratic party lose its single majority in the municipal assembly, though it is still by far the dominant party with 19 seats out of 45. Compared with most other municipalities, the Left (former communist) party is small with only one seat. Instead, the traditionally agrarian Center party is uncommonly strong and heads the opposition coalition, now working in a spirit of overall common purpose. In the last elections, local parties gained influence and presently hold nine mandates in the assembly.

Linköping – regional centre[6]

The city of Linköping lies 230 kilometres south-east of Stockholm, in the fertile central part of the county of Östergötland. The municipality has about 130,000 inhabitants and the city itself about 90,000. Today, Linköping is the sixth largest city in Sweden. In 1860, only 1 per cent of the county's total working force was employed in Linköping; in 1996 35 per cent of the county workforce was in Linköping.[7]

In 1996, 60 per cent of the total working population of Linköping were employed in the private sector (compared with 64 per cent of the national average) and 40 per cent in the public sector (compared with 36 per cent of the country average).[8] As far as the distribution between agriculture, industry and services was concerned, Linköping demonstrated the same percentages as Sweden as a whole – 2 per cent worked in agriculture, 27 per cent in industry and 71 per cent in services in 1996. The somewhat larger percentages of the total working population employed in the public sector in Linköping, compared with Sweden as a whole, can be explained by the existence of a considerable number of public employers. These include Linköping University, the University Hospital and the Defence Research Organization (FOA). Linköping has an exceptionally high percentage of inhabitants with post-high school education – 33 per cent, compared with the national average of 25 per cent.

Linköping is home to a number of the county's largest employers; the municipality of Linköping employed 8940 people in 1996, the county council employed about 6000 people, SAAB employed 5500, Ericsson telecom AB employed 1900, Linköpings University employed 2800 (and hosted around 20,000 students), and FFV Aerotech AB employed 1500.[9] If SAAB's employees, who constitute about 50 per cent of the workers engaged in manufacturing and extraction, are included, then the number of people whose jobs are directly or indirectly financed by state, county and municipal taxation amounts to at least 27,710, 45 per cent of the total workforce. This state of affairs makes Linköping vulnerable to changes in national political policies. The development of the distribution of employment in different areas is presented in Figure 6.1.

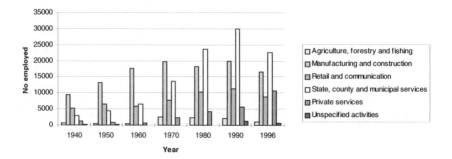

Figure 6.1 *Employed in Linköping by sector, 1940–1996*

Perceptions of sustainability-related issues

We conducted a broad survey in the municipalities involved in order to map perceptions about interest in societal development, environmental questions and approaches to local power.[10]

Quality of life
The respondents in Linköping did put a higher priority on proximity to work in their personal situations than those in Åtvidaberg. On the other hand, they considered 'a feeling of affinity with neighbours' to be less important than the Åtvidaberg respondents. This may well reflect the more evident urban character in Linköping. The inhabitants of Åtvidaberg also already made a judgement of balance in their private lives. Commuting every day to Linköping, with its access to the broader labour market, and at the same time having 'a good life' in comparatively less expensive Åtvidaberg during free time is regarded as a justifiable combination.

In both municipalities, 90–95 per cent rated factors concerned with housing as important. Highlighted factors were 'the cost of accomodation', 'clean air, land and water', 'to avoid activities dangerous to health' and 'beautiful surroundings', thus voicing general concerns among Swedes. At the margin, those in Linköping who rated 'clean air, land and water' as important were somewhat less in numbers than those in Åtvidaberg, although both were at a high level.

Regarding the question about important factors for leisure, there were significant differences between Linköping and Åtvidaberg in the categories of 'spending time in nature', 'animals' and 'hunting and fishing'. These factors were rated lowest by the Linköping respondents, who stressed 'relaxation', 'spending time with friends', but also 'spending time in nature'. Furthermore, 'exercise and sport', 'computer and technique' and 'culture and entertainment' had high Linköping ratings, mirroring different leisure preferences when compared with those of Åtvidaberg respondents. It is reasonable to refer to the Linköping pattern as 'urban-influenced leisure interests'.

When considering the factors that are more generally important for quality of life, nine components can be distinguished. These form a common core since the two municipalities demonstrate a relatively high degree of agreement concerning these factors. The factors are 'health', 'clean air, land and water', 'natural environment', 'good accommodation', 'rewarding leisure time', 'economic independence', 'to be left alone', 'other people', and 'employment which enables personal development'. Significant differences can be seen among the Linköping respondents for two factors outside of this list: these respondents gave a high rating to 'a high material and technical standard' and to 'good communications'. In the countryside, the importance of 'communication' and 'technical and material standard' are more disputed.

Environment

Linköping is considered by the respondents to offer a worse environment for its inhabitants than Åtvidaberg. The factors that are considered to a greater extent 'bad' by Linköping's respondents are 'air quality', 'noise levels near homes' and 'water quality in lakes, rivers and streams near accommodation'. Comparatively many Linköping residents have 'roads with heavy traffic', 'airfields', 'railways' and 'entertainment' so near their accommodation that they 'notice it or are affected by it'.

The Linköping respondents, as well as those from Åtvidaberg, viewed nature as an inheritance to be protected and conserved, as a resource for survival, a place for leisure activities and a source of pleasure and interest. Technology was seen as the key to progress and development. The respondents in Linköping felt, to a greater extent than those in Åtvidaberg, that nature was a place for leisure activities, and that technology was a source of pleasure and interest. Furthermore, a larger percentage of the Linköping respondents rejected the statement that 'nature is something threatening'. An examination of the more general questions about problems and threats to the general welfare demonstrated that less of the Linköping respondents perceived that general welfare was threatened. Those problems that were perceived as most acute were not concerned with environmental issues but with Sweden's economic circumstances and the lack of employment opportunities in the country. However, the Linköping respondents were less worried about the economy and employment than those in Åtvidaberg.

Involvement

In a comparison with Åtvidaberg, a lower percentage of Linköping respondents had been involved in environmental issues. In Linköping 74 per cent of the residents stated that they had changed their behaviour in order to influence the environment in a positive way, which is less than in Åtvidaberg, where 77.7 per cent of the respondents made the same claim. The percentage of Linköping respondents who kept themselves informed about environmental issues by watching TV or listening to the radio every day or sometimes during the week was also less than in Åtvidaberg. If a conclusion can be drawn about which political issues people try to influence, how often they inform themselves about environmental issues, and to what extent they have changed their behaviour in order to improve the environment, then it would seem that the Linköping respondents are somewhat less interested in environmental issues than the Åtvidaberg residents.

Methods used in the two cases

Although our interest in sustainability and democracy equally concern Åtvidaberg and Linköping, these areas are different in size, structure and social problems. We therefore approached the two cases in a somewhat different way, adapting our style of investigation to the specifics of the cases.

What is most obvious is the difference of scale. Åtvidaberg (population 12,000) is a limited, industrially oriented area with some forestry activity, whereas Linköping (population 130,000) is in itself one of the central areas of employment in Sweden, as well as the seat of a major university.

In the methodology, we placed emphasis on participatory observation in many of the often small groups devoted to LA21 work in Åtvidaberg. In this way, the aim was to penetrate a social structure using methods close to social anthropology. In the much larger city of Linköping, the approach was devoted more to the public debate in a broader sense. Here, the selection of focus groups was chosen to reach a deeper understanding of civic sentiment. In addition, the role of the media continues to be more important in the larger city context than in Åtvidaberg, although local press coverage is also worthy of note.

In addition, the structural connotations of the two cases are different. Åtvidaberg stands for the mini town of Åtvidaberg itself and the municipality region Åtvidaberg (Åtvidabergs Kommun). The municipality region consists of many small dwellings where the citizens do not always consider themselves Åtvidabergans. Linköping is characterized more by a city culture with less emphasis on micro-identities. Instead, any one person can exhibit several different identities which express themselves in different contexts. As a result, our investigation about Åtvidaberg also tries to penetrate these 'plural' identity dimensions based on competing localities and their identities. This aspect becomes less important in Linköping, where different professionality aspects may provide more fruitful hunting grounds for investigation.

ÅTVIDABERG – TRANSITION AND RENEWAL[11]

The local organization of sustainability in Åtvidaberg

In a draft conceptual model for the Åtvidaberg municiplity's LA21, four elements feed into the action programme: education, information and feedback; development and innovation; the natural landscape; and individual responsibility (labelled 'clean your own doorstep'). Based on these elements, the community can become potentially an ecologically sustainable society. Several documents give the impression that such a society is a reality that Åtvidaberg can achieve (the year 2020 appears to have been chosen for goal satisfaction). This notion notwithstanding, visioning has been an important part of the process so far.

In June 1997, Åtvidaberg reinforced its efforts for sustainable development when the municipality replaced a part-time LA21 project coordinator with a permanent full-time employee. The structure of governance surrounding that coordinator can be divided into four segments:

- a steering group of politicians;
- a working group, with representatives from several agencies of the municipality;

- an LA21 network of representatives primarily from business and civil society (this group meets regularly to share information);
- environment representatives in many of the work places of the commune.

An application for funding towards investment in sustainability projects has been sent to the Swedish government. Interestingly, while much background work for this was prepared by the LA21 coordinator, the agenda takes a broader approach to sustainable development than most LA21s in Sweden. Included in Åtvidaberg's strategy are issues such as employment, development of 'green' technology and gender equity. As of March 1999, positive feedback, but no decision on funding to Åtvidaberg, has been given by the government.

Paths to diversification

This section, dealing in more detail with Åtvidaberg, is based on empowerment, identity and political process. The argument is that these aspects combine at the local level according to new principles. The study shows how local internal identity and external constraints interplay in a way that depends upon both local competence to act under new circumstances and the external impacts. The process leading to these adaptive capabilities holds potential for involvement and mobilization, concerning issues such as those expressed in LA21. Such processes are often deeply rooted in social and cultural life and may frequently support formal political operation.[12]

The national left/right (or growth/green, or other similar dimensions) concerns is not a key political issue in Åtvidaberg. Instead, autonomy versus integration with the rapidly growing city of Linköping is vital. Identity, vulnerability and motivation were, in the earlier phases of the project, seen to account for a general softening of top-down structural links. The study, however, through its empirical investigations, revealed a more complex process in which national local ties are both weakened and strengthened by national ties.[13]

The issues of economy and scale seemed to be a key in the erosion of the earlier macro–micro relations. While the political parties 'manage' relations at East Gothian and national levels, industry goes international. The once multinational Facit concern has set the tone for international cooperation.

A seemingly long-term downward spiral for the community has generated major new trends. One spin-off of the Facit collapse was the establishment of a large number of small-scale enterprises that are highly profiled within very narrow niches, and which operate directly at the international markets in many cases via a link through Stockholm or Brussels.[14] In contrast, the economic activities of the small group of merchants in central Åtvidaberg are highly local in character, with major competition emerging from the modern commercial centre in Linköping. The net effect of all the changes has been towards an increased diversification of economy and production.

There are more actors who operate the Åtvidaberg development than those with political and industrial mandates. Merchants refer to the importance of autonomy when trying to convince their customers to purchase consumer goods in Åtvidaberg and not in Linköping. Teachers combine on the interest in community development with conventional environmental issues. The Linköping-based regional newspaper has a section on Åtvidaberg six days a week.

Against this background it is interesting to note that diversification in Åtvidaberg comes in two ways. Economic diversification is connected with spreading risks in an enterprise perspective. Diversified social networks open up other linkages. 'Belonging' is a concept that gives both an entry ticket into social networks for the individual, and an ascribed status as seen from the outside. The conventional view is that only in small-scale circumstances would this phenomenon appear (this relates to the distinction between *Gemeinschaft* and *Gesellschaft*). However, the observation in Åtvidaberg is that 'belonging' is established not only on the basis of community membership but also on the basis of locality as an attitude among the like-minded. Consequently, there is a heterogeneous blend of several social–local identities.

Local democracy in town and country

While the study touches on the quality of local and national connections, a key concern is the political processes which may influence the transformation of Swedish society as a whole – identities, risk management and self-esteem included. There are both old and new features of community development in national development, and the issue is how such features may relate to mobilization and knowledge formation.

One aspect of the analysis is: who has access to what type of knowledge and where are creative initiatives located? A few key issues are of particular significance in understanding how a new type of local identity emerges.

- Class structure: Åtvidaberg is an old industrial growth centre, a traditional Swedish *bruksort* with a large representation (even today a significant one) of large-scale industry. It exhibits a class structure in line with mainstream industrial development in Sweden as well as elsewhere in Europe (it may even be unusually outspoken for Swedish circumstances).
- Feudal structure: a peculiar feature of modern Åtvidaberg is the legacy of a medieval baronage and the social stratification that surrounds it. Although the exception from taxation has been abolished, the impact on cultural development and on problem perception remains significant.
- Actor structure: the dynamics of power structures are exhibited through a number of groups that manoeuvre with a corporate prefix. The Baroniet Inc is, of course, one key actor; others include small-scale enterprise, merchants, party politicians, civil servants, teachers and the mass media.

- Internal centre–periphery structure: the villages within the commune exhibit a mix of industrial and agricultural traditions and operate with their own political mandate. This is exemplified in competition over commune resources, but also in the highly politicized formation of knowledge on LA21 issues.
- Historical context: with its highly interesting history, particularly with regard to industrial creativity, the local folklore interest (*hembygdsintresse*) is rich and, as a conservative factor, impacts on perceptions of LA21-related issues. This occurs naturally at the community level but also at the national level due to an early presence by Åtvidaberg top industrialists in forming early social democratic traditions in Sweden.
- Archetypal context: identity and the perception of self in Åtvidaberg are based on a few archetypal factors. One is sports (high-quality football and golf), another is the garden city concept. A third is the political issue of autonomy versus integration with nearby Linköping, one of the major cities in Sweden and an expansive high-tech centre in the country. Kinship, and the significance of having roots in the community, is viewed as important.

The background study builds on these six issues by relating them to the question of power structures. The focus was not only identity, but also the capacity to gain knowledge in order to mobilize environment and development issues.

The combined class and feudal structure leads in two directions: one is the significance of political process for empowerment, and the other the sense of belonging as a recruitment basis. The latter type of development occurs at the extreme micro-level, even within the individual.

The political power structure as represented by parliamentary political parties proved not to be the most effective analytical approach. Class analysis provides a more 'effective' point of departure, although it does not constitute any significant part of today's Swedish political language. In terms of shaping identities, which in turn form a base for political mobilization, membership of class or other social categories in the community were shown to be decisive. Thus, even at this micro-level we need to distinguish between several 'Åtvidabergs' since information flow, knowledge formation and group identities look different.

A major debate during the 1990s revolved around the proposed installation of district heating, a political process culminating in severe turmoil for the Social Democrats in Åtvidaberg. The top politicians were ousted for exercising too much political power, and combined political–civil servant alliances de facto moved purely political issues. Decision-making on this scene continues to be solidly top-down. Meanwhile, rural–urban ties within Åtvidaberg show a potential for bottom-up approaches with some grass-roots initiatives in *umland* villages. And yet, passivity seems to dominate, restoring the locality concept of the past.[15]

These seemingly contradictory processes confirm a hypothesis, namely that the dynamics behind an emerging Åtvidaberg identity are found neither within the formal political system, nor in an agrarian or historically-based tradition. Instead, the key operators of change are those individuals who move between local, regional, national and even international contexts. They can be seen as the progressive Åtvidabergians in that their activities inspire new frames of reference that are brought back to Åtvidaberg and reshape a notion of locality. In particular, small-scale enterprises have a contribution to make to the Åtvidaberg case.

Vulnerability and local changes

Such a process is not isolated to this particular case. On the contrary, it may be claimed that Sweden as a whole is turning into a stratified society that is marginalizing its rural inhabitants.

One commonplace view of Åtvidaberg has been that of a collapsed community in the wake of the dramatic decline of Facit. Our empirical evidence challenges this view; the situation today is instead of a community that has moved from a one-off disaster and from vulnerability towards diversified production.

Small-scale enterprises in Åtvidaberg are an entry point into the social and cultural principles that are part of the community and which form the basis for mobilization and identity. The success or failure of small-scale enterprises, for example, depends largely on socio-cultural patterns..

The presence or lack of practical entrepreneurship has forged Swedish development into a dual trend. Where a culture of modernization prevails, people are in control. Conversely, where development stalls, we find the vulnerable. For the municipality, this means looking beyond social services, infrastructure and the like, in search of how identity and sustainability combine.

Identities and sustainability

In the case of Åtvidaberg, this project has concluded that specialization and the emergence of a new category of LA21 experts undermine popular participation in sustainable development. The LA21 civil servant within the municipality has created significant room for political manoeuvre. A full-time LA21 information officer, whose role is to involve the general public and initiate private enterprise, was employed in February 1999. This will probably add to the impact of the earlier informal reference groups in a move to connect LA21 issues with positive public opinion.

The more dynamic networks in the community, however, are those that are not issue oriented. They are action-oriented networks (the same individuals are small-scale entrepreneurs, attend football matches, rely on private Montessori nurseries for their child care and are highly mobile nationally and internationally). While the LA21 reference group operates in a fairly conventional manner, based on representative interests and reporting back to 'a constituency', action-oriented networks are individually centred, easy going and highly creative, but also more socially fluid.

Another way of looking at community life in its efforts to combine environment and development is to highlight social categories instead of networks. Relating to nature is one example. This generates three categories: basing quality of life on wilderness, using gardening as a mode of taming nature, or denying and avoiding nature. Three icons can be used to symbolize the positions: wilderness as an individualized nature relationship; the garden city as controlled nature, and class membership as a denial of a link to nature. Each represents different relations to the environment through views on what constitutes a natural resource.

These three styles express potential differences in identity and, by implication, in ideology. The first one is a conservationist outlook, the second one emphasizes a utility dimension of nature and the last one highlights nature as anything from an aesthetic experience to a non-entity. But the styles also vary in how they relate to Swedish society as a whole. They offer one basis for the development of LA21 in Åtvidaberg. Each social category requires its own LA21 approach.

Community development combines three paths to sustainability in ecological, production and social terms. This harmonizes with the three 'life styles' (wilderness, garden city and working-class orientated). If taken in isolation, they may lead to different strategies. Seemingly sustainable goals may have destructive implications. Nevertheless, the point of departure for improved environmental knowledge has to be from experience. Included in this is not only environmental knowledge but also the need for communally-based institutions for environmental management.

It has been clear over the past decade or two that new methods for project implementation must be utilized in community development, and that a different 'package' of knowledge must be incorporated for proper problem identification along with mobilization. This is demonstrated in how the Swedish government's planning of LA21 was received; in spite of the emphasis on integrated approaches, most commune applications were technologically and single-issue oriented.

Local identity and the identity inherent in locality

This study addresses how an Åtvidaberg spirit unites and mobilizes key community strata, and how a garden city concept can be used externally to ascribe a unique profile to the municipality. Åtvidaberg is one of a few Swedish urban places modelled at the turn of the last century after the ideas of Ebenezer Howard. It had all the ingredients of a garden city concept: proximity between home and work, the green ideology in living close to nature, the small scale and the social services of an urban place. In spite of technological creativity, economic development brought the place to both fame and disaster. Early high-tech inventions generated a creative atmosphere where, among others, the Facit transnational emerged until subsumed by global-scale IT technology. Today, Åtvidaberg is a seemingly typical Swedish municipality struggling for its existence.

At the onset of the study in 1997, Åtvidaberg experienced high unemployment rates, severe deficits in the municipality budget, outmigration, a political leadership with long-term internal conflicts and a significant populist opposition. Two years later that gloomy picture has altered. Unemployment rates in 1999 ranked among the lowest in the region (eastern Gothia), a revitalization of an Åtvidaberg spirit is now commonly discussed, the municipality budget is in surplus and a consensus approach to municipality politics has brought efficiency into the management of many key administrative issues.

The hypothesis is that a base for common identity is a prime asset for the sustainability of Åtvidaberg. This identity has two sides: self-esteem, generating a sense of togetherness (the internal side), and locating Åtvidaberg in the fields of regional, national and international interaction (the external side).

Enough individuals need to agree on a common identity in order to establish a sense of belonging. Social networks (neighbourhood, kinship, organization membership such as with sports clubs and schools) must also be utilized for internal resource mobilization. This is a typical trait of small-scale communities. Today a new kind of local ideology has emerged, drawing on global as well as local networks. The Åtvidaberg spirit is a conscious concept among small-scale entrepreneurs, drawing on the north Italian positive experience from clusters of such enterprises. It was built in the early days of community development and exploited by the Facit concern, among others, and its investment in the football team (twice Swedish champions in the 1970s).

The garden city concept has been transformed from Kropotkin's anarchistic thinking into today's suburban-style posh surroundings as a means of attracting taxpayers. This image holds the potential to supply a fundamental element to a new, individually oriented LA21 identity. The garden city concept today appears in two contexts: the history writing of early industrial culture, and the municipal launch, attempting to put Åtvidaberg 'on the map'. Internal identity based on an Åtvidaberg spirit, and community relations to the *Umland* under the garden city flag, thus serve the dual purpose of maintaining coherence and attracting outside resources. This approach has great potential for mobilization and empowerment since the concept of a garden city is a powerful cultural construct that underscores locality and sustainability.

Bridging the Åtvidaberg and Linköping cases

The question of whether the Åtvidaberg community will prosper or not is answered in terms such as: 'it depends which strata in society you are talking about'. The dynamism, the coping capacities and the adaptive creativity all exist but are unevenly distributed in a local society where people perform multiple roles and develop a differentiated set of capabilities.

Therefore instead of delivering a clear-cut 'yes' or 'no', our investigation in Åtvidaberg provides a myriad of partially contradictory trends, many of which have to do with sustainability. In the Åtvidaberg case, identity formation and consolidation processes, reformulation of alliances and political goals or diversification of the small industry base all point at maturing factors for coping with supra-modernity and globalization.

LINKÖPING – BUREAUCRACY AND MODERN TECHNOLOGY[16]

As was stated earlier, Linköping is characterized by its function as a regional centre but also by its connection to modern industrial technology. Based on the strong emphasis on specialization and social and organizational differentiation, Linköping expresses, in contrast to Åtvidaberg, a more urban mentality.

After the 1998 elections, Linköping was politically managed by a coalition headed by the Social Democrats. This management regime is based on a system that draws a clear distinction between the units that order services and those that provide them. Municipal services are organized in a 'buying and selling' system. Work with LA21 was, until the 1998 elections, managed by a group of politicians in the LA21 committee (Kretslopps-kommittén). The committee members represented most, although not all, of the political parties of the municipal council. The committee's aim was 'to achieve a balance in the ecological system and [to] accept our respons-ibility for the global environment' (Johnsson, 1998).

The local organization of LA21 in Linköping[17]

The municipality's LA21 strategy has been characterized as a three-pronged fork aimed at supporting the move towards sustainability in the munici-pality itself, in the business community and among members of the public. The process was initiated by two motions to the municipal board in the spring of 1993, and the effort took off after a decision taken by the municipal council in autumn 1993.[18] In 1994, an LA21 coordinator was employed with responsibility to be the executor of the LA21 process. The official task of the committee, together with the coordinator and his staff, was to initiate and improve contacts with inhabitants in the municipality, with local industries and NGOs and with associations and rural groups. Formalizing this ambition in 1997, the eco-cycle committee decided that the Linköping municipality should open an LA21 secretariat in close connection with the municipal information office.[19]

During 1998, LA21 implementation took the form of a local action plan. Diverse projects started in the realm of the LA21 process and a number of important attempts were made to involve citizens. These included invit-ations to special LA21 meetings organized by the municipality, participation by LA21 representatives in other meetings, newsletters, a home-page on the Internet and information campaigns utilizing 'environmental days' at central city locations and public libraries. Furthermore, the municipality organized a major campaign, the Planet Caretaker Campaign, involving 'promise cards' in which citizens were encouraged to sign an agreement with themselves that involved improving their environmental behaviour.

In January 1997, the LA21 committee presented new and more detailed visions as a base for the local LA21 action plan as follows:

> *This action plan is an important step in the local process for a sustainable society that will be realized in the municipal organization as well as in the whole local society. The action plan should contain comprehensive visions for a sustainable Linköping, long-term goals and a catalogue of ideas and measures.*[20]

With the adoption of Linköping's LA21, the visionary work culminated. This does not mean, however, that the work is finished. Administrative measures were decided upon at the end of 1996 in order to ensure the continuation of the work with the integration of broad environmental problems. Local authorities have stated that to be successful, these ideas have to be spread all over the municipality.[21] One means of ensuring this is the enrolment of 200 environmental ombudsmen, represented at different work places in the municipality. Their task is to inform their colleges about environmental questions and to improve environmental work. Moreover, 700 individuals, enterprises and organizations were (at the end of 1996) involved in an LA21 network that continues to be informed about the LA21 process through a monthly newsletter.

Despite these efforts, the number of citizens participating in LA21 in the municipality has, according to both politicians and civil servants, been disappointing. The approach adopted by city authorities towards LA21 has generally been technocratic and science-based, and most of the civil servants working with LA21 have a background in the sciences.

Another stark example of this approach to sustainable development is Linköping's management of 'green' services production. A company owned by the city – the Tekniska Verken (Technical Works) – provides most of the municipal services that are connected with issues of sustainability in Linköping. The company's concept is to 'provide the inhabitants of Linköping with a clean, warm and bright existence that may also spread to other parts of Sweden'. The Tekniska Verken provides electricity, district heating, potable water and methane gas for city buses. It also takes care of waste and sewage, runs a wind generator, manages the streets and city gardens, and experiments with a major project for treating waste water in a wetlands system. The company is innovative and lucrative for the city, and runs one of the most modern waste incinerators in Sweden. The incinerator provides heat and electricity, and burns waste from as far away as Germany as well as from Linköping and other towns and cities in the region. Tekniska Verken is well thought of by politicians, civil servants and the public, and most approve of the large-scale technological approach taken by the company. However, there is a large distance between the expert-level supply system and the seemingly non-involved citizen.

The public discourse of sustainability

The Swedish political system has been characterized traditionally by people's movements (*folkrörelser*) and by high levels of participation in national and local elections. During recent years, however, the people's movements, such as workers' movements, amateur sports clubs, senior citizens, etc, have lost ground and electoral participation has decreased. In 1998, the turnout in the national elections was just over 80 per cent, which, although still unusually high by international standards, was the lowest in Sweden in over 40 years. The existence of popular movements has not, however, led to the development of a strong civil society and individual empowerment. On the contrary, the high levels of organization and central-ization of these movements may have discouraged citizen participation in many issues and led to a public dependency on political and organizational solutions to societal problems. Sweden has adopted an ambiguous approach to implementing LA21. On the one hand, public participation is welcomed, while on the other, the implementation of the initiative is seen as primarily the prerogative of central and local government.

In an effort to probe into the civic dynamics about environment and development, we created ten focus groups. Age groups ranged from 18-year-old high school students to senior citizens. Socio-economically, the groups included unemployed persons enrolled in government projects, students, workers at a local factory, air force pilots, senior technicians and managers.[22] During the focus-group interviews, the participants were given copies of two newspaper articles dealing with LA21 and were asked first to read and then to discuss them. Many felt that they did not have the knowledge necessary to understand the technical details reported. Others commented on the style of the articles and questioned the way in which they seemed to be reproducing municipal information. A common reply was that they were not the kind of items that they would bother to read and that they would move on to other items after glancing at the headlines.

Regarding the role of the information and views provided by the mass media, several members of the groups felt that this effort was mostly to provide knowledge of far-away environmental problems; it fulfilled no significant function as a provider of knowledge and attitudes concerning local environmental issues. Instead, personal experience exerted a strong influence on the intensity of the discussions. The public transport system in the city, for example, of which almost all participants had direct exper-ience, was an issue that generated strong negative feelings and animated discussion. In general, group discussions about environmental problems tended to focus on individual problems more than on societal problems, and the point of departure was often the ways in which participants had been personally affected by these issues. Three issues dominated in this respect: cars, public transport and waste treatment. It was felt that our modern life style was destructive and needed to be changed. A high school student expressed the worry that many felt, saying:

> *. . . our way of life has changed in some way . . . we destroy things for ourselves. In the future . . . you hear those horror stories about how we're all going to die out, and nature dies, and we're going to die too. It's like, it's our own future that's destroyed.*

The younger and better educated tended to talk more about global problems, the ozone layer, global warming and pollution of different kinds, but also about local and personal issues such as recycling. Although many groups brought up water, air and land pollution as problems, these issues did not generate discussions in the same ways as waste, recycling and car transport. These three issues created lively discussions in almost all groups, though in different ways. Most of the participants separated their rubbish, although not all felt that they were making a contribution to the environment by doing so. In fact, many of the groups felt that waste separation and recycling were a hoax. The disappointment on this aspect of environmental behaviour expressed in the group discussions was one of the most striking results of the focus-group interviews. Almost all the groups discussed spontaneously the negative aspects of waste separation and recycling, although waste separation was also sometimes seen as a way of soothing a bad conscience for environmental degradation. A mature student said:

> *. . . there's a common belief that if you're environmentally friendly in one way, then you've been so clever so you can give yourself a pat on the shoulder and allow yourself to behave environmentally badly in another way . . . people are crazy about separating their rubbish and sending it to be recycled, but then they get in their car to go to work, instead of taking the bus.*

A notable result of the focus-group interviews was the fact that almost none of the participants knew much about LA21, and that sustainability was only directly mentioned *once* by a participant during the 15 hours of discussions. Participants felt that they lacked sufficient and satisfactory information about local environmental issues and LA21. They felt that the information they received was too sensational and difficult to relate to their own lives. The scientific content of much of the media coverage on the environment was also a problem for many participants. They felt that the coverage did not help them to understand what they could do to improve environmental issues where they lived, and instead of functioning as a tool for empowerment, the mass media coverage of the environment seems to have led to feelings of hopelessness and disempowerment.

The most striking result of the group discussion analyses was the lack of power and ability to influence important decisions felt by almost all of the participants. Many felt themselves 'powerless' and 'depressed' regarding environmental issues, and some had 'lost confidence in the environmental way of thinking and in decisions being steered over our heads' (for instance, a military representative spoke of military decisions). The power of money was stressed in a number of groups. For example, a worker in an electronics factory said:

> *This is how it is; everybody's aware that the environment is most important really, but it's still money that rules. In the end it's them that decide. And mostly it's the things that are horrible for the environment that are cheapest as far as money's concerned.*

The groups felt strongly that this was wrong, and that 'it's true that everyone should take part in making decisions, everyone's a part of society really' (high school student). Many also felt that they should have more involvement in political decisions, and that 'it's people who should decide about their own environment and use politicians as a tool to solve things. And it's pressure from below that decides that completely' (response from the military). Many were doubtful about their ability to influence even simple things such as consumer policy. All of the groups felt that LA21 was out of their control, and felt that 'Agenda 21 is already decided. It's a group of politicians who have decided a plan for Linköping . . . it's a group of experts who have decided. They're experts in different areas and they just decide' (response from the unemployed). Many of the participants were aware that their work places were vulnerable and dependent upon forces outside of their control, such as state procurement policies and political decisions that affect levels of spending on welfare. This is perhaps not surprising considering the role that the state plays in Linköping's employment market.

The mass media discourse

The Linköping area is dominated by one newspaper, the *Östgöta Correspondenten* (ÖC). The ÖC claims to be a 'free liberal' newspaper, and is the fifth largest morning newspaper in Sweden. It is published six days a week. A recent survey conducted in the region has shown that over 50 per cent of the respondents in Linköping stated that they read articles about environmental issues in the newspapers almost every day or at least a few times a week.[23] Earlier studies have also shown that the press functions as the major source of information on local environmental issues in the area.[24]

All copies of the newspaper, including articles, letters and debate sections in all issues were analysed between 3 November 1997 and 30 May 1998. A total of 478 items were found to treat environmental issues in one way or another. Of these, only two items made the front page, and these did not deal with LA21. Only 35 items specifically mentioned LA21, although a number of items also dealt with issues that were related to LA21, without explicitly mentioning the initiative. Nine of the 20 items about LA21 in Linköping were letters sent to the newspaper by members of the public or politicians. Three of these were written by the chairman of the municipality's *Kretslopp* committee, which was formed to coordinate LA21 issues in Linköping, two by other local politicians and one by members of the board of the local chapter of the Swedish Nature Protection Society. Members of the public wrote the remaining three letters; two of them complained about cutbacks in public transport, and the third complained about the harsh pruning of trees by the local river. The media's presentation of LA21 in Linköping can therefore be considered almost as much driven by the readers as by the editorial and journalistic staff of the newspaper. Of the articles written by the staff of the newspaper, five only briefly mentioned LA21, while six dealt specifically with LA21.

The themes used in the general environmental items can be roughly organized into three main groups: equity, sustainability and destruction. The solutions proposed in the items can also be ordered into three groups: economic, political or technological. The concept of 'sustainability' was used in 32 of the items, although, interestingly, only in two of the items that specifically mentioned LA21. 'Recycling' was used in ten items, seven of which specifically mentioned LA21. A dimension of conflict, which is normally a basic ingredient of much media coverage, was utilized in very few of the articles. Many of the articles concentrated on a basic presentation of information, often in a correct but unimaginative way, especially when concerned with LA21. Exceptions to this style of presentation included catastrophe frames such as 'threat to the world's existence', which described the 'unscrupulous preying on fish, poisonous chemicals and nuclear fallout that threaten the world's oceans and therefore the very basis of life on earth'.[25] Describing the way in which 'the oceans function as enormous depots for greenhouse gases' further developed the picture. The article containing these images was, however, based on information provided by the environmental organizations Greenpeace and the World Wide Fund for Nature (WWF), and was not concerned with LA21.

Considering the emphasis placed on democracy in the LA21 incentive, it was expected that democracy would be an important aspect of these issues. Local democracy was, however, an issue in only three of the LA21 items, and all three items were letters sent by local politicians, two by the same person. Politicians and representatives of authorities were otherwise often depicted as a problem in the journalists' articles. In one of the few articles concerned directly with Linköping's LA21 plan, it was reported that 'there was a great deal of whispering and gossiping going on in the chamber by politicians who were following the debate with only one ear'.[26]

The study of the newspaper coverage shows that few of the frames or 'stories' usually used in environmental issues could be identified in the articles about LA21. Two dominating themes could, however, be recognized. The first was that the issue was treated as inherently technical and the second was that LA21 was presented as the responsibility and domain of the municipality's civil servants. The role of the municipality in LA21 was stressed in the items. The items on LA21 also presented a technological approach to environmental problems, highlighting emission limits and technical goals more than citizen participation and social equality. 'Environmental audits',[27] 'consumption of electricity per inhabitant',[28] 'both modern and old building techniques'[29] are among the terms used to describe LA21.

The relatively high level of education in Sweden facilitates understanding of environmental issues, however, the public must first notice environmental items before they can understand them, and this does not happen when the presentation of the material is excessively technical. LA21 represents an attempt to move the focus of responsibility from the political to the civil sphere in order to involve the public in the move towards sustainability. The newspaper coverage did not emphasize the role of citizens in LA21, instead, the framing of the issue stressed the role of representatives of the local municipalities and civil servants.

This is not surprising, considering how general media research has shown official agencies of the state to be one of the most cited sources of information in environmental news coverage.[30] Government departments and regional and local authorities enjoy a privileged position as definers of key issues, a position they achieve through their access to information, their position in society and their availability to journalists in need of the information that they possess. Here, the local municipality and other governmental authorities were quoted as a source of information in 43 per cent of the items, and in 30 per cent of the items other media were used as a source of information. In the 35 items that specifically mentioned LA21, the local municipality was the source of information in 16 cases. The privileged role of authorities and politicians in the mass media's communication process should not, however, as this study has shown, be taken to mean that these actors can always determine the ways in which the public receive and translate information. Despite the efforts of the authorities working with LA21, they did not succeed in catching and encouraging media attention to any great extent. The politicians and civil servants were well aware of the importance of the mass media as a source of information for the public, and many were dissatisfied with the ways in which they had managed to persuade the media to cover LA21 issues.

Contradictions in political culture

This study has shown that the Linköping public was badly informed about LA21. This does not mean that the public is uninterested in environmental problems. The public's lack of knowledge of LA21 is probably more a result of the following factors. First, although not treated comprehensively by the local press, some coverage of LA21 did exist but had gone largely unnoticed by the group participants. Second, the LA21 project itself seems to have failed to capture the public imagination. Despite the aims of official proponents that the project should be based on a 'bottom-up' ideology, the implementation of LA21 in Sweden has mainly been characterized by a 'top-down' process. Central political authorities have dictated this process and have 'encouraged' sub-central governmental authorities to initiate it on a local level.

The contradiction of Swedish political culture, with its emphasis on collective solutions to individual problems and the official view on the importance of local authorities, does not seem to have empowered the public or to have created the necessary prerequisites for public participation in LA21. It is notable that the local municipality of Linköping attempted to instigate ten round table groups of citizens, and the only one of them that failed completely was the group that should have dealt with democracy. It was not possible to initiate this group due to the total lack of public interest.

The study indicates that sentiments of powerlessness are leading to a backlash against official environmental policies. Many of the participants expressed exasperation with the ways in which the authorities concentrated on what they felt were minor problems while major problems were left unaddressed.

CONCLUSION

The 'green dimension' is important to Swedes. A sound and beautiful environment is part of the local identity: 'We are happy to live here because we have a wonderful nature in our locality.' At the same time, there are sudden eruptions of disgust over occurrences such as contamination of groundwater from individual plants or fights to restrict speed limits on the new fine road from Åtvidaberg to Linköping. Part of what is considered quality of life is to live in Åtvidaberg due to its environmental attractions. On the other hand, some individuals want to commute to Linköping with its more sophisticated labour market.

The environmental dimension is high on the ideological agenda and is almost elevated above party political controversy. Conflicting political issues concern what methods and consequences there are in relation to alternative environmental options and within which general political paradigm problems should be handled. The environmental agenda, and in broader terms, the sustainability agenda, has to conform to political reality: namely, the economy, jobs and transportation infrastructure.

Globalization and locality – space for manoeuvring

A blunt way of describing the direction in which environmental issues are moving is from the local to the global. However, local empowerment is out of pace with what really occurs. The examples are many. The local butchery in Åtvidaberg has moved to another region. Farming has been permeated by the new and grander centralization schemes. Local hydro-power production has been sold to a national company (Vattenfall), which also operates consortia on an all-Scandinavian basis. Therefore, the movement goes from the micro to the macro in terms of control.

The sensitivity of the Linköping high-tech products for air fighters (the Saab company) to both national, and increasingly to international, markets is clear. What has happened to Ericson telephones and to Volvo cars in terms of new international business partners will occur potentially to several of Linköping's major companies. Again, the control level moves upwards into a globalized world.

On the other hand the historical experience of Åtvidaberg-based industries with regard to more decentralized but also high-tech endeavours reflects an engineering tradition or an identity that was never lost irrespective of formal structures. Globalization has hit the local economy very hard and may lead to further local economic and social vulnerability. However, this same globalization has for some individuals in these small municipalities opened new ad hoc niches, enabling executives from Åtvidaberg or Linköping to move back with new ideas as they settle with their families in their old home areas.

This 'local in the global' also comprises a sustainability context. Linköping has involved itself with German commercial transactions, securing an inflow of burnable waste for the big centralized communal heating system. Åtvidaberg has (together with the regional small town of Mjölby) engaged itself in a 'missionary' activity in the Baltic States area, and more specifically in Estonia, selling know-how and 'democratic solutions' regarding sustainability challenges in the spirit of LA21. So these local spots in Sweden suddenly appear as 'centres' with a much broader geographical and political network map. The high-tech companies surrounding the University of Linköping, with its more global network of joint ventures, is another example.

This deeply changed socio-economic landscape that provides the conditions for economic prosperity also creates the means for further environmental improvements. Without reasonable economic prosperity, there are fewer possibilities for further 'green' investments.

Identity and politics

The Swedish official system has strongly adopted the LA21 framework. There is a strong top-down signal to the local level that this is an important political priority. But there is also the signal that development of LA21, the exploitation of its possibilities and its basic financing and organization are local. This is true despite substantial central-innovation project funding that supports local initiatives in the LA21 realm.

The local level has absorbed the challenge from above and has established formal measures for implementation. This should, however, be seen in the light of a local perception to move independently from national centres in a globally benign way. In addition, other regions of Sweden have recently moved to add a multicountry identity to the basic national one. This holds true for the regions in the far north as well as for Skania in the far south, with its close connection to Denmark.

Most of the municipalities (*communes*) have loyally followed central directives and have acted according to the strong political signals of what is to be considered good development, including being stimulated by potential economic bonuses to the municipality. Thus, in both our case municipalities, an elaborate system has been designed for participation, including 'forum' mechanisms, working with youngsters in schools and using the traditional system of Swedish semi-official NGOs. This is all well. However, we highlight a distinct style of top-down control in all of these efforts.

What we see is a 'professionalization' of a mandate that has become so complex and technical that it is difficult to penetrate by amateurs. What remains within the democratic frame is support in terms of groups of interested citizens running the control nodes of governmental processes geared to the preparation of local democracy, as connected to local government although to meet the same objective.

By supporting these technical operations in terms of benchmarks, professional advice from centrally positioned consultancies and new national legal goals, they have been pushed forward at the local level. Furthermore, municipalities are not just concerned with working in these fields. Most are competing strongly at the national level to be leaders in this domain.

However, mobilization at the grassroots level is more problematic. Not that it would be fair to say that people, in general, are unconcerned with environmental matters. But it is the professionals who are handling these issues on behalf of the local population and under the guidance of the upper ranks of the local political party. The language in which these issues are discussed is highly technical. Most problems are viewed through a scientific perspective and according to technical economic rationales.

The young are still not creatively involved in LA21. There is only active interest by youth for more emotive issues such as animal rights. More traditional issues such as waste handling, green electricity and good food processing are the concerns of those in progressive top-sanctioned schooling. Swedish society seems saturated by what is officially deemed 'right' behaviour. At the same time, the issues involving conflict are kept hidden. Sustainability is still off the political agenda.

The issue of identity

The issues of identity and vulnerability in Swedish society are addressed here. Identity issues seem to grow in importance in circumstances of increasing global challenges. An interesting facet of this is to what extent environmental issues are woven into the fabric of local identity. In Åtvidaberg, the identity facet seems to be even stronger than in Linköping, where other factors of economic loacalization may compete with identity.

It seems difficult at this stage to provide a prognosis about the future interplay between local identity and the future of sustainability. What can be said, however, is that the form of professional democracy we are encountering in the LA21 domain (among other fields) may, in the long term, lessen the population's willingness to undertake hardships for the sake of abstract environmental goals. Perhaps a move away from environmental and sustainability issues may reintroduce new efforts by the public at large, although in other participatory forms. This is the conclusion offered by the UK report at the end of Chapter 10.

ENDNOTES

1   Rubensson, Stefan (1998) *Miljöbalken*, Nordstedts Juridik, Stockholm
2   This legal instrument has been made a part of the new Environmental Code. Mahmoudi Said (1998) *EUs miljörätt*, Nordstedts Juridik, Stockholm

3   This paragraph is based on a background study by Johanna Alkan Olsson

4   The two communes/municipalities chosen for study in our EU-project, Linköping and Åtvidaberg, have so far not been given any project support of the kind that has been referred to above, despite efforts to call for such support on their behalf. However, the process of distribution is continuing

5   This section was contributed by Jakob Ström

6   This section is based on a special report made for the project by Geoffrey Gooch

7   In comparison, the percentage of the county's workforce employed in the town of Åtvidaberg was 2.3 per cent in 1996. Linköping statistics are taken mainly from SCB (1996) *Statistical Yearbook of Administrative Districts in Sweden 1996*, Stockholm, Statistiska centralbyrån, Statistics Sweden

8   SCB (1996) *Statistical Yearbook of Administrative Districts in Sweden 1996*, Stockholm, Statistiska Centralbyrån, Statistics Sweden

9   Kommun, L (1997) *Företagsfakta*, Linköping, Linköpings Kommun

10   The survey was conducted by Karolina Isaksson and Sofie Storbjörk at Tema, University of Linköping, during the spring of 1997. 2100 survey formulae were distributed to 700 randomly chosen inhabitants in each of the municipalities of Linköping, Valdemarsvik and Åtvidaberg. After two reminders, 1517 responses were received, ie a response of 72.2 per cent of the total distributed invitation bloc

11   Anders Hjort af Ornäs is the main author of this section

12   The main background study concerns the interplay between empowerment structures and local identities, including the local–global interface. This study forms the basis for the current chapter. These phenomena are further dealt with in two supplementary background studies concerning political process. One of them concerns the political machinery in the Åtvidaberg core centre, written by Christina Björnelf. The other one is devoted to mobilization and identity in the rural surroundings, written by Mats Lundberg. In total, three background studies were carried out.
  – Two brief background studies supplement the one on power and identity. One study concerns the main villages in the Åtvidaberg *umland*; Björsäter, Grebo, Hannäs and Falerum. The issues raised were:
    • Survival and development of the village and parish; advantages and disadvantages of living in a rural area
    • Grassroots democracy and contacts with local politicians
    • Environmental issues and engagement in Agenda 21
  – The other brief background study dealt with the local management of politics. It did so by highlighting one of the main political issues during the study period, and looked into how goals were set and political support was sought. The issues raised in that study were:
    • the policy process that lead to the formation of an energy company for district heating

- where the motor of such a policy process is located
- what political arguments were utilized

13 The main study is based on participation and interaction; ie close observation and involvement in relevant political and social processes. This method has been extended to pure action research concerning certain aspects during the course of the field study. The intention has not been to manipulate an object of study for the sake of the current project. The researcher has increasingly been part of the process, living in the community with his family. Accordingly, this study is also normative in that it seeks to contribute to concrete local goals that harmonize with the global ambition to achieve a sustainable world. Prominent among the techniques is also a rapid appraisal approach

14 This refers to the bankruptcy of a dominant industry in Åtvidaberg, described in section 1 above.

15 For a more elaborate discussion, see Björnelf (1999) and Lundberg (1999)

16 Geoffrey Gooch was the main author of this section

17 This section partly builds on a background study for the project, written by Johanna Alkan Olsson

18 Protocol from municipal council 1993-08-31. Dnr 92.0986

19 ibid, p 1

20 Protocol from the municipal council 1997-01-28, Dnr 97.0037 (translation by Alkan Olsson)

21 Kretsloppskommitténs verksamhetsplan (Work programme of the LA21 Committee), 1997

22 Each interview took about one and a half hours to conduct, and the interviews were conducted at workplaces, schools, and club meeting-rooms, places that the participants were used to through their normal daily activities. All interviews were tape recorded by an assistant and transcribed

23 Isaksson and Storbjörk (1997) *A survey of Linköping, Åtvidaberg, and Valedemarsvik*, Linköping, Tema Institute, Linköpings University

24 Gooch, G D (1996) 'Environmental Concern and the Swedish Press: a Case Study of the Effects of Newspapers Reporting Personal Experience and Social Interaction on the Public's Perception of Environmental Risk', *European Journal of Communication* 11(1) 33–55

25 ÖC 1998-01-19, p A5: Water is threatened from many directions (Vattnen hotas från många håll)

26 ÖC 1998-04-02, p B2: Fresh herbs for the politicians (Färska kryddor till politikerna)

27 ÖC 98-04-17, p B3: Households are better at sorting waste (Hushållen sorterar allt bättre).

28 ÖC 1998-03-30, p B4: Coal and Oil will be replaced (kol och olja kommer att ersättas)

29 ÖC 1998-05-19, p A13: Ecological village established in Skeda (Ekoby anläggs i Skeda)

30 Greenberg, M R and Sachsman, D B (1989) 'Network evening news coverage of environmental risk', *Risk Analysis*, 9(1) 119–126. Hansen,

A (1991) 'The Media and the Social Construction of the Environment', *Media, Culture and Society,* **13** 443–458. Nohrstedt, S A (1991) 'The Information Crisis in Sweden after Chernobyl', *Media, Culture and Society,* **13**(4) 477–97. Gooch, G D (1996) 'Environmental Concern and the Swedish Press: a Case Study of the Effects of Newspapers Reporting Personal Experience and Social Interaction on the Public's Perception of Environmental Risk', *European Journal of Communication,* **11**(1) 33–55

7 OPPORTUNISM VIA SUSTAINABILITY IN AUSTRIA

Andrea Grabher and Michael Narodoslawsky

AUSTRIAN BACKGROUND

Austrian constitutional reality has been defined since the end of World War II by three pillars:

- a federal structure of the state;
- a large role of social partners in political decisions;
- neutrality as the base of international relations.

At the moment, all three pillars of Austrian constitutional reality have come under severe pressure that may lead to a different nation in just a few years from now.

The federal structure of Austria

Austria is partitioned into nine federal provinces (*Bundesland*), which are in turn split into provincial districts (*Bezirk*), which again consist of municipalities (*Gemeinde*). A breakdown of these different entities is given in Table 7.1.

The provinces have been in place since the end of World War I. Most of them, however, have much deeper historical roots and have always enjoyed a high degree of sovereignty. The same holds true for many of the municipalities, especially the larger ones, as our case study town of Graz will show.

From all these political entities on different hierarchical levels, most are democratically legitimated. On the federal level, Austrians vote for the parliament (*Nationalrat*) every four years, which then approves the government. Austrians also directly elect the president of the republic (every six years). This is largely a ceremonial position that has, however, some important powers in times of crisis.

Table 7.1 *The administrative division of Austrian federal territory in 1996*

Federal province	Area km²	Provincial districts	Municipalities
Burgenland	3 966	9	168
Carinthia	9 533	10	131
Lower Austria	19 173	25	571
Upper Austria	11 980	18	445
Salzburg	7 154	6	119
Styria	16 388	17	543
Tyrol	12 648	9	279
Vorarlberg	2 601	4	96
Vienna	415	1	1
Austria	83 857	99	2 353

On the provincial level, the parliament (*Landtag*) is voted for directly. The *Landtag* subsequently sets up the province governments and elects the *Landeshauptmann*, the premier of the province. The *Landtag* also appoints members for the second chamber of the federal parliament, the *Bundesrat*, that has limited power in the legislative process.

On the municipal level, the assembly is voted for every four years. Depending on the province, the mayor is either elected by the assembly (*Gemeinderat*) or by direct vote through the citizens.

The only level with no democratic representation is that of the provincial districts. In the Austrian constitution, this is constructed as a solely administrative level that forms a bridge between provincial and federal lines of command and is responsible for a great part of operational administrative duties vis à vis the citizen.

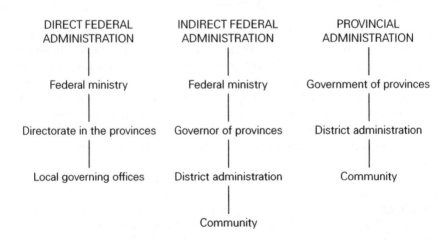

DIRECT FEDERAL ADMINISTRATION	INDIRECT FEDERAL ADMINISTRATION	PROVINCIAL ADMINISTRATION
Federal ministry	Federal ministry	Government of provinces
Directorate in the provinces	Governor of provinces	District administration
Local governing offices	District administration	Community
	Community	

Figure 7.1 *The hierarchy of administration in Austria*

Figure 7.1 shows the different lines of command defined by the Austrian constitution. One feature that is important from the point of view of implementing LA21 is that municipalities and communities are at the receiving ends of all these flows of power in Austria.

The dwindling role of social partners

Austria's politics after World War II has been characterized by a very active role by social partners. In a way, the prominent position of the social partners was meant as a safeguard against partisan politics of the type that brought dictatorship between the wars and eventually led to the demise of Austria's First Republic through the hands of national socialists. The intimate partnership between the different chambers representing workers, employees, entrepreneurs and farmers has served as a stabilizing factor of Austrian politics in times of rebuilding the nation from the material and moral damage of World War II. This partnership was the very basis of economic growth that started in the mid-1960s and served as a means to avoid the social unrest that was experienced in other European countries during the 1960s and 1970s.

During the last ten years, however, the power and problem-solving capacity of social partnerships in Austria have been in constant recess. As successful as this system has proved in distributing the fruits of growth in the past, it is becoming inadequate in organizing the share of burdens and the redistribution of social duties that accompany Austria's move towards European Monetary Union (EMU) and the general pressures of globalization. The old system of obligatory membership and the patronizing conception of the chambers has become obsolete. Recent power-structure analysis shows that institutions of social partners are no longer regarded as representative of their members and that their power has reached an all time low in public esteem. The increasing rift between institutions of social partners and their constituency, and the progressing loss of power of social partnership in the general political process, have led to a power vacuum that has yet to be filled.

Nevertheless, a new glory for social partnership might come about with the establishment of NUTS III Regions for planning by the EU, which are not congruent with Austrian provinces. Because these very often have no elected political representatives such as the Austrian districts, a committee consisting of the social partners may play an important role in future planning.

The neutrality discussion

Since 1955, when Austria became free again after ten years of occupation by allies, it pursued a policy of voluntary 'active' neutrality in the middle of a continent separated by the Iron Curtain. This neutrality allowed Austria to play the role of a bridge between East and West during turbulent decades in Europe. It also allowed Austria to maintain its historical links with the countries of central Europe, with whom it shared centuries of common culture.

With the collapse of the Soviet Union and the fall of the Iron Curtain, neutrality became an awkward position in the heart of a nearly unified continent. Austria's role as a bridge between East and West lost its importance. So too did the basis for Austria's special global positioning. Large sectors of the political spectrum in Austria are currently clamouring for Austrian accession to the North Atlantic Treaty Organization (NATO). This loss of international importance is one cause for a shift in the self-perception of Austrian citizens. They no longer perceive themselves as citizens of a country with a mission within Europe but as inhabitants of a small and increasingly vulnerable nation.

The profound change in Austria's self-perception adds a good deal to the devolution of power from the national to the supranational level. The discussion at the moment is characterized by whether or not large domains of national sovereignty should be transferred to supranational control.

Austria's economic situation is influenced strongly by foreign trade development, running parallel with the European cycle. Growth was very sluggish until late 1996. While gross domestic product (GDP) had grown by 3 per cent in 1994, the growth rates fell to 1.8 per cent in 1995 and further to 1 per cent in 1996. Starting with the fourth quarter of 1996, demand and production have begun to recover. However, this recovery is likely to be slow relative to the usual patterns of the past. Real growth amounted to 1.4 per cent in 1997 and 2.2 per cent in 1998.

The statistics in Table 7.2 give a general view on Austria's basic economic and population data.

Table 7.2 *General information on Austria*

Population		Economy	
Inhabitants	about 8 million one-fifth live in Vienna 800,000 foreigners 400,000 Austrians live abroad	Economic sectors	Today: 1.5% primary 30.5% secondary circa 68% tertiary sector in 1950 each economic sector had one-third
Religion	80% Roman Catholic (1914: 94%; 1967: 89%) 5% Protestant 10% other religious groups	Inflation rate	less than 3% (since 1994)
		Economic growth	2.4% (prognosis 1998)
Language	predominantly German 1% Croatian, Slovene, Hungarian, Czech, Gypsies	Unemployment rate	6.8% (EU calculation)
		Employees Self-employed:	nearly 3 million 13% of the working force (1992); in 1956: 32%
Area	83,855 km²	Average income	ATS 22,670 (EURO 3110)

Two topics have dominated the political discussion about Austria's membership since its accession to the EU in 1996: preparation for the EMU and enlargement of the EU.

The necessity to transform a free-spending welfare state to meet budgetary restrictions of the late 1990s has thoroughly altered the foundations of Austria's political system. A general trend of devolved power from the federal government, either upwards towards Brussels or downwards to the municipalities, can be noticed. In fields such as health, job security, education and the environment, the municipalities have to take responsibility for a great number of new tasks. The role of localities and *Bezirke* has become more and more important, especially for the sustainability transition processes. As EU policy funds 'disadvantaged regions', a new situation emerges for communities and initiative groups in order to get 'European money' for their own interests. At the moment, nearly 80 per cent of the Austrian area is registered as one or the other group of target regions of EU structural funds.

GRAZ: ECO-CITY IN TRANSITION

Graz is the capital of the province of Styria. Covering an area of 127.5 km², the city of Graz had 237,810 regular inhabitants in 1991, the year of the latest Austrian census. This number increases to about 300,000 if numerous people who live in Graz but whose regular places of residence are elsewhere, such as students, are added. There is a considerable numerical superiority of the age groups from 20 to 30 caused by the high number of students (more than 40,000 in total). The quota of foreigners in the population of Graz is about 5 per cent, most of them from the former Yugoslavia.

There was a continuous population growth until 1971. Since then the number of inhabitants has stagnated below 250,000. The reason for this is suburbanization: people move from the centre to the surroundings, causing a remarkable growth of population in the communities around Graz (about 10 per cent). Two major consequences of this process of suburbanization are:

- the rise in the ratio of old people to total city population;
- ecological problems caused by transport and daily commuting into town.

Graz is situated at the south-eastern edge of the Austrian Alps and at the boundary of the eastern hills, which causes temperature inversions in winter. The attractive surroundings of Graz (mountains in the north and lowlands with hills in the south) increase the quality of living in the city. Due to its strategic location in the south-east of the Alps, it has always been a bridge to the eastern and southern part of Europe.

The economic structure of Graz follows the typical development of medium-sized cities. The secondary sector has dramatically lost jobs in the years from 1981 to 1991 (6700 jobs were lost). Meanwhile industry and trade jobs increase continuously in the surroundings of Graz because of availability of place, fewer traffic problems (but still excellent infrastructure) and less resistance against industrial projects by local residents. In contrast, the service sector in Graz has been on the rise and compensating the job losses of the secondary sector.

However, Graz is still more or less a traditional industrial town. The enterprises are relatively large, and the ratio of industry to the total economy of Graz is one of the highest in Austria. The industrial products are mostly of a middle technological standard (such as cars). The fraction of high-tech companies is relatively low. The interlacing of different industrial branches in Graz and between Graz and its hinterland is very weak. There appears to be very little cooperation between the enterprises, and common marketing is not yet developed – though it has started within an automobile cluster.

With its high variety of universities, research centres, firms and institutions Graz can point to many years of experience in high-tech solutions in engineering. There are several 'alternative companies' in Graz that create new forms of work and try to reintegrate unemployed people within society and the labour market. These people are helped according to their social problems and are usually at the same time educated professionally.

Table 7.3 *Graz: basic economic data*

Economic sectors	Main branches	Unemployment rate	Average income
Today: 1% primary 31% secondary 68% tertiary sector	Mechanical engineering Steel construction Environmental technology Road and rail vehicle construction Banks and insurance companies	6.4% in 1996	ATS 22.276 (EURO 3065) in 1995

Environment

The location of Graz in a basin exacerbates air pollution problems. The 'smog winter of 1988–1989' initiated various attempts to improve the environmental quality of the city: GREIF (Graz Energy Information), Ökodrive, Ökoprofit, etc. The city joined the *Klimabündnis* (Climate Alliance) in 1992 and has committed itself to halve CO_2 emissions by the year 2010 compared with 1987. In this context, it should be mentioned that Graz was awarded the Climate Protection Prize by Greenpeace in 1993.

All of these activities led to the Ökostadt 2000 Programme, which is primarily a cluster of environmental measures with specific objectives and schedules. Separate plans of action are centred around relevant environmental issues and related areas. With the approval of this programme, Graz has become one of the first cities in Europe to include the objectives of

LA21 into its general planning. In September 1996 Graz won the Sustainable City Award granted by EU.

New land-register maps relating to environmental issues (online air-quality information, land-register map relating to traffic noise for the main street network, environmental information systems, Graz emissions land register) help to evaluate the ambitious environmental parameters of the programme.

A feature of Graz is the Grazer Umweltfest (environmental party). Once a year, the department of environmental affairs offers all environmental protection and nature conservation organizations the opportunity to provide information at an environmental party.

In May 1973 the *Gemeinderat* of Graz passed a resolution to establish an office for citizens' initiatives (Büro für Bürgerinitiativen) as a department of the municipality. At the time, this office was the first in Austria and has been an example for other institutions since then. The main task of this office is to link citizens' groups to politicians and the civic bureaucracy. The office has very good contacts to all levels of the civic administration.

Institutional structure and power-structure analysis

Power-structure analysis divides a region into subsystems representing different 'memberships' in regional society, where 'powerful' positions are anticipated. These are politics, administration, representatives of interest, media, societal platforms, economy, history and demographically distinctive groups. In one such analysis, 25 interviews were held with local 'players' of different typical Austrian power positions to ask, among other things, about their perceptions of power in the case study region.

Graz itself is a *Statutarstadt*, which has the same administrative duties as a district (*Bezirk*); however, it unifies these administrative duties and an elected political power structure. Figure 7.2 shows the most important interrelations between the different authorities of Graz.

The *Gemeinderat* is elected by citizens but is perceived to be 'powerless'. It is seen to hold a 'pretence of political power'. The real centres of political power rest with the *Stadtsenat* (city council) and the conference of the *Klubobmänner* (heads of the parties in the *Gemeinderat*). The *Gemeinderat* has some controlling function.

The administration, the *Magistrat*, is considered to be more powerful than the political representatives because it directly administers public money. It is closely linked to the '*Stadtrat*', who 'sells' the department's work. Departments such as the environmental agency or the department for city's development are driving forces for coordinated development and key players for sustainable development.

Every group interest has its own provincial and regional office in Graz. This should guarantee contact with their constituencies and the implementation of strategies of the respective national headquarters. The perception of their role in society is disillusioning. There is a big decrease of influence; the former important role in social partnerships is becoming less important.

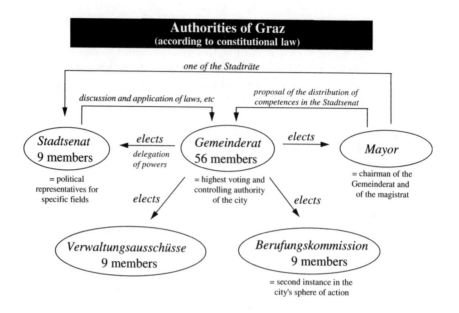

Figure 7.2 *Authorities of Graz*

In interviews, there was the common refrain that 'unions and chambers are paralyzed and no longer represent the opinion of members'.

The obvious lack of interest in local politics and problems is significant for entrepreneurs of large influential companies, especially in the city. The duty of politicians and an active administration is to build a reliable framework for the growth of economy. Though the influence of economy on regional decisions is not an obvious institutionalized one, it is related to their importance for the job market. Larger companies, in particular, influence regional political decisions indirectly. They exert systemic power: politicians are forced to anticipate economic interest and act explicitly according to the economy's desires. The larger numbers of jobs at stake, the bigger corporate influence can be.

Citizens' initiatives are often characterized as playgrounds for active citizens who want to realize their ideas. The perception is that they pursue 'fixed solutions' without discussing them in a broader context. The correlation between education and membership in initiatives is very high. Although Graz has been a forerunner in establishing institutionalized contact between citizens' initiatives and the administration, it is interesting to see that this institution is not held in high esteem by those who promote the initiatives themselves. Lately, this group have felt abused by the political power struggles that control the outcome of public referenda on controversial environmental issues.

The national NGOs on environmental issues are members of a committee for environmental municipal planning (eco-team). The influence of this group on regional life and decision-making is not strong because of the predominant influence of national offices and their objectives.

The politics of Eco-city 2000

The sustainability transition process in Graz is linked closely to the Ökostadt 2000 Programme and is driven mainly by the administration. Many municipal brochures advertise the progress. These brochures, as well as the involvement of authors in the process through different projects, are the main sources of evidence in this chapter.

The Ökostadt 2000 Programme was an attempt to provide an integrated concept to the city of Graz concerning all environmental topics, problems and framework conditions in order to achieve a new kind, and a new quality, of local environmental policy. It can be seen as an environmental guideline for the local decision-makers and it is, in fact, an enumeration of municipal authority actions and activities in the field of environmental policy. Many projects, either small- scale or large-scale, are integrated in this Ökostadt 2000 Programme.

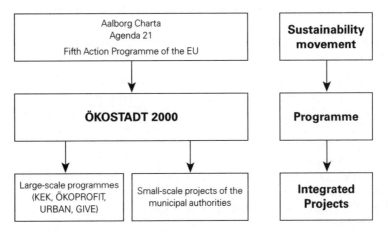

Figure 7.3 *Concept of the Ökostadt 2000 Programme*

The Ökostadt 2000 Programme consists of nine different action programmes and suggested measures in the following fields of action:

- private households;
- public facilities;
- enterprises;
- agriculture;
- water, nature and green areas;
- traffic;
- noise;
- the earth's atmosphere.

The implementation of these measures as an integrated whole depends heavily on the cooperation of all offices, authorities and civic institutions involved.

The cooperation in the planning process was worked out by the Inter-disciplinary and Inter-University Centre of Research in Graz in cooperation with the environmental department of Graz. Since the participation of concerned citizens is one of the necessary preconditions to make the programme work, several discussion and information meetings were organized, and some ideas and propositions to improve the planned programme from different internal and external institutions were inte-grated. In total, 146 institutions were invited to give their opinion on the proposed programme.

To evaluate the programme, the eco-team of Graz was founded; it included external experts, environmental groups and NGOs, citizens' initiatives and members of the local government institutions. In 1998–1999 the first evaluation of the progress of the activities, based on the quantitative goals of the programme, took place. A newly created administrative position within the municipality shows the importance of this process. These quantitative goals (called 'sustainability parameters') are defined for the following areas: air, noise, energy and climate, traffic, waste, water, soil, and green areas.

Many larger and small-scale projects are integrated within the Ökostadt 2000 Programme:

- KEK (municipal energy concept) has to be seen as a basic guideline with recommendations for the future energy policy in Graz. This includes minimizing the use of fossil fuels and the resulting pollutant and greenhouse gas emissions by increasing energy efficiency and using renewable energy sources.
- GIVE (Integrated Development of Traffic and Public Transport in Graz): the mobility of all citizens of Graz should be improved (for all means of transport) while generating as little pollution and nuisance as possible. This programme is based upon guidelines for the 'gentle mobility' of Graz. There are three principles of action: security for all road users, efficient and ecologically-friendly transportation and emphasis on the public places and parks in Graz.
- URBAN (place for people): the living conditions and the quality of the economic and ecological circumstances in an inner-city urban district should be improved. About 11,000 inhabitants live in the URBAN project area. The proportion of children and teenagers is below average, whereas the share of the over 60 age group is too high. The percentage of foreigners and the numbers of people receiving income support or unemployment benefits is remarkably high. The proportion of sub-standard flats is high, households that generate high incomes are moving away and social classes with a lower income, partly also with a low educational level, are moving in. The area has a well-developed red-light scene and a disproportionately high crime rate. The unfavour-able location in the city causes worse environmental conditions and there are few green areas.
- Three particular fields of support have been selected: district develop-ment and district renewal; job creation and intensification of the social net; participation of residents, project management and technical aid.

Besides the large-scale projects there are a lot of other municipal activities. In light of the importance of the social dimension for every sustainability movement, some of the activities mentioned in the Ökostadt 2000 Programme concern social questions. The following institutions are involved in these projects:

- social welfare office;
- health office;
- office of women's affairs and commissioner for women;
- commissioner for children;
- bureau of citizens' initiatives;
- bureau for freedom and development.

Some of these institutions are mandated by law (such as the social welfare office and the health office). Others were installed by the city council and are charged with specific actions, such as the bureau for freedom and development and the bureau of citizens' initiatives.

From this point of view, these institutions act as mediators between authorities and concerned organizations or citizens. Some of these institutions were, in fact, created to 'build a bridge' to the city council. However, in some cases, they lost their intended 'linking' image and are no longer accepted by the public.

Graz: an economic attraction

The combination of urbanity and variety, and the vibrant relationship between tradition and cultural openness, characterize the image of this second largest metropolitan area in Austria. There are high-tech and farmers' markets, ancient quarters and modern architecture. Its importance as a business centre in the south-east of Austria is demonstrated by 40 per cent of the Styrian workforce, who are employed in the central region of Graz. One-third of the Styrian industrial output is created there. Graz offers free access to EU markets, together with immediate vicinity to the countries of southern and eastern Europe and top-quality infrastructures and highly qualified labour.

The economic structure is fairly equally distributed among industrial branches and enterprises: 379 industrial plants and large manufacturing enterprises employ about 28,000 individuals; 2000 SMEs employ another 20,000.

The University of Graz and the Graz University of Technology offer a large research capacity; the Industrial Liaison Department of the TU-Graz coordinates the technology transfer so that research results are made accessible to business enterprises.

There are 130 different companies classified as Leader companies of Graz by the municipality. These companies have a certain importance nationally as well as internationally and are mostly big employers that give an economic stability to the business location of Graz. They are classified according to the main achievements as seen by the Graz economic visioning exercise.

Response strategies and scope for evolving institutional redesign

The sustainability transition process, and the claim to be an environmentally friendly town, are both pursued by local authorities with an attitude focused on planning. The general public does not even notice much about the city's internationally accepted activities. There is a clear need for better public participation. Two mainstream policies reflect the effort of the municipality to modernize Ökostadt 2000 into a full-blown sustainability programme:

• the integration of the socio-cultural dimension to fulfil the LA21 objectives;
• the support of local environmentally sound SMEs to follow the vision of an eco high-tech region, which is an important objective in economic visioning development.

In 1996 the local department of environmental protection began to summarize activities and results within the Ökostadt 2000 Programme. To achieve all the objectives of LA21, other departments were asked for their collaboration within the municipal authority.

In a first step, activities by these departments concerning sustainability issues were considered for the sustainable city award. A second step was taken during the period of programme evaluation in 1998. While environmental parameters had framed the ecological progress, social sustainability objectives were not even defined. The municipality therefore started to discuss socio-cultural parameters for the new period of the Ökostadt 2000 Programme together with the research team.

A survey of all socio-cultural activities of the different departments formed the basis for a discussion with the involved authorities. By using LA21 objectives, the activities were organized to cover different topics, such as housing, leisure, education and work, in which different types of sustainability parameters were defined.

In discussion with the authorities, it was not possible to draw a clear picture of various social activities and their overall objectives. Most social services in the city are focused on the 'acute' necessities of people. The overall objectives of these services have not been discussed. However, without clear public participation on visions and goals, it is not possible to create vital socio-cultural sustainability parameters.

The process of integrating the social dimension within Ökostadt 2000 is in its infancy. There is a need for a social consensus comparable with the results of the environmental discussion in the 1970s and 1980s. Its progress is most important for the sustainability transition process in Graz.

In an EU context, Graz and its hinterland want to become an 'ecological region'. The ability and the potential for development in this field is high because of the following factors:

- qualified research institutes;
- well-educated employees;
- political support;
- innovations in the field of pollution prevention, renewable energy resources, ecological house construction and recycling;
- multiple production and consulting enterprises in environmental fields.

At the moment, technically well-developed companies (eco high-tech) suffer from a weakness in marketing and cooperation. Few activities have been directed towards strengthening the know-how transfer between research institutes and companies (such as the industrial liaison department of Graz University of Technology).

The province of Styria and the city of Graz have agreed to finance a 'networker' in order to stimulate cooperation between different companies. The main target groups are the 'ecological service enterprises' in the fields of bio-gas, bio-mass, low-energy houses, bio-diesel/fuel oil and recycling. Enterprises within a field are connected to smaller subject-oriented networks. Often an analysis of this 'branch' is made that can show weak points within the production and management of products, such as missing stages and lack of knowledge. Before these networking activities started, many enterprises worked in a regionally confined area.

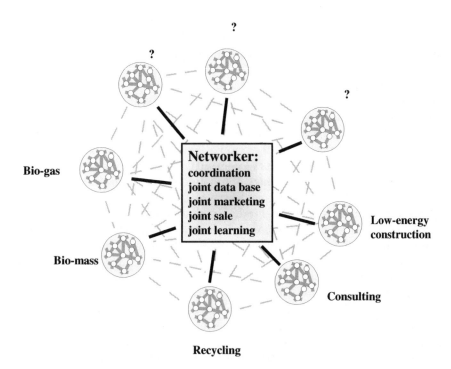

Figure 7.4 *Structure of the eco high-tech cluster*

The objectives of work within the cluster of service enterprises is to:

- offer possibilities for a joint database to initiate more communication;
- support cooperation through collection and mediation of offer and demand;
- exchange knowledge between companies through seminars or workshops;
- undertake joint public relations.

The main instruments are marketing through the Internet (such as homepages and chat rooms), and coordinating and leading the process of a joint future development.

FELDBACH: RURAL REVIVAL

Population and landscape

Feldbach is a district of 727 km^2 in the south-eastern part of Styria in Austria. It is situated close to the Slovenian and Hungarian borders. In 1997 Feldbach's population was 67,566 inhabitants. The region shows steady population development during the last 100 years despite various factors which could have led to a significant decrease:

- a remarkable decrease in the number of jobs in agriculture, which lost about one-quarter of jobs from 1981 to 1991;
- an increase in the number of commuters attracted by the nearby urban area of Graz because of a lack of regional jobs.

It is significant that the educational standard of Feldbach's population is below the Austrian average. Only 6.5 per cent of the regional population older than 15 years finished high school (the Austrian average is 13 per cent), and only 55 per cent of the population finished Austrian elementary school (the Austrian average is 43 per cent).

With regard to the percentage of foreigners, the Feldbach region at 1.1 per cent is far below the Styrian average of 2.6 per cent, although there are some sectors such as the leather industry, abattoirs or construction industry that employ more foreigners, mainly in low-quality jobs. Most of these people commute from their homes across the Hungarian border.

The job situation in the Feldbach region has been subject to significant changes during the last decade. A rather strong decrease in the primary sector, a nearly constant situation in the secondary sector and a remarkable increase in the tertiary sector are the main elements of change over the last decades. The increase in the tertiary sector is mainly caused by growth in the public sector and in trade.

The predominance of agriculture has lessened. The number of farms has decreased from 8461 in 1980 to 7944 in 1990. The tendency is generally towards larger farms; older farms in this area were relatively small, with an average area of 13.78 hectares. Today, 60 per cent of farms are in second occupation. Agricultural income in Feldbach, measured in terms of the income of one 'family worker', is higher than the Austrian agricultural average because of fertile soil, long hours of sunlight and good possibilities for farming in the valleys. The insecurity about the consequences of Agenda 2000 is high because of the pattern of small farms and because local products are coming under increasing price pressure. Maize, corn, oil seed rape, meat (pork, chicken), milk and eggs are the main products. The cultivation of fruits and wine is extensive because of the small structure of most farms.

Most of the enterprises in industry, trade, agriculture and tourism are small sized. There are many varied medium-sized enterprises in production, handicrafts and trade. Agricultural products form the basis of some companies.

The Feldbach region is characterized by a high number of commuters who are attracted primarily to the urban area of Graz. The number of daily commuters is still rising. The decrease in the number of weekly commuters might indicate a trend, namely that people with jobs in remote areas tend to move into these areas in the long run.

Table 7.4 *Feldbach: basic economic data*

Economic sectors	Main branches	Unemployment rate	Average income
Today: 27% primary 32% secondary 41% tertiary sector	Machines: structural steel Minerals: construction Food and wood products Leather, textiles	6.8% in 1995; 25.6% (youth)	ATS 18,136 (EURO 2496) in 1995 (Austrian average: EURO 3110)

Environment

An ecological footprint of 1.6 means that the area needed to service Feldbach's demand is 1.6 times higher than what is considered sustainable. This is based on the equivalent amount of natural resources to fuel the economy of Graz.

Consumption of renewable energy can be documented by one of the highest global concentrations of solar collectors and by several bio-mass district-heating systems in several municipalities.

In order to identify the relative importance of key economic activities and how they relate to ecological impact, regional material and energy flows were balanced. The timber industry and its associated activities, abattoirs, transport and traffic are all important when interpreting regional economic–ecological links.

Environmental pressures in the agricultural industry which are considered to be moving towards sustainable development include the following:

- the pig stock, which is four times too high;
- nitrogen emissions, which are three times too high (2000 tonnes of nitrogen seep into ground water annually in the region);
- the dominance of maize has decreased;
- the pesticide use in monocultures and fruit cultivation has been reduced.

Several local initiatives (such as the use of bio-mass for district heating, self-marketing of products by farmers and trade cooperations) have produced a positive response from regional farmers with regard to globalization and a willingness to reduce environmental pressures.

Institutional structures and power-structure analysis

The administrative head of a rural district (*Bezirkshauptmann*) is not elected by citizens but appointed to his office by the government of the province. The only vaguely democratic platform is the regional *Planungsbeirat*, where the mayors and representatives of interest groups meet. The political power of this platform is perceived to be very low, however, because of regional discussions within the EU, its importance has been increasing in the last few years.

A partition of the district into six sub-regions (*Kleinregionen*), depending on the planning interests of communities, was decreed by the Styrian administration some years ago. These *Kleinregionen* can be platforms of a district's interests, and their representatives (the speaker of the other mayors of the involved communities) have some influence in the district.

These two platforms – *Kleinregion* and *Planungsbeirat* – should support a political homogeneity in the rural district, though each lord mayor is still able to negotiate local problems directly with the political or administrative units of the province. The political power of mayors can be considered 'dominant' in their towns and villages. This close contact can cause a rapid change of the lord-mayor and his party's importance in small municipalities. Their activities are strongly orientated towards the interests of their citizens.

It is not easy to separate the political and administrative sub-systems at the local level because they are interwoven. The mayor is head of the local administration and in smaller communities he even does manual public work such as, for example, cleaning snow from roads. Mayors do not consider themselves to be 'real' politicians. In the rural district, politics is generally perceived to act at the 'higher hierarchical level'.

A district cannot present its interests as monolithically as the representatives of the city can. This depends on the aptitude and influence of individual mayors at the level of provincial politics.

Only a few companies in the Feldbach area are owned by multinational conglomerates; most are still owned by local entrepreneurs. There is much variety in the types of companies that exist. Economic decisions are made mostly by local economic players, though their decisions are influenced by the global economy.

Identification with locality and with local society is generally very high in Austria. Examples of this are the relative immobility of the workforce (compared with other European countries) and the very high percentages of commuters in the workforce. Many people prefer to endure the long daily journey to and from their workplace rather than to resettle. There is also a tendency to accept economic disadvantage rather than to settle in areas with higher chances of economic progress. This sense of 'belonging' is even stronger in rural areas and is clearly a dominant factor in the life-style decisions of people in the Feldbach region.

This sense of identification and 'belonging' is, however, rarely expressed at the political level. This is the case, even though the strong position of the municipality (and by extension the mayor) in the political and the social lives in the area is a direct consequence of it. Identification with locality is expressed by membership in various associations that play a dominant role in rural social life. Voluntary fire brigades, sport clubs and cultural associations (music bands, singing circles, dancing associations, etc) are the main social evidence of this local identification. Membership is strictly local (no citizens of neighbouring communities need apply), and these associations are more or less the driving factors in local–social life, organizing everything from balls to dancing parties to funerals. As a case in point, Feldbach has more voluntary fire brigades than municipalities and all are equipped with state-of-the-art engines. Any town council would certainly be hard pressed if it had to decide whether to upgrade equipment for the fire brigade or to renovate the school building.

Conversely, the important players at the municipal level include the mayor (who very often plays an important role in the fire brigade or other local associations), the leaders of the local associations, such as the fire brigade, and traditional social players in rural areas, such as the priest, the doctor and teachers.

Regional visioning process

The visioning process was undertaken in cooperation with active citizens and organized by the regional planner in cooperation with the Austrian SUDECIR research group. Results highlight the main topics of the local transition process and the goals for the future. Different procedures were used in the vision development process. The 'rules of the game' describe the 'organizational and communicational frame' and guarantee an open, transparent and evolving process with a concern for negatively affected citizens. A SWOT analysis (strengths, weaknesses, opportunities, threats) was the basis for defining the current regional situation in the fields of economy, ecology and social structure. In the next step there was room for visions, for critics and for ideas on implementation.

The visioning process (*Leitbild*) of the region began two years ago. It is subsidized by the province of Styria and the regional *Planungsbeirat* is responsible for drawing up the *Leitbild* and its implementation.

Altogether, five workshops were carried out with some 20 to 30 participants (the local and regional actors of Feldbach) within four months from March to June 1998. This *Leitbild* was complemented by the official *Leitbild*, worked out for the political representatives by the regional planner.

The results of the workshops show the top ten strengths of the region:

- landscape: cultural land;
- human resources;
- leisure possibilities and thermal springs;
- quality of agricultural products;
- cultural heritage;
- intact social structures;
- small-scale and innovative business enterprises;
- potential for 'gentle tourism'; healthy tourism;
- good price:service ratio;
- distinct seasons (spring, summer, autumn and winter).

The most obvious weaknesses turned out to be:

- lack of cooperation in many fields;
- low educational possibilities;
- weak connections to main traffic lines;
- high numbers of commuters.

These aspects clearly describe the situation and resources of the rural district.

The risks are seen in discussions on enlarging the EU: the development of traffic; large-scale projects; problems concerning financial support; European fiscal restructuring; small-scale structures; and supraregional coordination and organization.

The results of this workshop were summarized in the *Leitbild*, an economic and social development model for the region of Feldbach. It transpired that the most important influence on the region will be the enlargement of the EU, consequently the region of Feldbach has to face a reorientation in the future. The region will develop from a 'border region' into a core region of the EU. This was felt by the participants to be both an opportunity and a risk. An early orientation of the regional economy versus this expansion that will include close neighbours will become an integral part of future development.

Agricultural initiatives as 'scouts' in the sustainability development transition

Qualitative interviews are an appropriate method of reconstructing the logical organization of systems of behaviour (the individual perception) and of social interactions. This technique is based on systemic, theoretical cybernetic models of thinking and was used first in psychotherapy.

The interviews were based on the following format:

- introduction describing the basis of the interview, such as the role of the interviewer, who commissioned the project, the role of interviewees, the treatment of information, the collection of data, project results;
- questions to gain information about the interviewee's involvement in the 'game' (the topic), the partners, the business, the interviewee's motives, etc;
- questions designed to use the interviewee as an adviser for future developmental trends and visions;
- conclusion about answers to questions and other possible interviewees.

Seven interviews with representatives of different agricultural initiatives were conducted in the summer of 1997. The examined 'initiatives' represent small enterprises such as farmers' shops and bigger enterprises such as cooperating abattoirs. All the results were summarized by the interviewers and later presented and discussed with interviewees and members of the participating EU research groups, INSURED and SUDECIR, in a workshop in December 1997.

The interviews reflect the most important circumstances necessary for sustainable initiatives to grow:

- The surroundings in which sustainable initiatives evolve are family orientated and some areas work in direct cooperation with the whole family. The family is one of the most used key words in all interviews. It is defined as a source of creativity and support. In some cases, the heritage was the impulse to return 'home' (to farms) and work there again after gaining education and being employed in a very different vocation. Only a few initiatives were subsidized by public funds.
- The distinction between farming and commerce/handicrafts is beginning to disappear. In the emerging 'grey area' (there are not yet many legal regulations), new structures and innovations occur. Every initiative represented in each interview comes from either commercial or agricultural traditions.
- The strategy for each successful initiative is to produce a final product and to 'control' the production line. Companies work like switchboards between farms and customers where there is a need to organize the breeding and feeding of chickens, the quality of stables and the selling of eggs, meat and processed chicken meal of varying quality to wholesalers or, if possible, directly to customers in shops. In another example, farmers organize shops to sell their own produce but also to sell those of other farmers in order to increase the choice of products. The global trend of labour division is somewhat reversed in these locally-based sustainability initiatives. A new type of 'cooperative vertical integration' is emerging, where key players double as vendors, farmers and managers but are still part of a closely knit production network. These networks clearly exhibit different characteristics compared with 'normal' farmer–wholesaler relations. Interactions between vendors and

producers are much closer, with producers feeling directly responsible for the success of vendors. This, of course, stipulates high-quality products.

- For the most part, local people work within small structures, even though the global tendencies in agriculture and commerce lean towards larger structures. Thus the foundations are being laid for new democratic and service-orientated associations. These voluntary associations are able to inform and serve a bigger market than could any individual initiatives.

Response strategies and scope for evolving institutional redesign

Considering the situation, the sustainability transition process shows some interesting results on the district level. Institutional arrangements, such as the *'regionale Planungsbeirat'* or the *'Kleinregionen'*, become stronger because of a new 'political' feeling for more cooperation combined with a stronger awareness of local and regional problems and solutions. The three response strategies presented here support these tendencies.

The LA21 process in the region

At the local level, challenges to decision-makers come from a high administrative level and are increasing. There are many new responsibilities, such as job creation, care of the elderly and health care, and a new attitude by people who do not accept imposed plans for environmental improvements or for other specific issues. The uncontested authority of mayors is gone. In its place is public participation through LA21.

At the moment, the national level is not very active in the LA21 process, except for the production of an LA21 manual in Austrian communities and for some data collection on sustainable best practices. The province of Styria started an initiative for LA21 implementation, together with the *Gemeindebund* (a representative association of the municipalities). In the meantime, LA21 promotional meetings, which addressed district mayors, took place in half of the districts. The reaction of mayors is widely differing:

- Type 1: some mayors say that they have always organized their community as suggested by LA21. They will continue doing so, but for their own interest and not for any international agreement.
- Type 2: some mayors are interested in the suggested process but do not see the international connection as necessary.
- Type 3: other mayors are not remotely interested and try to continue the traditional way.

Although implementation of LA21 is part of the *Leitbild* of the region, mayors in Feldbach are overwhelmingly 'type 3' mayors. There is a clear rift in the region. Some progressive mayors are either following the LA21 line intuitively (without naming it) or are in the process of adopting LA21. Others are passionately opposed to any change and rely on their political strength and good connections to provincial political and administrative networks. A new facet in this development will be introduced by establishing a regional research centre that will dedicate a considerable part of its activities to speeding up LA21 processes in the region.

The foundation of a centre for locally applied research

In 1997, one of the sub-regions (*Kleinregion Feldbach*) was led by an exceptionally ambitious duo consisting of a mayor and a civil servant, founded a regional educational centre and called *Haus der Region* (house of the region) in Kornberg. Very early in the development of this centre, it was conceived that it should be complemented by an active research unit. This unit should directly address problems (in technological as well as socio-economic areas) that arise from the sustainability transition in the Feldbach region. The idea behind this centre was that research may offer interesting solutions to local problems. Since there is always a greater resistance to bringing actual problems to the attention of the proper research institutions, it is necessary to bring research closer to the region.

The centre acts in three different ways:

- It helps local enterprises, communities and individuals to find research institutions in order to solve their problems.
- It organizes cooperative, innovative projects between enterprises in the region and research institutions.
- It conducts active research on strategically important problems for the region.

One important research topic will be the implementation of LA21. The *Kornberg Institut* will act in this respect both as a consultant to regional communities and as a scientific centre for the LA21 process in the whole province of Styria.

The regional development programme

This regional development plan is a product of the regional *Planungsbeirat*, the meetings of mayors in the different *Kleinregionen*, and a regional group of active citizens who work on future development in the district. It is officially called a programme for regional sustainable development. A platform will be responsible for the coordination and implementation of the plan.

The name of the plan, Feldbach Fit for the South-East, suggests the active and positive push to prepare for the enlargement of the EU in order to develop from a 'border region' into a core region of the EU. The programme runs under the motto of the 'Volcano Country', which represents regional closeness to the natural resources caused by volcanism. Volcanism is perceived as the source of new economic benefits (hot springs) and represents energy, the harvesting of nature, human connection to nature and a holistic attitude towards life.

Suggested projects include improving educational possibilities for people and the house of the region as a centre for regional development. Other initiatives include: the preservation and cultivation of nature; the revitalization of housing; the creation of conservation areas in the volcano land; tourism and leisure attractions (biking, hiking and horse riding roads; adventure parks; signposted roads on specific topics, such as vineyards and castles); cultural attractions (which combine tourism and local handicrafts); and agriculture (concerning quality of produce and health aspects).

CONCLUSION

General statements about the sustainability transition process in the Austrian case study regions summarize the topics covered in this chapter:

- The idea that sustainability involves more than projects for a better environment is a new one for people and politicians. The process of jointly worked out regional development plans and discussions on social sustainability characterizes this new approach.
- Since Austria joined the EU, new layers of governance have appeared that are more flexible than traditional structures. It has become possible to revalue regional 'parliaments' or new partnerships for regional project funding.
- The complexity of 'sustainable decision-making' strongly supports cooperation. The solutions are increasingly found in consensus-building processes. Networks and clusters are the new organizational institutions, as indicated in Chapter 3.
- The future of the EU – Agenda 2000 – will bring about opportunities and risks.
- EU enlargement improves possibilities for Graz as a traditional bridge to the south-east, however, as an agricultural region, Feldbach will have to reorient itself. Though Austrian farm structures do not fit into the EU norms for innovative initiatives, there will be an active search for new arrangements.

On the whole, it can be said that the transition towards sustainability coincides with a thorough change in the overall structure of society in Austria, caused by its newly acquired membership in the EU and its transition from a country at the 'dividing line between east and west' to a country at the core of an even more uniting continent.

REFERENCES

Amin, A and Thrift, N (1994) 'Living in the global' in A Amin and N Thrift (eds) *Globalization, Institutions and Regional Development in Europe*, Oxford University Press, Oxford, pp1–22

Becker E (1997) *Sustainability: A Cross-Disciplinary Concept for Social Transformations*, MOST-Policy Paper, UNESCO, Paris

Bundesministerium für Umwelt (1995) *Nationaler Umweltplan, Österreich – Ein Wegweiser in die Zukunft*, BMUJF, Wien

Capra, F (1996) *Lebensnetz-Ein neues Verständnis der lebendigen Welt*, Scherz Verlag, Bern, München, Wien

Drewe, P (1967) 'Techniken zur Identifizierung lokaler Eliten', *Kölner Zeitschrift für Soziologie und Sozialpsychologie*, vol 19 Jg., pp721–734

Ecker H, Grabher A, Narodoslawsky M and Retzl, H (1998) 'Leitfaden zur Umsetzung der Local Agenda 21 in Österreich', Bundesministeriums für Umwelt, Jugend und Familie

Grabher, A, Haiböck D and Narodoslawsky M (1998) *Cooperative ways into the future: Local Agenda 21, a joint vision development process*, The Second European Social Sciences Conference, Europe: Expectations and Reality: The Challenge for the Social Science, Bratislava, Slowakia.

Grabher, A, Haiböck D and Narodoslawsky M (1998) *Institutional structures – a help in sustainable developement?*, Second International Conference of the European Society for Ecological Economics, Geneva, Switzerland

Grabher, A, Narodoslawsky, M, Krotscheck, C, Wallner, H P and Eder, P (1998), 'City Hinterland Relations – environmental responsibility as a guiding concept' in I Gabriel and M Narodoslawsky (eds) *Proceedings of the International Symposium on Regions – Cornerstones for Sustainable Development*, Austrian Network for Environmental Research, Austrian Federal Ministry of Science and Transport, Vienna, pp243–262

Grabher, A, Wallner, H P and Narodoslawsky M (1996) 'Islands of Sustainability – Seven Hypotheses', Discussion Paper, The Fifth International Conference of the Greening of Industry Network, Heidelberg, Germany

Krotscheck C (1998) 'Quantifying the interaction of human and the ecosphere: the sustainable process index as measure for co-existence' in F Müller and M Leupelt (eds) *Eco Targets, Goal Functions, and Orientors*, Springer Verlag, Berlin, pp71–85

List, D (1996) *Lokale Agenda 21 Graz: Ökostadt 2000, Globaler Konsens – Lokale Umsetzung*, Auf dem Weg zu einer lokalen Agenda 21, Wien

Melbeck, C (1987) *Kommunale Machtstruktur und community power structure – Eine vergleichende Analyse anhand einer deutschen und einer amerikanischen Gemeinde*, PhD thesis, University of Kiel, Germany

Moser F and Narodoslawsky, M (1997) *Bewußtsein in Zeit und Raum: Einblick in die Spielregeln Gottes*, Inselverlag, Graz

Narodoslawsky, M and Krotscheck, C (1998) 'Graz principles: the role of research in the sustainable regional transition' in I Gabriel and M Narodoslawsky (eds) *Proceedings of the International Symposium on Regions – Cornerstones for Sustainable Development*, Austrian Network for Environmental Research, Austrian Federal Ministry of Science and Transport, Vienna, pp281–295

Neisser H (1996) *Unsere Republik auf einen Blick – ein Nachschlagewerk über Österreich*, Ueberreuter, Vienna

Nick, R and Pelinka, A (1996) *Österreichs politische Landschaft, aktualisierte Auflage*, Haymon Verlag, Vienna

Retzl, H (1988) *Interdisziplinäre Gemeindeforschung zur Verbesserung der Partizipation der Bürger und als Grundlage für Kommunalpolitische Entscheidungen*, PhD thesis, Salzburg University, Salzburg

Retzl, H (1998) 'Expertenbericht für den österreichischen Beitrag des "ECE Workshop on encouraging local initiatives towards sustainable consumption"' *im Auftrag des Bundesministeriums für Umwelt, Jugend und Familie*

Schlippe A and Schweitzer J (1997) *Lehrbuch der systemischen Therapie und Beratung*, Vanderhoeck und Ruprecht, Göttingen

Schwendter R (1997) 'Drehpunktinstitutionen und ihre Rolle für soziale Innovationen', *Forum Sozial- und Gesundheitspolitik*, pp79–85, Salzburg

SUSTAIN (1994) 'Forschungs und Entwicklungsbedarf für den Übergang zu einer nachhaltigen Wirtschaftsweise in Österreich (Verein zur Koordination von Forschung über Nachhaltigkeit)' *im Auftrag der BBK, des BMWF und des BMUJF*, Institut für Verfahrenstechnik der Technischen Universität Graz, Graz

SUSTAIN (1994) 'Leitfaden zur Projektbeurteilung nach dem Gesichtspunkt der Nachhaltigkeit (Verein zur Koordination von Forschung über Nachhaltigkeit)' in *Auftrag des Bundesministeriums für Wissenschaft und Forschung*, Institut für Verfahrenstechnik der Technischen Universität Graz, Graz

Wallner, H P and Narodoslawsky, M (1996) 'Evolution of regional socio-economic systems towards islands of sustainability (IOS)', *Journal of Environmental Systems*, vol 24 (3), pp221–240

Weber, R (1985) *Politische Partizipation in Österreich unter besonderer Berücksichtigung der Bürgerbeteiligung in Graz*, PhD thesis, Universität Wien, Vienna

Willke, H (1997) *Supervision des Staates*, Suhrkamp, Frankfurt

Feldbach reports

Eder, P (1996) *Evaluating the ecological sustainability of regional economies*, PhD thesis, Institut für Verfahrenstechnik der Technischen Universität Graz, Graz

Graßl, H (1995) *Der ökologische Fußabdruck Feldbachs*, TUSCH-Diplomarbeit am Institut für Verfahrenstechnik, Technischen Universität Graz, Graz

Kraus, H (1998) *Naturräumliche und ökologische Grundlagen für den Bezirk Feldbach*, Diplomarbeit am Institut für Geographie der Karl-Franzens-Universität Graz, Graz

ÖKOFIT (1995) *Ökologischer Bezirk Feldbach durch integrierte Technik*, BM: WVK, BMUJF, Amt der Steiermärkischen Landesregierung, durchgeführt am Institut für Verfahrenstechnik, Technischen Universität Graz, Bericht aus der Energie- und Umweltforschung des BM: WVK, October 1995

SUDECIR (1996–1998) *Sustainable Development of European Cities and Regions – A Concept for Local Actors*, Forschungsprojekt der Europäischen Kommission DG XII/D-5, Umwelt und Klima, Contract No ENV4-CT96-0271

Steirische Statistiken (1991) *Volkszählung, Ergebnisse I*, Amt der Steiermärkischen Landesregierung, Präsidialabteilung – Referat Statistik

Graz reports

Magistrat Graz (1990) *Stadtentwicklungskonzept 1990*, Graz

Magistrat Graz (1994) *Grazer Lärmkataster*, Graz

Magistrat Graz (1994) *Statistisches Jahrbuch der Stadt Graz 1994*, Graz

Magistrat Graz (1995) *GIVE – Grazer Integrierte Verkehrsentwicklung*, Graz

Magistrat Graz (1995) *Kommunales Energiekonzept Graz – ein Konjunktur und Umweltbelebungsprogramm für Graz*, KEK Berichte Nr 2 und Nr 10, Graz

Magistrat Graz (1996) *Verzeichnis der Organe der Stadt Graz*, Graz

Magistrat Graz (o.J.) *Graz – Substanz einer Stadt*, Graz

Magistrat Graz (o.J.) *Europaregion Graz – Leitbetriebe*, Graz

Magistrat Graz (1995) *Ökostadt 2000 – On the way to Sustainable City Development in Graz, European City Award 1996*, Einreichungsunterlagen der Stadt Graz für die EU-Auszeichnung Zukunftsbeständige Stadt, Graz

Magistrat Graz (1995,1996,1997) *Jahresberichte des Grazer Büros für Frieden und Entwicklung*, Graz

Magistrat Graz (1996) *Graz: Data of a City*, Graz

TRIGON (1999) 'Netzwerk für Ökotechnik' in *Auftrag der Stadt Graz und des Landes Steiermark*, Graz

8 COMING TO TERMS WITH GLOBALIZATION IN PORTUGAL

Valdemar Rodrigues and Fátima Direitinho

INTRODUCTION

Local communities in Portugal still believe in the power and capacity of the nation state to drive major changes in the locality, namely those imposed by globalization and sustainable development. The Portuguese nation state is simultaneously trying to cope with the deleterious consequences of economic globalization while taking advantage of emerging opportunities at various levels. However, this response requires more holistic approaches. Globalization cannot be addressed solely in its economic dimensions, and sustainability cannot be regarded exclusively as an environmental challenge. Perhaps as a consequence of this bias, national strategies to overcome the impacts of a globalizing world on sustainable development and on democracy are still lacking in Portugal. The Portuguese case studies examined here are the local community of Peniche, a coastal fishing town in the western region of mainland Portugal, and Vale do Ave, a region in the north-west heavily dependent upon the textile and clothing industry. In the last decade, both fishing and textile industry activities have been affected by challenging policies towards free trade and market liberalization, as well as by policies that might be seen in the global economic context as somewhat protectionist. This is the case of the CFP. The huge investments made in Portugal in the fisheries and textile and clothing sectors between 1989 and 1998 brought significant improvements to the communities of Peniche and Vale do Ave, mostly in terms of infrastructure. However, they had low or even negative impacts in many sustainability indicators of those local communities.

NATIONAL BACKGROUND AND PERSPECTIVES

In Portugal there is a growing concern about the possible impacts of globalization on the national economy and, to a lesser extent, on domestic politics and sustainability. The faceless phenomenon becomes tangible in the lively discourses that take place on the deleterious effects of some EC policies on local economies. The basic assumption is that such policies must and do occasionally sacrifice some more marginal regions or local markets to favour opportunities for other more competitive markets or regions within the EU. This discourse emerges not exclusively at local level, and policy-makers often give to public opinion an image of struggling when involved in EC negotiation processes. Negotiations under the auspices of CAP and the recent Agenda 2000 discussions are just two examples of this. Such discourses support the idea of those who see the EC and EU as a genuine regime or system of governance that reduces or limits the authority and power of the sovereign member states (see Schmitter, 1998).

Reflections about the most frequently cited features of globalization – namely, the increasingly *stateless* character of big business, the growth of international money markets, the so-called global communications revolution and the growing importance of global institutions and international law – can be found here and there in the Portuguese literature as well as in some legal documents or plans produced in the 1990s. However, holistic views comprising globalization, sustainable development and the implications for local democracy are very rare.

Globalization, European integration and the Portuguese economy

The Portuguese economy, with a contribution in 1994 of about 1.2 per cent to the GDP of EUR15 (the 15 member states of the EU), has been stimulated by European integration, a consequence of the accession of Portugal to the European Economic Community (EEC) in 1986. The removal of protectionist barriers against the competition of imports, and preferential access to EC and European Free Trade Association (EFTA) markets, were the first challenges that the national economy had to cope with in the 1980s. Some agreements between the EC and developing world countries in force at the time of accession were detrimental to specific sectors of the national economy. The sardine canning industry, for instance, was affected adversely by the agreement established between Morocco and the EC in 1976 (Elias, 1996).

In the 1990s another threat appeared. This was the world liberalization movement, inspired in the ideas of freedom of circulation of people, goods, services and capital. At this stage Portugal was not an isolated nation, and its economic interests had to be protected in a new context. The EC, acting as a single country for its member state interests, committed itself during the Uruguay round to the progressive reduction of customs rights for fisheries' products in a period from five to ten years, beginning in July 1995. The integration of the textile sector in the rules of the World Trade Organization (WTO), with the total liberalization of market forces for 2005, is another policy that the EU must address internationally as a single voice.

Economic globalization and European governance thus transformed the Portuguese fisheries and textile industry sectors. To varying degrees, the Portuguese government has negotiated trade and compensation deals with the EU in an effort to maintain the social and economic functions of these sectors.

Coping with the challenges

The Portuguese concern about globalization and its major economic implications is rather obvious in the EC RDP (regional development plan), the framing of which was defined in the Strategic Options for the Development of the Country for the period of 1994–1999 (SODC).[1] Concerns about the environment, sustainable development and people's quality of life were expressed, but no mention was made of global problems such as AIDS or drug smuggling. The focus of attention was on economic globalization, with no explicit references being made about the possible effects of globalization at local level. In Article 4, SODC recognizes the need to strengthen the national identity by valuing the country's historical and cultural inheritance through conservation, efforts through the country's artistic and cultural creativity, and through the promotion of great events with international scope. The last was obviously a reference to Expo 1998, an event that took place in Lisbon between 22 May and 30 September 1998.

Together with these legal interpretations of the damage posed by globalization, some of which led to major institutional adjustments in central government,[2] there have been visible signs from various governmental as well as non-governmental sectors about the possible impacts of a globalizing world on democracy and on the ability of the nation state to cope with its development strategies (for example, MPAT/DPP, 1995; Ribeiro, 1995; Alves, 1998). One important non-governmental event was the symposium held in Lisbon in 1997 on Portugal in the Transition of the Millennium (PP/IHC, 1998), with quite valuable contributions on the interactions between globalization, democracy and the democratization of Europe, and national identity and sovereignty. For instance, Mário Soares, a socialist politician well known across Europe, paid attention to the increasing power of multinational corporations and the possible social conflicts that may arise with the overshadowing of nation states by such global forces beyond their control (PP/IHC, 1998,173-181). The link between democracy – in its ethical, philosophical and sociological dimensions – and the environment has also, in Portugal, relevant research contributions such as those of Soromenho Marques (Alves, 1998, pp421–428) and Sousa Santos (1994).

In the environmental policy arena, there is little of reference to globalization or its environmental consequences. The National Environmental Policy Plan (NEPP) refers to globalization just once (NEPP, 1995, p290), and only then in a totally different context. Also interesting is the difficulty with which environmental authorities address the concept of sustainable development. The state of the environment reports that have been published annually between 1987 and 1998 show systematically no references to social or economic indicators (for example, REA, 1998). Yet, in economic sectors such as agriculture and industry a more comprehensive definition of sustainable development is now evident. This included the incorporation of social problems such as employment, economic problems such as market liberalization and deregulation, and environmental problems such as water and waste management.

Sustainable development entered the Portuguese constitution after its last revision; Article 81 states:

> *[It is a priority duty of the state to] promote the increasing of social and economic well-being and the people's quality of life, in special of those more disadvantaged, in the framework of a sustainable development strategy.*

In the same year a National Council for the Environment and Sustainable Development (NCSD) was created as an independent consultative organ operating close to the ministry of the environment.[3]

The national government, through the ministry of the environment, and environmental NGOs have paid little or no heed to the LA21 process. By the end of 1996, just ten cases of LA21 in Portugal were reported by the International Council of Local Environmental Initiatives (ICLEI) (1997). In all cases, the academic influence of the Portuguese environmentalist schools was a factor. Issues such as water quality, waste-water treatment, solid wastes, air quality and noise (schools of engineers); nature conservation and biodiversity (schools of biologists); and land-use planning and management of natural landscapes and green areas (schools of architects and urbanists) formed typically the substance of such environmental agendas. The focus of LA21s on the environmental aspects of sustainable development can be, in part, explained by the lack of basic infrastructure as well as by the weak implementation of post-materialist values in Portugal, as noted elsewhere by Ribeiro and Rodrigues (1997).

Manifestations of governance in Portugal: some examples

As noted in Chapter 1, governance, understood as the overall administration of social affairs that takes place in any society, is said to be slipping away from national governments to be partially relocated at sub-national or supranational levels. That was the case, for instance, of the blockage of the 25 de Abril Bridge in Lisbon in June 1994, a protest led by truck drivers against the new tolls proposed by the government. A more recent controversy still rages over the ministry of the environment's decision to locate two hazardous waste coincineration systems in two cement plants in Portugal. The decision came to public attention in December 1998 and was contested severely by local people and authorities. Until now the government was forced to empower an independent committee of experts to supervise the operation of these plants, with a mandate that gives them the capacity to stop the process if any risk for public health is perceived. Various local movements have also been formed when decisions were taken on the location of waste disposal or waste treatment facilities, particularly sanitary landfills, in the pursuit of the governmental commitment to eliminate the sites of uncontrolled municipal waste disposal by the year 2000.

Other governance signs at sub-national level include the recent electoral boycotts and, perhaps more interesting from the political point of view, the emergence of local referendums. Electoral boycotts take place to call the attention of government and public opinion to local problems or needs. In the elections for the European parliament of 1999, there were ten cases of electoral boycotts involving 44 voting places mainly in the northern region of mainland Portugal. Two local referendums have also taken place in the last two years, and the idea of the last one, held in Tavira (a municipality in the Algarve region), was to decide about the future of an old water reservoir much loved by the local community. The community won, democratically, against the alternative of using the area for the construction of a cultural centre, as proposed by the local government.

Local authorities (municipalities) in Portugal, since being elected directly by citizens, tend to avoid central administration control in their local development strategies. An exception occurs when local projects require direct support from central government. The responsibilities of local administration have grown tremendously in recent times, especially after the 1974 revolution. Local authorities can decide on issues regarding sanitary works and services (waste management, water supply, waste-water treatment), land-use planning, municipal transports, primary and adult education, culture and sports, environmental protection and quality of life of their populations. Probably because of this, water prices to the domestic consumer can range in Portugal between 0.03 and 0.75 Euro per cubic metre, depending on the municipality. The same variations are present over water and waste treatment taxes collected by local authorities. The recently created institute for the regulation of the environmental market, as far as water and wastes are concerned, recognizes the immense difficulty of cooperation with all municipalities to achieve a greater uniformity of prices (Serra, 1999).

METHODS

The general methodological background of this study is discussed in Chapter 5. Research included the study of several written documents, a literature review, discussions and interviews with key people (mainly at the local level but also at the national level), informal contacts and local observation. Research also included the organization of a seminar, open to public participation, on sustainability, locality and democracy.

The Peniche community research study included three types of questionnaires, four FGMs and one local seminar. Fishermen, Peniche III quarter residents and women-focused questionnaires were performed at various stages. Focus-group meetings were planned as summarized in Box 8.1.

Box 8.1 *Summary of focus-group meetings held in Peniche*

FGM1

This includes fishermen from the different arts of fishing (for example, coastal, siege, long-range). This focus group included *mestres*, *contra-mestres*, the owners of fishing vessels and the general *camaradas*.[4] It included also representatives from the professional associations based in Peniche, namely AMAP.[5]

FGM2

This focus group was more related to land activities which are a subsidiary of fishing. It included the first-hand customers of fishing products (those who buy fish in the *lota* and those who buy fish directly from the fishermen),[6] the owners of small shops and restaurants located in the urban area of Peniche, and the representatives from the local fish-processing industry.

FGM3

This focus group meeting was comprised exclusively of women, namely fishermen's wives or fishermen's closer relatives of the female gender, and the group of women employed in the canning industry of Peniche.

FGM4

Young people from Peniche aged between 18 and 25 made up this group. The overall idea was closer to a visioning exercise rather than a focus-group meeting exploration. As a result, the issue of fishing was not raised during this meeting.

For Vale do Ave, because of the social complexity of the whole region, three levels of analysis were used:

- regional (the four most industrialized municipalities of Vale do Ave region);
- local (two parishes: one with urban characteristics and the other with more rural features);[7]
- company (six companies considered representative of the region's textile and clothing sector).

The questionnaires were administered in Pevidém (210 questionnaires were completed) and Barco (111 questionnaires were completed).

CASE STUDY: PENICHE

Socio-economic characteristics

Peniche is one of Portugal's smallest municipalities, with an area of 77 km² and a population of about 26,000 residents in 1991 (10,000 of which are economically active), and with an unemployment rate of 7 per cent in 1991 (INE, 1991). In the town of Peniche, about 27 per cent of the active population is dependent directly on fishing activity, whereas for about 23 per cent that dependence is indirect. Most of the infrastructure and fishing-related activities are located near the fishing harbour, the second most important in the country (DGP, 1995).

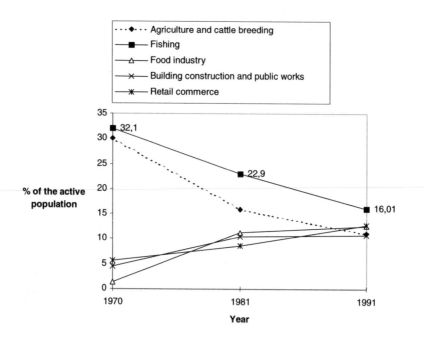

Source: Adapted from Leitão and Vicente (1993)

Figure 8.1 *The changing proportions of Peniche's active population per activity sector between 1970 and 1991*

Peniche has been historically a community dependent upon activities related to the primary sector (Calado, 1991). In terms of employment, the contributions of agriculture and fishing have declined tremendously between 1970 and 1991. In the same period, the growing importance of the local food industry and some service-related activities has been clear (see Figure 8.1). However, the importance of the fishing sector is rather more visible in terms of local gross-added value.[8]

The canning industry (sardine, tuna, chub mackerel and other fish), as well as the frozen fish industry based on long-range catches, both assume particular relevance for the local economy of the village. However, these industries sometimes had to rely on non-local markets for their fish supply. Cardoso Leal (1993) notes an increasing quantity of imported raw material to supply these companies. For instance, in 1993–1994, when the Morocco sardine prices were lower, local companies gave a clear preference to importation.

Sardine species have a very important contribution to the total quantity of fish landed in Peniche (see Figure 8.2).

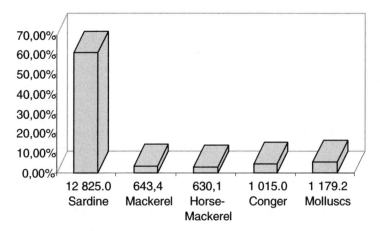

Source: DGP (1995b)

Figure 8.2 *Amounts (in percentage and in tonnes) of the major species landed in Peniche fishing harbour in 1995*

Fishing, a traditionally male preserve, employs directly about 2600 people (see Table 8.1). With regard to indirect employment, the canning industry employed about 1260 individuals in 1991 (INE, 1991).

Table 8.1 *Direct employment in the fishing sector in the community of Peniche*

Fishing method	Approximate number of employees in 1996
Siege fishing	1100
Traditional coastal fishing	1200
Long-range fishing	300
Total	2600

Source: INE (1991); Leitão and Vicente (1993)

Major actors and their role

Fisheries policy in Portugal is conducted by the central government through the Directorate General for Fisheries, a department under the Portuguese Ministry of Agriculture, Rural Development and Fisheries. This centralism is also noticeable in other scientific, technical and local administrative aspects.

The major restrictions that have been imposed by the EU to the fishing activity, namely to avoid situations of overfishing, are often justified with the argument of sustainability. However, as Ferreira (1997) points out, neither awareness nor information dissemination campaigns have been carried out in Portugal to shift public opinion towards the need to protect fisheries. One of the most important institutions at national level that pursues scientific objectives regarding sea-resources research is IPIMAR – the Portuguese Institute for Sea Research. Once more, this institute is under the control of central administration through the Portuguese State Secretariat for Fisheries.

The NEPP (NEPP, 1995) has a section concerning sea resources and identifies the main institutions committed within their management.[9] By that time a special mention was made to the former ministry of the sea (a ministry that was extinguished after the election of the new socialist government in October 1995), whose services were in the meanwhile transferred back to the Portuguese State Secretariat for Fisheries under the Portuguese Ministry of Agriculture, Rural Development and Fisheries.

Other institutions involved with sea resources management include the ministries of environment and planning and territory administration. However, these ministries are more concerned with coastal zone management than with fishing policy. Quite different is the condition of the ministry of defence which is responsible for sea and coastal surveillance, a responsibility that has been sometimes criticized for being a military instead of, as would be preferable, a civilian service (Ferreira, 1997).

From the point of view of fishing control and management, the most important institution in Portugal, as well as to Peniche at a local level, is DOCAPESCA – Portos e Lotas, SA. DOCAPESCA is a society of public capital that is responsible for managing fishing harbours and the *lotas*.[10]

At a local level, the Association for the Development of Peniche (ADEPE) is an NGO involved in several local projects and activities, as well as in the creation of a network, supported by the worldwide web, of people concerned about Peniche and its future.

Local sustainability impediments: the case of Peniche III Quarter

Peniche III is the code name for a very peculiar slum located in the heart of the urban zone of the city of Peniche, with 623 inhabitants in 1997.

For historical reasons related to the origin of an important percentage of its population, which is predominantly composed of immigrant people, and to a considerable extent of people that came in the past from other fishing communities in Portugal, Leiria district has the highest number of socially disadvantaged quarters and the highest rate of dwellings. In the beginning of the 1980s, Peniche III quarter was built in order to accommodate the residents of Fonte Boa quarter – a very degraded quarter both from urban and social points of view – as well as a community of citizens who came from the Portuguese ex-colonies in Africa and who were formerly living in deplorable conditions in the Peniche fortress.

As in Mile Cross, in Norwich, the Peniche III quarter presents many social problems that originated in the past and have been aggravated by the scarcity of family ties in the surrounding community (see Table 8.2).

Table 8.2 *Perception of the existing problems in Peniche III quarter by its resident population*

Problems in the quarter	Percentage of respondents who perceive the particular problem as . . .	
	Very important	Not very important or unimportant
Drug addiction	97	2
Poverty	92	3
Lack of cleanliness	83	7
Unemployment	80	8
Noise	75	8
Prostitution	75	10
Lack of a police force	72	21
Alcoholism	68	9
Criminality/delinquency	54	24
Lack of medical assistance	26	55

Despite the recognition of these problems, the unemployment rate in this quarter was not very pronounced (8.5 per cent of female unemployment and 2.7 per cent of male unemployment). About 12 per cent of the population in the quarter are aged 9 or less, and almost 40 per cent are under the age of 18.

Field survey results and interpretation

Fishermen in Peniche are typically aged 35 or over and are rarely educated beyond the first school. Approximately 56 per cent are employees, 20 per cent are self-employed and 16 per cent are retired but still work. Unemployment is mentioned only by 6 per cent of the respondents. Fishermen below the age of 35 have a slightly higher level of education and typically attend a job-training course, in some cases not related to fishing.

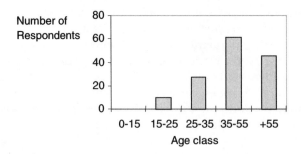

Figure 8.3 *Fishermen-oriented questionnaire: distribution of respondents per age group*

The generalized practice of informal businesses was confirmed mainly by the group of self-employed and among the retired fishermen who catch in small launches near the coastline. The catches are sold in about 40–45 per cent of cases mostly in the *lota* (70 per cent), but also to local fish buyers (17 per cent), restaurants (9 per cent) and to friends or neighbours (3 per cent).

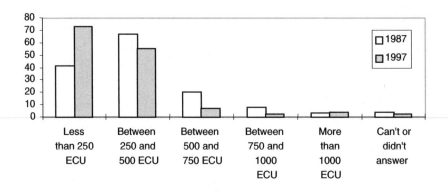

Figure 8.4 *Average monthly wages in 1987 and 1997, as estimated by the respondents*

With respect to the current wages compared with those observed in 1987, respondents believe the situation is worse than it was in 1987, except for those who claim to earn more than 1000 Euros per month.

In general, fishermen perceive fisheries policy, insofar as it means the reduction of fish catch, as a combination of several factors. About three in five recognize a combination of resource scarcity, political and commercial interests of foreign countries, and incompetence of the Portuguese government when negotiating the national interests.

When asked to rate their trust in different institutions, respondents from Peniche III quarter claim to trust their family (87 per cent), military forces

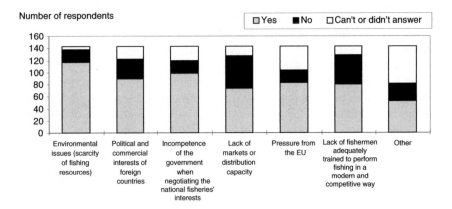

Figure 8.5 *Results for the multiple-choice question: 'Which are, in your opinion, the main reasons for constraining the activity of fishing in Portugal?'*

(48 per cent) and the Church (38 per cent) – see Figure 8.6. The high level of confidence in military forces can be explained by the image of heroes associated with military men when the government released political prisoners who were arrested in Peniche's prison at the time of the 25 de Abril Democratic Revolution in 1974.

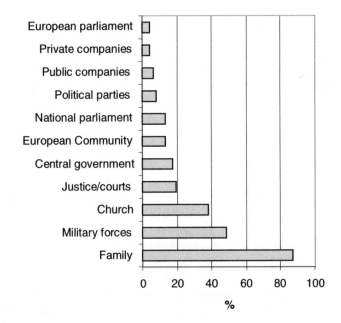

Figure 8.6 *Percentage of respondents from Peniche III quarter who place trust in the corresponding institution*

The percentage of those who would rather live elsewhere for reasons of individual development or for the sake of their children's future is quite high in Peniche III quarter (54 per cent), particularly among women. About half would like to leave the quarter but not the locality of Peniche.

In Peniche III, 20 per cent of the respondents aged 18 and over are affiliated with a political party. Local government elections are participated in the most regularly (54 per cent), followed by national government elections (51 per cent), presidential elections (50 per cent) and the elections for the European parliament (46 per cent). The majority of the respondents do not know the name of the parish councillor (82 per cent) or the mayor's name (57 per cent). However, about 70 per cent stated correctly the name of the Portuguese prime minister.

When asked about the institutions people felt were more able to solve local problems and thus to influence the future of the locality, local government came in first place (47 per cent), followed by central government and the police force (both with 35 per cent of responses).

About 70 per cent of the fishermen currently active in Peniche have *quinhão* as a major complement to their livelihoods.[11] This *quinhão* is hard to estimate either from quantitative or from qualitative viewpoints. Despite this uncertainty, a rough estimate of 40 kilogrammes per working day per fisherman is suggested.

With respect to the technological and human resources allocated, the sea-based fishing sector in Peniche shows some important shortages, many of them a result of an inadequate training policy for fisheries. There are vessels with advanced (and often expensive) technologies installed aboard, but without people prepared to use them. On the other hand, the governmental training programmes such as FORPESCAS, at least in the first years of their existence, were found to be at cross purposes with the needs of the sector. Perhaps the most important outcome of this evidence is the proportion of FORPESCAS trainees who are actually working in the sector: for each group of 15 trainees who have successfully finished their courses, only about 2 are today active in the fishing sector.

About 80 per cent of the *camaradas* earn less than the minimum national salary.[12, 13] An estimate of the fishermen's average incomes is 200 Euro per month, plus the *quinhão* – the latter obtained each time the vessel is landed.

Three-quarters of the women currently working in the local fish-processing industry are in a situation of precarious employment (short-term contracts, usually for a period of six months and sometimes even for shorter periods). Of these women, about 70 per cent obtain extra sources of income in the local informal economy.

The forced reduction of the local fishing fleet is not accepted by the participants of the focus groups. The official justification of a reduction of 50–60 per cent is considered too high, even fictitious. The participants point out strategies involving associations with Moroccan shipowners, one of which consists of making an association with a Moroccan fishing unit, which is a legal procedure. The Portuguese shipowner gets the compensation for the abatement of the vessel while, at the same time, he sells it to a third country. This third country, in his turn, is licensed to fish in the Portuguese coastal waters, so that fishing effort remains more or less the same. Moral of the story: some shipowners get rich rapidly, the fishing pressure is not considerably changed (contrarily to the objectives of the CFP) and the EU pays the bill.

Because of the low salaries obtained aboard of a fishing vessel, some fishermen prefer to run their own fishing businesses, many of which are illegal. This procedure – locally referred to as *candonga* – has grown significantly in the last decade and also involves retired people who fish in small launches near the coast. These illegal catches go directly to the black market. The owners of local restaurants used to worry about the scarcity of fresh fish at good prices in the market. Today this is not the case – it is much easier to get fresh fish at suitable prices. The proportion of legal to non-legal fish bought by the local restaurants is revealing: an estimated ratio of about 1:15.

As far as recreational fishing is concerned, there is also agreement on its predominantly illegal character. For each group of three boats fishing legally, there are 20 operating illegally. This recreational fishing takes place during the weekends, and an estimated catch of about two tonnes per week was suggested during the focus-group meetings. The destination of this product is mostly the local black market.

In order to assure a minimum income for fishermen, CFP created a new figure – locally referred to as *report*. In practice, *report* means the storage, for a period of six months, of sea products that show no quality (and hence get no price) to be sold in the *lota* and that are therefore used for other purposes, for instance as bait. In this process, the state pays about two-thirds of the price (for example, 0.2 Euro per kilogramme) and the fish buyer (who must have an adequate storehouse for fish products) pays the remaining third (for example, 0.1 Euro per kilogramme).[14] *Report* buyers should maintain the fish stored for a minimum period of six months, but in practice this rarely happens; some sell the fish at higher prices soon after purchase.

With regard to the most important fish species landed in Peniche – the sardine – all the participants in the focus-group meetings agreed on the necessity of a proper close season to protect the breeding period of November to January. This view confirms, to a certain extent, the ecological conscientiousness of Peniche fishermen.

By interpreting the descriptions of the participants, as far as fish catch is concerned, one can conclude that the population of the sardine is undergoing a process of overexploitation (catch at a level exceeding the maximum sustainable carrying capacity of the fish). This conclusion is based on the general agreement on the behaviour of the sardine catch during the more adequate periods of the year. Such unsustainable behaviour is illustrated in Figure 8.7.

A great percentage of the young people in Peniche think of fishing activities as the last alternative for a job. The low salaries, the uncertainty of payments and the hard working conditions have pushed them away from the sector or created in them an image of something to avoid. However, if alternative employment were available, many young people would prefer

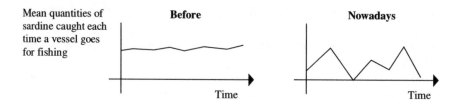

Mean quantities of sardine caught each time a vessel goes for fishing

Figure 8.7 *Illustration of the evolution of sardine catches 15–20 years ago (left) and today (right)*

to stay in Peniche. Despite a considerable social identity with the locality, young people have a great deal of political apathy: only about 35 per cent vote regularly in any elections.

Drug addiction and smuggling are two problems constantly raised as paramount for the community of Peniche, in particular by women and the young who refer to several cases of disrupted families. There is a general agreement about the worsening of drug problems in recent years and a feeling that the local community is becoming more vulnerable in this respect. Another factor relates to drug smuggling, since a considerable percentage of the drugs crossing Portuguese borders are said to be landed in Peniche seashores.

CASE STUDY: VALE DO AVE

Socio-economic characteristics of the community

Vale do Ave is a region in the north-west of Portugal with about 460,000 inhabitants in 1991 (about 5 per cent of the country's total population), spread over an area representing 1.4 per cent of the national territory and including six municipalities: Fafe, Guimarães, Póvoa de Lanhoso, Vieira do Minho, Vila Nova de Famalicão and Santo Tirso.

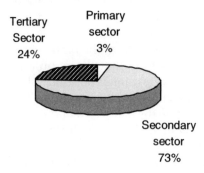

Source: INE (1991)

Figure 8.8 *Distribution of employment per economic sector in the four most industrialized municipalities of Vale do Ave (Guimarães, Vila Nova de Famalicão, Santo Tirso and Fafe)*

From the mid-1960s onwards, a specific model was adopted in Vale do Ave, based on specialization in a single industry sector – textiles and clothing – and involving nearly 70 per cent of the active population dispersed throughout the region. Natural water resources were used to wash away industrial effluents. This industrial growth has taken place within the existing urban structure, made up of small, separate neighbourhoods. This creates a three-sided working structure or, in other words, the combination of industrial and agricultural activities near the home.

The arrangement facilitates the taking on of various activities by the economically active members of the population, creating worker–farmers who, together with their families, carry out subsistence farming on tiny farming plots next to their homes, adjacent to their small textile workshops.

The development of Vale do Ave is notable, first, for the premature integration within the workforce of many young people who have not completed their compulsory schooling and, second, by the integration of a large female workforce within an unskilled industrial process (see Figure 8.9). Third, it is notable for the competitiveness of the textile industry, resulting from the devaluation of the Portuguese currency which has been suppressed by the integration of the Escudo within the EMU. Fourth, it is distinguished by an antiquated industrial-production system with inadequate cash flow for capital investment, reinforcing the image of an industry dependent upon outside technology at all levels, from design to international marketing.[15]

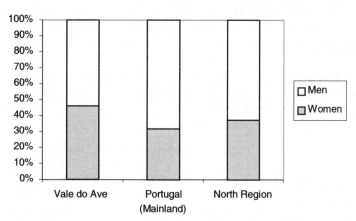

Source: INE (1991)

Figure 8.9 *Comparison between the percentages of men and women employed in the secondary sector in Vale do Ave, mainland Portugal, and in the north region (1991)*

Employment in Vale do Ave is to a great extent associated with the secondary sector, while the unemployment rate in the region is relatively low when compared with the national average (3.9 per cent in 1991 against 4.8 per cent).

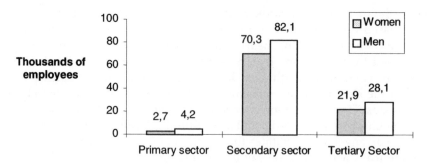

Source: INE (1991)

Figure 8.10 *Employment distribution per economic sector and gender in the four most industrialized municipalities of Vale do Ave (Vila Nova de Famalicão, Santo Tirso, Fafe and Guimarães)*

The extent of the informal economy in the region is considerable, involving sub-contracting in the productive process. These are illegal company structures, most of them family sized, which often operate in annexes of private homes and that have been recurrently underestimated or simply ignored by the official statistics (Fernandes, 1994). Asymmetries are also noticeable in the Vale do Ave region, where municipalities show a strong industrial tradition while others maintain predominant rural features and reduced industrial activity (such as Póvoa de Lanhoso and Vieira do Minho). The two parishes selected for field survey aimed at reflecting this rural–urban duality (see Table 8.3).

Table 8.3 *Some indicators of Barco and Pevidém, the two parishes of Guimarães municipality where questionnaires were put to the local population*

Indicator	Parish	
	Barco (Rural)	Pevidém/S. Jorge de Selho (Urban)
Area (hectares)	295	533
Population in 1991	1449	4163
Illiteracy rate (%)/unemployment rate (%)	10.2/3.0	8.3/3.4
Active population working in the secondary sector (%), mainly in textile and clothing companies	75.6	76.0

In Barco, farming takes place in local swamps, with small kitchen gardens for family subsistence and some cattle breeding, namely milk cows. The natives from Barco used to work in the most industrialized parishes in the neighbourhood, and agriculture often represents a complement to their normal labour activity. The traditional granite houses in Barco, together with recent residences, normally belong to local emigrants.

Pevidém is the most industrialized parish of Guimarães municipality, often called the heart of the textile industry in Vale do Ave. Its population is predominantly comprised of factory workers. Some of the oldest and biggest industrial units of Vale do Ave are located in Pevidém. This is the case with companies such as Coelima and Lameirinho, which were particularly affected by the market's liberalization of textiles. From the urban point of view, Pevidém shows a great mix of industrial and residential areas – a result of past uncontrolled growth without proper planning.

Major actors and their role

Local authorities, individually or collectively within the Association of Vale do Ave Municipalities (AMAVE), are the main political structures of the Vale do Ave region. However, the existing local NGOs are nearly always reliant upon local authorities both in terms of financial support and logistic assistance (Sol do Ave, 1994)

Central government is represented by its various local departments, of which the Coordination Commission of North Region (CCRN) and the Directorate General for Regional Development (DGDR) have been of major importance in implementing the strategies and priorities concerning regional development in the last decade.[16]

The Vale do Ave region is disputed by two major regional centres of political influence: Braga and Oporto. With the exception of Santo Tirso, all the other municipalities of Vale do Ave are territorially and, to a certain extent, administratively under the influence of Braga, the district to which they belong. The industry lobbies reflect this dichotomy: they are organized around two major industry organizations, one with its head office in Braga (AIMinho) and the other in Oporto (AIPortuense).

Another important regional institution is the NGO Sol do Ave.[17] Created in 1993 and with head office in Guimarães, its main priorities are related to social problems: employment, professional training, social exclusion and social solidarity. This very active NGO has been involved in several initiatives such as the elaboration of regional studies and the implementation of economic, social and culturally related programmes and projects. In one of its projects, it made an inventory of Vale do Ave NGOs (49 in total), identifying a number of different organizations (Sol do Ave, 1994).

With regard to the textile and clothing industry associations, APTV, the Portuguese Association of Textiles and Clothing is worthy of mention.[18] Together with some institutional proximity to AIPortuenese, APTV represents the strongest lobby of the textile and clothing sector in Portugal. Although of national scope, SINDETEX and FESETE are currently the most active labour organizations in Vale do Ave.

Local sustainability impediments: questions and examples

Invisible poverty?
In a study carried out in March–April 1995 by the Portuguese Ministry for Qualification and Employment (MQE, 1995), it was found that 18.3 per

cent of the families in mainland Portugal were living below the poverty line and 4.8 per cent were living in conditions of extreme poverty. In Braga, the district that includes the municipalities of Guimarães, Vila Nova de Famalicão and Fafe, those percentages are significantly lower: 16.3 and 4.1 per cent. When compared in terms of macro-regional distribution, situations of poverty and extreme poverty are significantly less frequent in the littoral north, to which Vale do Ave belongs, than in the other *quadrants* of the Portuguese territory (see Figure 8.11).

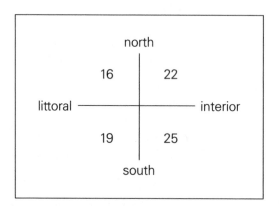

Source: Adapted from MQE (1995)

Figure 8.11 *Distribution of people living below the poverty line (values in per cent) according to the major two axes of development (north–south and interior–littoral)*

In comparison with other regions of Portugal where existing poverty is often visible, in the municipalities of Vale do Ave there is some sort of *invisible poverty*, in the sense that the most usual signs of it are not discernible.[19] This is an important distinguishing feature of a region where family ties seem to play a major role in mitigating the most immediate consequences of poverty. Yet, there is a generalized agreement (see Melo, 1997; Marinho, 1997; Guedes, 1997) that supports the idea that such family ties do contribute to a very significant reduction of a community's social vulnerability.

Wage discrimination between men and women
In Portugal, the disparity between male and female wages in the secondary sector of the economy is quite significant (see Figure 8.12), particularly in the textile and clothing industries.

Drug addiction and child labour
Drug addiction is a common problem in Portugal, particularly in the more economically disadvantaged zones, either rural or urban. There is also a

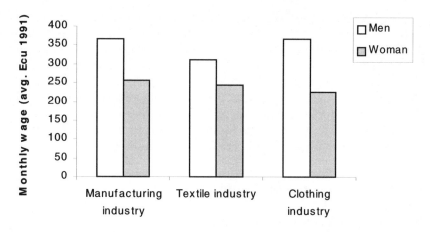

Source: Lima et al (1992)

Figure 8.12 *Average monthly wages (in approximate ecu, 1991) obtained by men and women working in the Portuguese industrial sectors of textiles, clothing and manufacturing*

generalized perception of a significant submerged market of child labour, whether as a persistent or a growing phenomenon, in the municipalities of Vale do Ave – primarily in Guimarães.

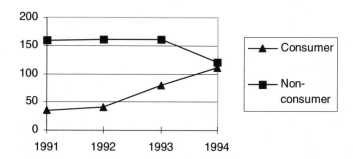

Source: Guimarães Prison, cited in CMG (1997)

Figure 8.13 *Number of prisoners who are said to be consumers or non-consumers of drugs at the moment of entrance to Guimarães Prison (1991–1994)*

Analysis of the data available from the various institutions dealing with drug addiction in the region has shown that such problems can probably be related to the unemployment generated in the textile sector in the last few years. Between 1991 and 1994, the number of prisoners who are said to be consumers or non-consumers of drugs at the moment of entrance to Guimarães Prison has increased substantially (see Figure 8.13).

With respect to child labour, in 1996 the Portuguese government created an interministerial working group for action against child labour.[20] Eleven municipalities in the territory were selected for the implementation of a pilot scheme, four of them from Vale do Ave (Guimarães, Vila Nova de Famalicão, Santo Tirso and Fafe). In a recent study based on school abandonment between 1993 and 1997, covering about 15,000 children, about 600 cases of child labour were detected just in the region of Guimarães. According to Freitas (1997) this figure would have been much higher if cases of informal domestic child labour were included.

Field survey results and interpretation

Barco and Pevidém local communities

In Barco and Pevidém, people in general feel insecure about local problems such as drug addiction, criminality and the insufficiency of security forces. These feelings have intensified during the last decade, with almost all respondents agreeing that delinquency has increased substantially in the last ten years. Unemployment is seen as a very important problem by two-thirds of the respondents, but poverty is referred to as problematic in only 28 per cent of cases. This confirms the existence of supplementary sources of income, especially among the group of employees. The institutions seen as responsible for existing problems are the city council, the central government and the police force in 79, 72 and 55 per cent of the cases respectively. The EU is mentioned only by 5 per cent of the respondents.

Table 8.4 *Perception of existing problems in the communities of Barca and Pevidém*

Problems in the community	Percentage of respondents who perceive the particular problem	
	Barco	Pevidém
Drug addiction	89	97
Unemployment	62	66
Criminality/delinquency	57	73
Poverty	24	34
Child labour	5	40

About 30 per cent of the respondents have found a new job in the last five years. Most of them are young people, aged 35 or less, and about 80 per cent are women. The percentage of those adults who would rather live elsewhere for reasons of individual development or for the sake of their children's future is substantially lower in Barco and Pevidém than in Peniche. In Pevidém, about 17 per cent of the respondents say that would like to leave the locality, a value that in Barco decreases to just 11 per cent.

In Barco and Pevidém, 9 per cent of the respondents aged over 18 are affiliated with a political party, a percentage that is about half of that observed in Peniche. However, participation in elections is comparatively higher. Approximately 80 per cent of respondents vote regularly in local government and general and presidential elections. The elections to the European parliament are less popular (70 per cent). Most of the respondents know the name of the parish councillor (76 per cent), the mayor's name (90 per cent) as well as the name of the Portuguese prime minister (93 per cent).

When asked about the institutions felt most able to solve local problems and thus to influence future development for the locality, local government comes in first place, followed by the police force and central government (44 per cent). The EU is mentioned only in 4 per cent of cases (see Figure 8.14).

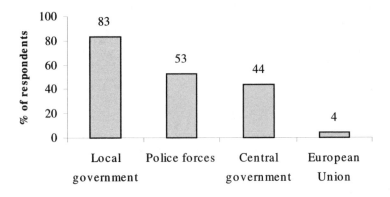

Figure 8.14 *Institutions felt more capable of initiating changes in the local communities of Barca and Pevidém*

Family ties play an important role in alleviating the social vulnerability of communities, which is interpreted through a general feeling of security. In the community of Barco, where family ties are more expressive, community vulnerability is perceived as significantly lower than that observed in the urban community of Pevidém. Another factor that supports this difference is economic. In Barco, people – especially the elderly – can all the more readily complement their subsistence needs with incomes obtained in agriculture.

The average household income of a family where both members of the couple work in the textile or clothing sector is not compatible with a sustainable lifestyle. Complementary activities are nearly always necessary, despite the number of working hours per week. In Pevidém, such activities can include domestic work, babysitting/child care and temporary sewing work.

The growing unemployment in Vale do Ave in the last years has motivated an increase in criminality and marginality in the region. When asked about their perception of the evolution of criminality and delinquency

Table 8.5 *Characteristics and some performance indicators of representative textile and clothing companies in Vale do Ave*

Indicator \ Company name:	ASA – Agostinho da Silva Areias e Filhos, Lda.	Lameirinho – Têxteis, S.A.	Freitas e Fernandes, S.A.	Bordarte, Lda.	Lasa and Filasa – Group Armando da Silva Antunes, S.A.	AMERTRADE – Têxteis, Lda.
Number of employees	430	1150	120	33	400	16
Turnover/sales (Mecu)	14.5	59	13.35	0,75	47.5	3
Main products	Sheets	Sheets	Knitted goods	Embroidery for sheets and underwear	Face towels, bathing gowns and baby clothes	Fashion trade
Preferential markets	US; Portugal; other EU member states	UK; US; Germany	Portugal	Portugal	EU; US; Canada; South Africa; Poland; ex-Soviet Union	France; Germany
Percentage of the production which is subcontracted to other firms or small companies	≈ 70%	?	?	< 50%	> 50%	100%
Approach to environmental issues	Production cost	Production cost/ competitive factor	Production cost	Production cost	Production cost	Production cost

Indicator	ASA – Agostinho da Silva Areias e Filhos, Lda.	Lameirinho – Têxteis, S.A.	Freitas e Fernandes, S.A.	Bordarte, Lda.	Lasa and Filasa – Group Armando da Silva Antunes, S.A.	AMERTRADE – Têxteis, Lda.
Technology development level†	C	A/B	C	C	A/B	B
ISO 9000*	nc-k	c	nc-k	nc-k	nc-k	nc-k
ISO 14000*	nc-k	nc-k	nc-i	nc-i	nc-i	nc-i
EMAS*	nc-k	nc-k	nc-i	nc-i	nc-i	nc-i
VAs**	No	Yes	No	No	No	No
How does the company face the future***	–	o	o	o	o	o

Note:
* nc: not certified
c: certified
k: knows the existence of certification scheme
i: ignores the existence of certification scheme
** Has the company adhered to any voluntary agreement (VA) for complying with the environmental legislation?
** o: optimistically
p: pessimistically
n: neutrally
† A: best available technologies; B: recent technologies; C: obsolete technologies

in the last decade, 98 per cent of the respondents from Barco and Pevidém, and particularly the latter, agreed that there was a very significant increase.

Child labour is limited to companies that produce low added-value products and is located mainly in small units belonging to the submerged economy. For cultural or economic reasons, parents often encourage child labour. This is much more visible in rural communities, such as Barco.

Neither local NGOs nor local governments represent the informational channels through which social, economic and environmental problems in Vale do Ave come to public attention. Friends, relatives and especially the media (mainly television) are the pathways of information dissemination at the local level. For the most part, people are poorly informed about the major threats that affect local economy and particularly the textile and clothing sectors.

Local textile and clothing companies

In the period between 1985 and 1994, the textile and clothing sector was subject to great adjustment in Portugal. Despite the proclaimed crisis, more than 2000 new companies were created. Machado (1996) refers to an increase of about 55 per cent in almost every segment, with an exception to spinning and wood-weaving units. The breakdown of several big companies with more than 500 employees took place simultaneously with the creation of small units, mainly in the clothing sector, with less than 20 employees. The collapsed companies, most of them capital intensive, have been replaced gradually by labour-intensive units, often operating in sub-contracting regimes. Most of these small units make extensive use of the female workforce, and informally sub-contract seamstresses who frequently work at their homes without declaring their activity to the tax authorities.

In Guimarães there is an intriguing coexistence of companies, some of which are winning the challenges of globalization while others are not and therefore are collapsing. The success stories involve strategies such as management decentralization, the increase of management profession-alism, quality certification, training and the increase of production-added value.

With regard to companies' environmental concerns, about 80 per cent understand environmental investments simply as additional production costs, while the remaining 20 per cent see some advantage in terms of a firm's image (Amorim, 1997). Despite this, environmental management systems (EMS) such as EMAS and ISO 14001 are viewed by many comp-anies as valuable for improving their image and for ensuring close links to their customers, insurance and finance institutions, and to the authorities. A still very limited number of companies understand the implementation of EMS in terms of competitive advantage in the medium to long term and see image improvement as linked to environmental pressure groups and the public in general (see Table 8.5). Overall, however, environmental management does not figure prominently at board level for the larger companies.

The globalization of the textile and clothing markets has not induced the diversification of regional economy as foreseen, for instance, by specific programmes such as SINDAVE. For example, during 1993 and during the first three trimesters of 1994, 53 per cent of the new manufacturing companies created in the region of Vale do Ave still belonged to the textiles and clothing sector (INE, 1995).

CONCLUSION

Holistic views or strategies to overcome the impacts of a globalizing world on sustainable development and on democracy are still lacking in Portugal, notably at a local level. Globalization is addressed mainly in its economic dimensions, and sustainable development is regarded primarily as a technical and scientific challenge that can be surmounted through the application of environmental knowledge and technology. The links between the environment and the economy seem to influence the latter more than the former towards critical aspects of sustainability. Portuguese environmental institutions have paid little or no attention to issues such as globalization, governance, LA21, or to the social and economic aspects of sustainable development.

Challenges are perceived by local communities as being driven by national and sub-national forces or interests, although in Peniche this perception extends to the influence of the CFP. Local communities tend to see the existing problems of the locality as a consequence of the deficient performance of national and local governments and corresponding policies. At the same time, trust in local governments depends on what institutions are believed to drive major changes in the locality. Confidence in the ability of the nation state to control the future of the locality is still high for both case studies, however, in Vale do Ave interest groups are more self-willed and feel, in general, more secure about their own capabilities to initiate the changes.

The existence of fish for the informal fisheries sector in Peniche is comparable with the availability of sub-contracted work for the informal textile sector of Vale do Ave. Comparable problems for the successful shift to sustainability can also be foreseen. Community subsistence can be assured and social problems can be alleviated in the short term. But in the medium to long term the share of a common resource with free access for everyone might pose a serious risk to sustainability. The key is a degree of local knowledge and informal regulatory arrangements that will control local overfishing.

The huge investments made in Portugal in the fisheries and textile and clothing sectors during the first and second community support frameworks (about 520 Mecu for the fishing sector and about 1100 Mecu for the productive sector of Vale do Ave, with emphasis on the textile and clothing industry) had few positive effects in terms of promoting local sustainability in Peniche and Vale do Ave (see Table 8.6).[21]

In Vale do Ave, the most visible positive effects relate to infrastructure building (for example, roads and basic sanitation facilities) and the growing number of people who are self-employed or engage in small businesses. Drug addiction and the feeling of insecurity are the most visible negative effects of this period. But even the investments in environmental infrastructure – about 75 Mecu in the framework of SIDVA – brought no significant improvements to the environmental quality of the Ave River, into which most textile and clothing companies from Vale do Ave discharge their effluents.

In Peniche, visible improvements have occurred regarding the increasing number of people who are self-employed or are engaged in small businesses. Community self-reliance, individual welfare and a feeling of

Table 8.6 *Evolution between 1989 and 1998 of several local sustainability indicators in Peniche and Vale do Ave (Barca and Pevidém)*

Peniche	Vale do Ave	Indicator
⤴	⤴	People's access to information
⤵	⇔	Active individual membership/political activity of the population
⇓	⤵	Community self-reliance/independence from resources under external control
⇔	⤴	Creativity and production of creative products
⇓	⇓	Individual welfare (independence from narcotics)
⇔	⇔	Effectiveness of political and social participation
⤴	⇔	Income equity (men/women)
⤴	⤴	Adaptability/adjustment of social norms and administration
⤵	⇔	Affection for the locality
⤴	⇑	Per-capita service capacity (roads, schools, hospitals, basic sanitation)
⇓	⇓	Personal happiness/feeling of security
⇔	⇔	Unpolluted water, beaches and soils
⇓	⇔	Renewable resource regeneration/ renewable resource-use rate
⤴	⇔	Self-organizing activities (NGOs)
⇓	⤵	Employment rate
⇑	⇑	Workforce self-employed or engaged in small business/adaptability of human resources

Note:
⇑⇓   manifest increase or decrease of the indicator, supported by objective evidence
⤴⤵: likely increase or decrease of the indicator, sometimes lacking the support of objective evidence
⇔:   imperceptible or non-relevant change in the indicator during the period of analysis

Source: Several indicators are adapted from Bossel (1999). The qualitative appraisal of indicators was based on local surveys

security, sustainability of marine resources (mainly due to the growing number of informal catches near the coast) and the falling employment rate are the sustainability indicators in Peniche that show manifest signs of decline between 1989 and 1998.

One could say that in Vale do Ave, the global balance for the period of 1989–1998 is almost neutral, while in Peniche it is chiefly negative. The winners in the process were, in the meanwhile, mainly those who had the knowledge or the opportunity to access available funds, subsidies and projects. Disempowerment in both case studies has proved to be nearly always related to the lack of education and professional skills of the active population. The disempowered are ultimately the losers in the adjustment to globalization. It is this systematic failure to reduce vulnerability that is the most notable characteristic of the formal Portuguese response. What is evident in both case studies, however, are the unexamined support networks for the more marginalized children, women, unemployed and displaced fisherman; these networks help them to escape from the gaze of tax collectors and to survive through the lively mix of social–local networks. In this adjustment to survival, sustainability hardly figures at any level of governance.

REFERENCES

General

Alves, J L (1998) *Proceedings of the International Symposium on Ethics and the Future of Democracy*, Lisbon, European Capital of Culture, 25–28 May 1994, João Lopes Alves (ed), Colibri/Portuguese Society of Philosophy

Bossel, H (1999) *Indicators for Sustainable Development: Theory, method, applications – a report to the Balaton Group*, International Institution for Sustainable Development, Winnipeg

ICLEI (1997) *Local Agenda 21 Survey: a study of responses by local authorities and their national and international associations to Agenda 21*, UCLEI and UNDPCSD, Freiburg

MPAT/DPP (1995) *Cenários da evolução estrutural da economia portuguesa 1995–2015*, Departamento de Prospectiva e Planeamento do Ministério do Planeamento e da Administração do Território, Lisboa

MQE (1995) *Caracterização da pobreza em Portugal: Março/Abril 1995*, Departamento de Estatística do Ministério para a Qualificação e Emprego, Lisboa

NEPP (1995) *Plano nacional de política de ambiente*, 2 vols, Ministério do Ambiente e Recursos Naturais (ed), Lisboa

PP/IHC (1998) *Proceedings of the Symposium Portugal na Transição do Milénio*, Lisbon, 5–8 November 1997, Pavilhão de Portugal, EXPO 1998 and Instituto de História Contemporânea (Org), Fim de Século (ed), Lisbon

REA (1998) *Relatório do Estado do Ambiente em Portugal: 1998*, Direcção-Geral do Ambiente (ed), Lisboa

Ribeiro, J F (1995) *Portugal 2010: Posição no Espaço Europeu, Uma Reflexão Prospectiva*, Departamento de Prospectiva e Planeamento do Ministério do Planeamento e da Administração do Território, J Félix Ribeiro (Coord.), Lisboa

Ribeiro, T and Rodrigues, V J (1997) 'Institutional adjustments to sustainable development strategies: the Portuguese case', *Environmental Politics*, vol 6 (1), pp110–130

Serra, P (1999) *Regulação do mercado de gestão dos resíduos*, Communication presented at the workshop 'A componente socio-ecnonómica na gestão de resíduos', Lisbon, 8–9 April, organized by the Portuguese Association of Environmental Engineers

Sousa Santos, B (1994) *Pela mão de Alice: o social e o político na pós modernidade*, Edições Afrontamento (6th edition), Lisboa

Schmitter, P C (1998) 'The practice of "democracy in Europe" and the prospects for the "democratization of Europe"', in *Proceedings of the Symposium Portugal na Transição do Milénio*: Fim de Século (ed), Lisbon, pp133–149

Peniche Case Study

Calado, M (1991) *Peniche na história e na lenda*, Mariano Calado (4th edition), Peniche

Cardoso Leal, M M (1993) 'Costs and benefits of European integration for the Portuguese fishing industry' in *Portugal and EC Membership Evaluated*, José da Silva Lopes (ed), Pinter Publishers, London, pp51–56

DGP (1995) *Recursos da pesca: série estatística*, vol 9A–B, Ministério da Agricultura, do Desenvolvimento Rural e das Pescas, Direcção-Geral das Pescas Lisboa, Lisboa

Elias, L N (1996) *A política comum de pescas: o caso português*, MSc thesis, Technical University of Lisbon (ISEG), Lisbon

Ferreira, M (1997) 'E quando os pescadores acabarem?' in *Jornal O Público*, 2 February 1997, vol 10 (Marina Ferreira was the former directorate-general for fisheries)

INE (1991) *Censos 91: Resultados definitivos*, Instituto Nacional de Estatística (INE), Lisboa

Leitão, A J and Vicente, D N (1994) *Plano de desenvolvimento local de Peniche*, Trabalho realizado no âmbito da Iniciativa Comunitária Pesca, Câmara Municipal de Peniche

Vale do Ave Case Study

Amorim, T (1997) Personal communication (Teresa Amorim is a senior researcher at the Department of Textile Engineering of the University of Minho at Guimarães)

Fernandes, A (1994) 'The Case of the Ave Valley, Portugal' in *Proceedings of the Seminar on Training, Employment and Competitiveness in the European Textile/ Clothing Industry: the Role of Local Authorities*, Terrassa (Spain) ACTE (ed), pp109–123

Freitas, M (1997) Personal communication (Manuela Freitas is the head of the social division of Guimarães municipality)

Guedes, G (1997) Personal communication (G Guedes is currently finishing her PhD thesis on the competitiveness of textile and clothing companies of Vale do Ave; she is at the University of Minho at Guimarães)

INE (1995) *Estudos relativos ao espaço OID Ave*, Direcção Regional do Norte do Instituto Nacional de Estatística

Lima, M P, Nicolau, I and Salavisa, I (1992) *Le secteur textile au Portugal: l'employ et les enjeux de la restructuration*, rapport realisé pour l'Observatoire Européen de l'Employ (CCE-DGV), DINAMIA (ed), Lisbonne

Melo, C (1997) Personal communication (Conceição Melo is an architect at the Planning Services Department of Santo Tirso Municipality)

Machado, C P (1996) 'Estudo sobre a indústria têxtil da região do Minho: Relatório de Progresso' in *Proceed. do Congresso da Indústria da Região do Minho*, Associação Industrial do Minho, Braga

Marinho, L (1997) Personal communication (Leonor Marinho is a social assistant at the Social Division of Fafe Municipality)

Quaternaire (1995) *Plano Estratégico do Sistema Urbano do Vale do Ave*, Quaternaire Portugal, Recursos Humanos, Junho

Sol do Ave (1994) *O tecido associativo do Vale do Ave: algumas pistas de análise. Sol do Ave*, Associação para o Desenvolvimento Integrado do Vale do Ave and Quaternaire Portugal, Recursos Humanos, S A (ed), Guimarães

ENDNOTES

1   Law nr 69/93, of 24 September 1993
2   This is notably the case of the creation of a new institution, the Ministry of Economy, whose responsibilities include the evaluation and follow-up of the costs and opportunities for the Portuguese economy of globalization and of European construction (Art 2, d), Decree-Law 222/96 of November 25)
3   Decree-Law nr 221/97, of 20 August 1997
4   The classification is not clear cut; for instance a *mestre* (the skipper) can, himself, be the ship owner, and can even participate actively in fishing, the latter meaning that he is a *camarada*
5   AMAP is the mutual association of Peniche's shipowners
6   These first buyers of fishing products have predominantly a regional action
7   In Portugal, parishes (*freguesias*) represent the lower level of the territory's administrative divisions
8   In 1991, the relative weight of the fishing sector in the local gross-added value (GAV) was about 50 per cent, compared with 22 per cent and 17 per cent of the corresponding contributions of agriculture and industry respectively (Leitão and Vicente, 1993)
9   NEPP was approved in the Council of Ministers by the former social-democrat government. Until now, the new socialist government (elected in October 1995) has ignored the document, and no mention has been made on the intention of binding it to the current environmental policy
10   *Lota* is the Portuguese designation for the official place where the fish is taxed and sold
11   *Quinhão* is the part of the vessel's catch that is shared between the crew after landing
12   *Camarada* is the term used to designate the fishing colleagues, regardless of their skipper, professional position or charge
13   This minimum salary is updated annually by the governmental employment policy and with the agreement (when it exists) of the major labour unions. In 1997 its value was about 280 ecu per month

14 The state grants to the buyer a payment term of four months without reckoning interest

15 In fact, most production was, and in part still is, merely the result of sub-contracting due to the lack of own labels and markets

16 Both under the Ministry of Infrastructure, Planning and Territory Administration

17 Association for the Integrated Development of Vale do Ave

18 APTV comprised in 1996 about 2500 companies from the textile and clothing sector

19 In the densely populated urban areas of Lisbon, Oporto and Setúbal the signs of poverty are clearly discernible

20 Grupo de Trabalho Interministerial para o Combate ao Trabalho Infantil – Joint diploma of the Ministry of Justice, Ministry of Education, MQE and MSSS (published in the Diary of the Republic, 2nd Series, nr 79, of April 2, 1996)

21 The values of the second CSF are based on investment estimates (DGP, 1995b; Quaternaire, 1995)

9 LOCAL IDENTITY AND SURVIVAL IN GREECE

Maria Kousis and Eugenia Petropoulou[1]

GREEK POLITICAL CULTURE AND SUSTAINABILITY

The end of the dictatorial regime in the 1970s was followed by socialist party dominance and the consolidation of democracies (Gunther et al, 1995). Students of Greek political culture have pointed to patron–client relationships in political exchanges, a powerless publich sphere, and the intense political struggles for the sake of the party (eg Demertzis, 1990, p74). During the past decade, however, the importance of these traits has decreased. Trends towards a more prevalent civil society, especially as regards the environment, are evident (eg Kousis, 1999). Simultaneously, a break from traditional views and practices, as well as signs of a political crisis have also been documented for the same period (eg Dodos et al, 1990).

However, trends towards more privacy and mass political participation are evident. Simultaneously, a break from traditional views and practices as well as signs of a political crisis have been documented in the past decade (see Dodos et al, 1990).

The development of state policies in Greece up to the 1990s has taken place within a highly concentrated administrative system, autocratic control and supervision of local governments by appointed prefectors (until very recently), as well as persistent power-dependent relations systems via party mechanisms and state job provisions. Rules are redefined each time a new party comes to power, with little continuity in state actions (Kioukias, 1991, p25). Prefectors and local governments become the recipients of central-state policy choices because their domains and resources are deliberately limited (Getimis, 1993, p114). Since 1994 prefectors have been locally elected, taking all powers that belonged to the state prefector except those concerning national defence, justice, finance and foreign affairs. Although this may lead to better coordination between local agencies, locally elected governments may be more vulnerable to local interests, and hence should pay careful attention to the protection of the local environment (Fousekis and Lekakis, 1998). Local problems may still be solved through the mediation of a locally elected member of the parliament, but in a controlling and dependency-creating manner.

Greek local governments are of two types: at the high level there are communities and municipalities (OTAs) and at the lower level, prefectures or counties (NAs). Successive socialist governments attempted to ameliorate the situation by enacting legislation that would alleviate administrative dependency, for example, by making the prefects answerable to judicial authority (Kioukias, 1991, p302). Through the reforms, they tried to create a balance between state and civil society. Critics argued that the prefector (a government appointee until 1994) assumed even greater control of the distribution of economic resources to municipalities and communes. Although the socialist party initially increased state subsidies, grants and transfers to local governments, it did so for political purposes: that is, to promote its own policies. In essence, however, local municipalities and communes were still fully dependent on state resources (Kioukias, 1991, p316). Given the socialist party changes, local municipal and communal authorities used the ruling political parties as channels of access. Municipal authorities who were tied to opposition parties challenged socialist state policies, while the socialist party-affiliated local governments functioned as dominant party outposts (Kioukias, 1991, p329).

Some transfer of power over environmental matters has gradually been granted to municipalities and communities, with regard to the construction of water supply and waste management projects, provision of recreation sites, land management and physical planning. Nevertheless, these initiatives are all financially dependent on the central government. Administrative economic and other difficulties that may arise in the smaller communities may be handled through the 1995 establishment of regional councils comprised of OTA representatives with common geographical, economic and cultural characteristics (Fousekis and Lekakis, 1998).

Concerning LA21 initiatives, the Central Union of Local Governments in Greece (KEDKE) organized a conference in 1994 on European environmental policy and the role of local authorities. The planned actions included, among others, energy and waste management, health matters and local democracy via the establishment of mechanisms to enhance citizen–local government communications (Fousekis and Lekakis, 1998).

Environment-related power and responsibilities of key actors

Greece does not have a unique national plan for the environment. However, one of its ministries, the Greek Environment, Physical Planning and Public Works (YPEHODE), has coordinated environmental policies aiming towards merging ecology and sustainable development, environmental protection, international collaboration, as well as NGO cooperation (Fousekis and Lekakis, 1998). Serious obstacles to implementing sustainable development strategies in Greece remain. These include sectoral fragmentation and the absence of effective interministerial coordination (Fousekis and Lekakis, 1998; Pridham et al, 1995; Kokkosis, 1993, p378). Environmental protection has not been a primary concern of national policies. Consequently, pollution-control instruments were introduced only when environmental crises occurred, while 'green' taxation continues to be a threat to the secondary sector (Fousekis and Lekakis, 1998).

Greek trade unions are financially dependent on the state. More importantly, a singular, non-competitive hierarchical structure and the selection of single interlocutors to represent labour interests have been imposed by the state and by legal statute. Furthermore, since the 1980s, the state has unofficially intervened in the unions to regulate matters of leadership and representation (Kioukias, 1991, p134). Although some interest has been shown by the unions in sustainable development, workers seem to be concerned more about their economic futures (Fousekis and Lekakis, 1998).

The organizational structure of farmers' cooperatives has remained unitary and singular under the Panhellenic Confederation of Unions of Agricultural Cooperatives (PASEGES). Some of the most important developments since the 1980s have been the pervasive penetration of political parties within the non-governmental sector due to the effect of the socialist laws, the increasing financial reliance on the state, and an institutional dependence where the partisan origin of the leaderships made them more conformist in carrying out party orders for political control (Kioukias, 1991, pp214–223).

In Greece, social care (child care, care of the elderly, family services and care of the disabled) is not properly organized. Social welfare is the least developed aspect of the nation's social policy. Social care is characterized by a centralized bureaucracy, lack of planning, non-specialized personnel, lack of a contemporary, coherent institutional frame, and the establishment and reproduction of inequalities. At the local level, the absence of a legal duty to allow local interventions from within a community, and the development of an OTA social policy, decrease even further the coordinated opportunities for social care (Stasinopoulou, 1993, pp272–298).

Limited steps taken by businesses to ameliorate their deteriorative impacts on the environment points to a very slow but gradual change towards environmental protection. In the 1990s the Association of Greek Industrialists organized information centres and meetings and established the Hellenic Etairia for Recycling with other groups. There does seem to be an interest in eco-labelling and in eco-management and audit schemes (Fousekis and Lekakis, 1998). Growth versus the environment has materialized into a sensitive issue when high-tech environmental protection projects have been slowed down by the manufacturing sector since they otherwise threaten its competitiveness (Kousis, 1994, p133).

Various types of citizens' groups were created in the post-dictatorial period. Some were politically based, such as the neighbourhood councils. Others, however, arose more autonomously as a reaction to the problems with which they were faced. 'Cultural' *(politistikoi)* clubs or associations have been formed in urban as well as in rural communities with the aim of preserving local traditions. 'Movement' *(kinisi)* groups were organized to address problems relating to the environment. Struggle committees (*epitropes agona*) were set up to make more specific claims regarding a local problem, usually relating to environment and development.

THE CASE STUDIES

The two case studies were selected on the basis of criteria where EU competitiveness policies create serious problems of adjustment, and EU policies aiming for a more sustainable use of local resources also lead to local hardships. One case (Aegaleo) has more urban and secondary-sector characteristics, while the other (Timbaki) has more rural and primary-sector attributes. Aegaleo meets the 'competitiveness which leads to hardships' criteria, while Timbaki meets the 'EU initiatives for sustainable use of resources which leads to hardships' criteria. In addition, Aegaleo represents a working-class urban community in Athens with higher than the national average unemployment levels, economic problems in some industrial units, an influx of former Soviet Union Pontian repatriates, and a declining local textile industry. Timbaki is representative of a family-based agricultural community experiencing the differential impacts of the CAP. Most medium and small family units are forced to survive in the wake of a reduction in subsidies and the low final prices they receive for their produce. Thus, both areas have recently experienced economic and social hardships due to changes in EU policies, while for a longer time both have been feeling the impacts of environmental deterioration in their everyday lives.

The data set includes primary and secondary data from various studies, reports, dissertations, the printed media and statistical information, as well as interviews with informants who are either residents of the communities, municipality affiliates, key informants, key actors, representatives of target groups and focus-group interviews. Content analysis of the local newspaper of Aegaleo, the *Aigaleo*, was applied to code the issues under study since 1985.

Timbaki: a greenhouse-dependent community

Greek agricultural policy in the 1974–1981 period supported agricultural incomes, following European overproduction trends. Price protection by the government had created a false picture of prosperity for the Greek farmer. Fossil fuels were used to increase the production of food energy and agriculture was industrialized. However, the intensification of production led to an increase in production costs due to the structural deficiency in Greek agricultural development. In an effort to confront the problem of the increasing cost of production, and with state support mechanisms, the farmers responded by intensifying even more, aiming for a further increase in production.

The period from 1981 towards the end of the decade was characterized by the continuation of state expenditures for support, while subsidies were maintained at the highest possible level leading again to increases in production costs and subsequent overproduction. It has been recognized that the CAP policy needs substantial reform (see Daoutopoulos, Pyrovetsi and Petropoulou, forthcoming). Each member state was required to construct and implement plans to bring about a decrease in food production by employing environmental safety schemes. Successive reforms of the CAP resulted in the reduction of community support, both at the level of inputs and at the level of product prices (Louloudis and Maraveyias, 1997).

During the past few years, the local economy of Timbaki has experienced major adverse economic and social changes because of the entry to CAP. By the early 1990s, state subsidies for industrial inputs were reduced to zero, while successive reforms of the CAP led to the reduction of EC support, both at the level of inputs and at the level of product prices (Gardner, 1997). Thus, the farmers of Timbaki have seen a rapid increase in the prices of inputs while the product prices have remained stable or even declined. Therefore, during the past 15 years, the implementation of EU and national agricultural policy in Greece is now clearly demonstrated in Timbaki's crisis as well as in local perceptions and practices.

Key actors' perceptions of the agricultural crisis and possible solutions

According to the head of the agro-industrial cooperative in Timbaki, the main problem confronting agriculture today lies in the disposition of agricultural products. Competition with other Southern and developing world countries on Mediterranean products makes the marketing of traditional Greek products such as olive oil, tomatoes, cucumbers, etc) difficult in the EU and even domestically, due to their high prices. In order to deal with these problems, Timbaki's farmers try to produce crops as early as possible and of the best quality. This is achieved by choosing the right hybrid, together with frequent applications of synthetic fertilizers and pesticides. A vicious circle is therefore formed. The reduction in profit and income (found for 88 per cent of the targeted sample) has forced farmers to improve quality and increase production of the commercially produced vegetables through the use of expensive synthetic fertilizers and pesticides. Increases in the cost of production and overproduction have inevitably followed.

Farmer's initiatives towards environment-friendly methods of cultivation have begun but remain limited. Many young locals expressed the desire to adopt these methods but explained that these must be supported technically and economically by the state or the EU in order to succeed. Lacking the appropriate know-how, as well as not being able to take the economic risks, deters many locals from chosing a more sustainable form of agriculture.

Different local actors propose various solutions to the current crisis and perceive these transformations as the emerging point in the sustainability transition. For one representative of the municipality sustainability can be achieved through the transformation of the economic sector, via the development of alternative forms of tourism, such as yachting and agro-tourism. For the agro-industrial cooperative as well for the agricultural cooperative, the sustainability transition is seen in terms of a proper organization of 'producer groups' whose aim is efficient planning and the search for new markets to dispose of high-quality and 'less chemically infected' local produce. For the local media representative, many young people reject the idyllic picture offered by modernization, which is accompanied by anxiety and urban patterns of consumerism. For the informal institution of the Association for the Protection of the Environment in Kokkinos Pyrgos, the transition to sustainability is reflected in the current local concern for the environment and any future actions to be taken in collaboration with other local institutions (such as the municipality or informal institutions).

Local perceptions of the sustainability transition

In the pre-war and initial post-war period, there were two different social categories in Timbaki. The first and higher strata belonged to those households that ensured their survival through small family farming. The second category, belonged to those households that were able as farm workers on others farms to supplement the income from their own small agricultural holdings. The social distinction was clear and led to the development of defined relationships based on needs.

The economic development of the wider region of Iraklion, and particularly the introduction of the first greenhouses in Timbaki in the late 1960s, led to the disappearance of the second social category. Today, it is very rare to find locals who work as farm labourers. Due to its economic development, Timbaki has attracted waves of people living in the nearby mountainous areas, as well as foreign immigrants (Albanians, Bulgarians, etc) who usually work on a seasonal basis as farm labourers.

This rapid social transformation allowed the development of complex family strategies of social and economic ascent. Within a period of approximately three decades, the social sphere was radically transformed. Social stratification is now based upon a variety of criteria.[2] Property size remains dominant. However, the intensive cultivation of greenhouse vegetables has significantly broken the link between agricultural income and the size of landholdings. At the same time, new criteria have been added, such as incomes from non-agricultural activities (trade, services, construction, the public sector, packing, shipping, transporting, etc) as well as incomes from the many jobs held by young farmers and educated people.

The result of all these rearrangements was the creation of a large middle class of indigenous residents of Timbaki (constituting about 60 per cent of the overall population), made up of the owners of middle-sized holdings. These residents enjoy a relatively high standard of living, usually owning one to two houses and cars, and face problems of survival only after two or three consecutive years of bad yields.

The rich families of the village consist of little more than 100 people who own large-sized holdings. A bigger number is constituted by those migrants who returned to Timbaki after the introduction of the first greenhouses. They share an entrepreneurial spirit and are considered to be the most valuable farmers. Their main motivation is expansion. Small or subsistence farmers represent 15 to 20 per cent of the total population and produce mainly for self-consumption, while 10 per cent of them have outstanding loans. They face severe problems of survival if even for a single year their yields are not satisfactory.

The consumption patterns and beliefs of middle-class families show a significant degree of homogeneity. They work hard, but enjoy leisure pursuits during summer which is an 'unproductive' period for greenhouses. They adopt urban consumption patterns only when they have ensured the economic viability of their farms.

Furthermore, residents of Timbaki compare and contrast the current quality of their lives with that of their parents. Thus, new patterns of consumption (80.3 per cent), the changing diet (81.8 per cent), opportunities for women (86.4 per cent), and education (81.8 per cent) and better services, such as public nurseries, constitute areas of positive development. In addition, residents mention entertainment, labour-saving appliances, car ownership, reduction in animal fat and other new life patterns. Simult-aneously, however, the educational requirements of children have increased dramatically. To this end most parents feel they have to help their children with their schoolwork, either directly or simply through supervision, and they invest a good deal of time and effort in their socialization and education. Only 22.6 per cent of the 66-person sample (targeted at those on low incomes) wanted their children to become farmers. The other 75.8 per cent were strongly negative, an attitude which must inevitably be passed on to their children. This reveals a certain contradiction in the role of the rural household regarding the reproduction of family farms. The intense desire of most young rural children to escape agricultural work, and by both parents to enable them to do so, is most likely the consequence of the difficulties they themselves face from the agricultural occupation – such as international competition, overproduction and disposition.

Since the majority of the respondents represent age groups of people over 30, we invited a group of six young people aged 22 to 25 to talk about the positive and negative aspects of their lives in Timbaki and their perceptions of their village's future. Their conversation developed around issues regarding the effects of the rapid social and economic transformations that took place in the village during the last two decades.

The young reject the 'idyllic' picture offered by their elders concerning the existing quality of life. They emphasize that life today is dominated by anxiety and insecurity because of the rapid changes that have taken place over the last three decades. They see locals adopting urban consumerism patterns due to intensive competition between families. This has, they believe, contributed to a reduction in the quality of human relations, which in turn undermines the social life of the community. Most admit that competition between families increases anxiety, creates tensions in human relationships and hinders the development of a sense of communal sharing. Decreasing communication in social and economic relationships between rural households and the increased adoption of urban patterns of behaviour, in addition to social and political differentiation, lead to the fragmentation of the community. This, in turn, aggravates underlying problems that the community faces, such as drugs and family breakdown. The latter is due to the strong moral principles that prevailed in the village in the past. These could not continue to be absorbed smoothly with the new demands of modernization. To all of these insecurities, concerns have been added regarding the recent influx of foreign immigrants into the area. There are also complaints about the lack of information on various issues from both local and central government institutions.

This young group of people do not see much hope for the community's future unless there is a shift towards a shared communal identity. Some believe that local households must have a personal stake in order for this to occur, but all agree that there should be some form of cooperation among local people and local institutions encouraged by grassroots involvement. The youth group had no suggestions as to how this might happen. Their view may suggest, however, that the village in the future will survive partly as an agricultural community, partly as a tourist resort and partly as a pluriactive community (see Moisidis et al, 1994). Greenhouse production confronts the lack of support policies for the agricultural sector in Greece, leading to problems of overproduction, disposition, international competition, as well as increases in chemical input prices, related health problems, landscape degradation and pollution of local resources.

Local perceptions of global–local change

While the most common responses were related to economic and poverty factors, crime, drugs and new consumerism patterns constitute other anxieties. These contribute to insecurities in social identity, with subsequent uncertainties over jobs and family relationships.

The following list summarizes local perceptions of causal attributes and ways out of the problems that residents face:[3]

- Economic problems: nearly 90 per cent experienced a reduction in income. The main causes were seen as national policy (77.3 per cent), competition from the developing world (72.7 per cent), national economic decline (62.1 per cent) and competition within the EU (56.1 per cent). Sources of assistance with such problems were seen to be offered by the Greek state (75.8 per cent), local economic networks (56.1 per cent), local cooperatives (45.5 per cent), pressure groups (42.4 per cent), the Agricultural Bank of Greece (ATE) (30.3 per cent), local government (27.3 per cent), political parties (18.2 per cent) and no one (6.1 per cent). With regard to various coping strategies, people proposed social mobilization and demonstrations (43.9 per cent), pressure on politicians (39.4 per cent) and use of the mass media (36.4 per cent) to voice their concerns.
- Crime: 84.5 per cent of respondents had been victims of crime. Crime was attributed to insufficient policy (86.4 per cent), the influx of foreign immigrants (86.4 per cent), drugs (58.1 per cent), the influence of television (47 per cent) and poor government policy (31.8 per cent). Respondents looked to the mass media (36 per cent) for help, and also to political channels of problem-solving (24 per cent).

- Environmental problems: the prime issue of concern was soil and groundwater contamination by agro-chemicals (75.8 per cent), degradation of local natural resources (66 per cent) and ill health (59.1 per cent). Respondents regarded waste (77.3 per cent), and commercial agriculture (74.6 per cent) as the main sources of contamination, followed by excessive consumerism (56.1 per cent) and economic pressures arising from international competition (34.4 per cent). For coping strategies, they looked to a healthy diet (80.3 per cent), political pressure groups (40.9 per cent) and the use of the mass media as a means of voicing their demands (34.8 per cent). Help was sought from each other (72.7 per cent), rather than government (60 per cent) and environmental organizations (50 per cent).
- Structural problems were seen as inadequate sewage systems (83.9 per cent) and local activities (71.2 per cent), followed by the absence of any coordinated village plan (54.5 per cent) and illegal construction of housing (54.5 per cent). These problems were attributed to citizens' unlawful activities (74.2 per cent) and poor implementation of regulations (69.7 per cent). For assistance, respondents looked to the council (60.7 per cent), to the state (56.1 per cent) and to each other (17.3 per cent). For coping strategies, they proposed refuge in political pressure groups (47 per cent) and social mobilization (37.9 per cent).
- Political crises were a product of loss of faith in the state (81.8 per cent), nepotism and corruption (73.8 per cent) and international pressures (42.2 per cent). These were viewed as being created by interest lobbies (68.2 per cent) and citizen dissatisfaction and disillusionment (60.6 per cent). Again, the state (53 per cent) and social action by civil networks (51.5 per cent) were regarded as the best way forward.
- Psychological problems: nearly everyone (95.5 per cent) experienced anxiety and tension, while almost 70 per cent expressing insecurity and fear. The main causes were seen as income (86.4 per cent) and employment (66.7 per cent) related, as well as family pressures (60.6 per cent). Communicating within social networks constituted the primary source of coping strategies (69.7 per cent), followed by going to church (50 per cent) and visiting the doctor (42.4 per cent).
- Social problems: drugs were the primary worry (89.4 per cent), followed by 'loose morals' (62.1 per cent) and excessive consumerism. The primary coping strategy was to keep in contact with close family and friends (87.9 per cent), communicate better with children (87.9 per cent) and maintain local cultural traditions (72.7 per cent).
- Poverty was caused primarily by unsuccessful cultivation (90.9 per cent), excessive borrowing (87.9 per cent) and crop failure (54.5 per cent). The main causes of poverty were seen as family breakdown (72.7 per cent) and laziness (56.1 per cent). For help, the respondents propose family support (73.3 per cent), support from neighbours (30.3 per cent) and support from the Church (22.7 per cent).

These attitudes from the targeted sample imply that the question of agricultural modernization has brought with it an increasing overall concern regarding the future viability of farming in the Greek countryside. Along with this genuine anxiety is a threat to both economic and social security; social–local networks and family bonds are trusted to handle this threat.

There are new ways of 'alleviating' the current crisis (see, for example Damianos, et al, 1997) with regard to better-quality production, new forms of commercialization, organic transformation, organized and collective responses to economic, social and environmental problems, and diversification in economic forms of production. In order to address local problems, the farmers require assistance from the state. Indeed, when asked how they would help themselves, many people responded by making claims on the state, indicating the degree to which the state has come to be considered an important element of their strategies. It should also be noted, however, that the respondents indicated that other solutions could be implemented in conjunction with help from EU subsidized programmes, as shown in Table 9.1.

Table 9.1 *Help sought from the state/EU*

Help sought from the State or the European Union	*Per cent of positive responses*
Decrease in the cost of chemical inputs	100
Continuation of crop and livestock subsidies	95.5
Infrastructure for the better distribution of agricultural products	100
Farming-training seminars	100
Environmentally friendly technology	95.5
Economic and social motivations for young farmers	98.5
Research institutes for Timbaki	97

Source: Targeted sample interviews, summer 1998

Indeed, there is considerable and widespread interest in new ways forward and in finding new mechanisms capable of containing cost increases, as shown in Table 9.1. This interest reflects the organization of new forms of quality production, nature conservation, product innovation, commercialization and environmental control. Forgotten, obscured or institutionally blocked resources are being reactivated in individual and collective experiments. Taken together, they represent the many expressions of local innovation. Table 9.2 shows the institutions that the farmers believe can assist them in securing their future. Although they still highly value help from the state, local councils and agro-industrial institutions, the revitalization of the farmer's own resources stands out. This may mean the capacity to combine agriculture with other activities, a view also found in both key-actor and focus-group interviews. Local economy may be strengthened via nature and landscape conservation, the ability to create new networks to link production with consumption, the establishment of control over the resources lost when activities came under external prescription and sanction, and, finally, the common goal of using the benefit produced to further social–local identity.

Table 9.2 *Help sought from institutions for Timbaki's future viability*

Institutions and future viability	Per cent of positive responses (%)
EU	56.1
Greek state	66.7
Local councils	68.2
Political parties	34.8
Agro-industrial cooperatives	66.7
Agricultural Bank of Greece (ATE)	43.9
Pressure groups	59.1
Courts	18.2
Producers	80.3
Nobody	3.0

Source: Targeted sample interviews, summer 1998

Table 9.3 further reinforces greater reliance on a producer's own resources. What is being proposed is a more locally sufficient development that may contrast dramatically with the logic of modernization where the reorganization of farming is dependent on external resources. The critical question, of course, is whether this endogenous approach will lead successfully to a way out of the crisis.

Table 9.3 *Trust placed in different institutions*

Institutions	None	Little	Average	Very	Very much
EU	21.2	19.7	31.8	13.6	4.5
State	53.0	16.7	19.7	6.1	1.5
Local councils	34.8	15.2	30.3	13.6	3.0
Political parties	68.2	15.2	9.1	4.5	–
Cooperatives	19.7	10.6	25.8	30.3	12.1
Agricultural Bank of Greece (ATE)	39.4	9.1	25.8	25.8	1.5
Pressure groups	21.2	24.2	19.7	19.7	7.6
Justice	33.3	12.1	24.2	19.7	7.6

Source: Targeted sample interviews, summer 1998

AEGALEO IN TRANSITION

The understanding of urban 'problems' related to the sustainability transition requires a multidimensional aspect as part of a series of reinforcing processes. These do not stop at processes of impoverishment that derive from lack of income and low consumption. Processes that increase vulnerability and insecurity, described by Chambers (1983) as the 'deprivation trap', are just as important. These are processes that erode people's assets or prevent them from acquiring assets in the first place. In addition, processes of deprivation or social exclusion deny some groups full participation in social, economic and political life. Particular processes are specific to urban (and rural) contexts and need to be understood with reference to locality.

The case study of Aegaleo applies a combination of conventional approaches with qualitative and participatory assessment approaches.[4] These shed light on the process of deprivation, vulnerability, insecurity and social exclusion. They also present the current socio-economic and environmental circumstances of the municipality by reflecting the perspective of people who have experienced these processes most closely. The data describes Aegaleo's current socio-economic and environmental features, focusing on disadvantaged groups of people. Different actors and target groups identify possible policy responses to a variety of urban problems through community, municipal, governmental or EU initiatives.

A general profile of Aegaleo

Aegaleo is one of the largest municipalities, in area and population, of the western wing of the greater Athens area (GAA). It covers 620 hectares and includes part of the 'Olive Grove' (*Elaeonas*) which is excluded from the city plan. It has been a principal economic centre for decades that has been favoured for industrial development, with a concentration of industries in the 1960s which led to urban migration by many peasants. While in the 1980s population outflows from Aegaleo to other departments of Greece or abroad reached 9.75 per cent (ASDA, 1994, p57), influxes of Greek repatriates from the former Soviet Union republics or Albanians, Indians, Iraqis and Pakistanis have resulted in current population estimates of about 120,000. Overall, Aegaleo's population is young – only 7.8 per cent are 65 or older while 24.3 per cent are younger than 15.

Most industrial and manufacturing firms, as well as commercial businesses, are located among the houses of Aegaleo. These firms specialize in food and drinks, textiles, footwear, wood-processing, tanning, plastics, chemicals, final metal products, machinery, smelting works and ceramics. Together, these industries employ 3140 people from Aegaleo. Manufacturing and industry employs more workers than does trade (Marouli, 1992, p71). However, despite this concentration of industry, the nature of recent industry has a limited capacity to absorb labour, especially after the 1980s. For example, in the 1988 manufacturing establishments census, industrial and manufacturing units decreased to 1459 in only four years according to the 1984 census, with an overall loss of 200 jobs.

Increasing numbers of the economically active population are working in the local tertiary sector. According to a 1992 sample of 60 enterprises from different branches in Aegaleo, about 58 per cent employ from 5 to 20 workers. Interestingly, the majority (97 per cent) of workers are permanent employees. In the sample, the largest categories are those of workers and office personnel (Euroform et al, 1993). Over the last two decades a commercial centre has been established in the municipality, leading to increases in the tertiary sector, while some industries have moved to the Olive Grove.

Consequently a significant number of people employed in industry or manufacturing firms have lost their jobs mainly because of the shrinking staff which was substituted by inexpensive technological equipment due to international competition. Nevertheless, Aegaleo's residents are mainly industry workers and technicians (58.4 per cent). Most are salaried (75 per cent) and 19.6 per cent are self-employed (1991 ESYE Census). However, the expansion of services was due to a growth in the population employed in low-productivity activities (such as the repair and cleaning services), reinforced by very low educational attainment (more than 47 per cent of Aegaleo's residents have an elementary education and only about 6 per cent have some form of higher education, given the 1991 census).

This new trend of low monthly incomes (150,000 Greek drachmas, the equivalent of US$450) for almost half of western Athens' households (*Ta Nea*, 1993) reflects the urban unemployment not only in the municipality but in neighbouring areas as well. Although the official unemployment figure in 1981 was 6 per cent (Euroform et al, 1993), given the influx of more than 20,000 new residents in Aegaleo in the 1990s, some estimate it to be about 18 per cent (informal interview with municipal personnel, August 1997).

Environmental problems must be seen in the context of a model of dependent and unbalanced national development, which presents problems of structural unemployment and workforce exploitation, and works mainly for the benefit of industrial and financial sectors. These also profit from the concentration of population and economic activities in the municipality of Aegaleo (interview with the vice mayor of Aegaleo). The recent influx of approximately 20,000 Russian expatriates, and more than 5000 migrants from countries such as Albania, India, Pakistan or Iraq, may only marginally affect environmental quality via population growth.

Aegaleo was constructed with neither a plan nor the resources to accommodate large groups of newcomers. After local action pressured the government, most of their properties were included in the city plan (interview with municipal representative). It is very densely built, 200 inhabitants per hectare, with very inadequate land for administrative uses and social services. According to two newspaper reports (*Ta Nea*, 1996, pp12–13; *Exousia*, 1996, pp21–23), illegal and informally developed settlements without services and with limited and deficient facilities and self-constructed housing affect mostly foreign migrants. These migrants tend to live in low-income settlements along with those who had settled near industrial and manufacturing units during the 1960s in a time of increased unemployment.

The areas mostly affected are the *Damarakia* quarter, situated near a polluting glass industry, where Pondian repatriates from the former Soviet Union live. The area as stated by local informants is considered socially and environmentally degraded, without the appropriate infrastructure. The *Polykatoikies* quarter adjacent to the Olive Grove district is mainly inhabited by another repatriated group as well as industrial workers, since large firms such as AMSTEL (brewer) and DMC (textile) operate in the area. Finally, the *Sotiraki* quarter – not included in the city plan – attracts Iranian refugees and is regarded as an environmentally degraded area, hosting a large number of car repair shops and the industrial unit of STELLA (food processing). Both quarters lack proper sewage and water supply infrastructure.[5]

The municipality has also been facing a serious traffic problem. Sixteen different urban transport lines go through it in addition to two national (inter-country) routes (*Iera Odos* and *Leoforos Thivon*). These two routes cut Aegaleo into four equal parts. The road network covers about 25 per cent of the municipality's area. This creates a serious shortage of public transport facilities and inadequate connections between different transport systems in the city (Marouli 1992; 1995). Proposed changes in the road network will involve the construction of a highway by filling in the Kifissos canal and building an elevated highway over it.

Almost one-third of all person-trips take place in Athens' periphery where there are no subway lines with subsidized fares. To get to work, individuals living in these areas use increasingly overcrowded buses or collective taxis, whose prices have increased considerably in the last few years.

There is also a serious lack of parking space in Aegaleo. This leads to the use of the pavement for parking purposes, creating problems for pedestrians, in waste collection and traffic movement, etc. As far as traffic safety is concerned, Aegaleo has been facing serious problems relating to its main traffic routes, namely pedestrian safety and traffic safety during the night. In the three years to 1996 approximately 1000 traffic accidents have occurred, with 13 dead and 40 seriously wounded (Demetriadis, 1996, pp5–25).

Rapid and extensive industrial development has increased air pollution problems in Aegaleo. Industrial and manufacturing firms located in residential areas are creating an even more acute pollution problem. These activities are aggravated by lack of green areas which have been turned into schools, public buildings or athletic facilities (Marouli, 1992, pp70–73).

The large number of road vehicles and poor maintenance of their engines and traffic jams result in heavy pollution. Evidence from the municipal environmental protection agency suggests that 10,000 person-trips are registered daily from the Kifissos station. Automobile emissions account for 991.2 grams per litre of carbon monoxide, 81 grams per litre of hydrocarbons, and 14.5 grams per litre of particulates (TEE, 1982). Motor vehicles are the major source of carbon monoxide emissions in Aegaleo (28.3 kilogrammes per day), and industrial sources are responsible for the high levels of sulphur dioxide in the area accounting for 2132 kilogrammes per day (TEE, 1982; ASDA, 1994; EMP, 1995).

Atmospheric pollution caused by heavy traffic and local industrial activities, creates serious problems for the integrity of local ecosystems and the general public health of Aegaleo. In addition to the less heavy industrial units, plastic, final metal products and chemical firms in residential areas add pollution loads to the atmosphere which, given certain atmosphere conditions, make breathing very difficult. Other sources, such as high-voltage electricity poles inside the residential areas, also create an unsafe environment for locals (Marouli, 1992, p74), along with scattered solid wastes from domestic, commercial, industrial and institutional sources. A study made by ESDKNA (1984–1985) estimated that a total of 27,432 tonnes of solid waste was generated in the 1984–1985 period.

In the past two years, the central government has planned to construct a waste transport and storage unit in the 'Olive Grove' not only for local but for a considerable portion of Athens' domestic waste. Several actions have been taken by local groups to protect the olive grove and prevent the associated negative environmental and social impacts. Since early 1998, locals have been protesting about the deterioration of common property resources, and demanding the environmental management of green areas (press release of the Mayor of Aegaleo, May 1998). In October 1999, residents, parents associations, students, local businesses, representatives from different political parties, all municipal council members, and the mayor occupied the site where the station is planned to be established, and blockaded major routes around it. In January 2000 they also proceeded with more road blockades, protesting against the siting of the plan once more. In addition to these actions the mayor, along with local food industry entrepreneurs (who have been operating in the grove for many years) took the case to the Supreme Court. The recent ruling annulled the environ-mental impact study by the Ministry of Environment, Physical Planning and Public Works and asked for a new one. Thus far, local environmental activism has been successful in halting the siting of the station for a period of two years. In early March 2000, the mayor, in colloboration with six municipalities that are adjacent to the olive grove and have supported these local protesters, is organizing a workshop to inform all interested parties, including the government, on the different dimensions of the issue.[6] The outcome of this conflict is still unknown. The persistent activism and the formation of successful social networks are clearly indicative of a strong comtemporary community which has broken its ties with patterns of the past. It envisions, demands, and takes initiatives towards securing a more sustainable future far more than central authority does for its constituents.

A media view of the transition

In Aegaleo, one good quality newspaper, the *Aigaleo*, has been in existence for a long time (from 1985 to 1999). It has a leftist orientation and provides a continuous coverage of issues that affect the local community. Using content analysis, a 50 per cent random sample of all the newspapers was coded and analysed with regard to issues reflecting democracy, sustainability and local matters.

Figure 9.1 illustrates a time profile of the main issues that concern the local community. Although political mentions are more extensive, environmental, economic and social issues are generally more frequent. Since the late 1980s, there have been increasing upward trends regarding environmental and economic issues. These trends appear to dip in the late 1990s.

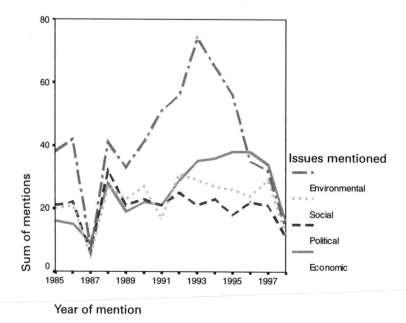

Figure 9.1 *Type of newspaper mentions in the* Aigaleo *by year (1985–1998)*

Table 9.4 presents local newspaper mentions of social, political, economic and environmental issues for two time periods, 1985–1991 and 1992–1999. Increases during the second period are especially noted in environmental issues related to forest protection, domestic waste, health and pollution; increases in economic issues refer to international and national economic policies, taxes, (un)employment, business survival and municipal economic problems. Similar increases are also found in political supranational and national issues, as well as in social issues regarding health, minority interests and transport.

By contrast, decreases are visible in political issues such as elections, clientelism, the internal politics of political parties, as well as local and municipal groups; decreases in social issues are related to health, and decreases in environmental issues are linked to nature protection, construction and traffic-related pollution.

Table 9.4 *Issues mentioned in the* Aigaleo *by time period*

ISSUES	1985–1991 (%)	1992–1998 (%)	Total (%)
SOCIAL			
Crimes	66.7	71.8	69.4
Drugs	57.4	43.6	50.0
Social welfare, poverty	60.6	61.5	61.1
Health	51.5	61.5	56.9
Education	72.7	56.4	63.9
Minorities	**18.2**	**51.3**	**36.1**
Transport	**69.7**	**71.8**	**70.8**
POLITICAL			
Elections	93.9	71.8	81.9
Supranational	**39.4**	**46.2**	**43.1**
State	**15.2**	**33.3**	**25.0**
Municipality	72.7	53.8	62.5
Local groups	30.3	7.7	18.1
Clientelism	33.3	23.1	27.8
Internal political party	45.5	28.2	36.1
Social protest	30.3	35.9	33.3
Political crisis/apathy	36.4	35.9	36.1
ECONOMIC			
International economy		**15.4**	**8.3**
National economy	**6.1**	**15.4**	**11.1**
Taxes	**21.2**	**64.1**	**44.4**
Civil service jobs	**30.3**	**41.0**	**36.1**
Problem industries	**21.2**	**38.5**	**30.6**
Business closures	**9.1**	**28.2**	**19.4**
Municipal economic problems	**24.2**	**35.9**	**30.6**
Unemployment	**18.2**	**28.2**	**23.6**
Economic survival	33.3	28.2	30.6
ENVIRONMENTAL			
Forest protection	**24.2**	**33.3**	**29.2**
Nature protection	48.5	23.1	34.7
Aigaleo industry	15.2	17.9	16.7
Building construction	57.6	28.2	41.7
Road construction	63.6	43.6	52.8
Traffic pollution	54.5	46.2	50.0
Domestic waste	**33.3**	**53.8**	**44.4**
Sewage problems	39.4	30.8	34.7
Health	**12.1**	**38.5**	**26.4**
Pollution in general	**54.5**	**64.1**	**59.7**
Air pollution	57.6	46.2	51.4
Noise pollution	**18.2**	**23.1**	**20.8**
Total per cent (N)	100.0(33)	100.0(39)	100.0 (72)

Figure 9.2 depicts global aspects from 1985 to 1999. Global issues include articles on immigrants, supranational political topics, global economy themes and international environmental issues. Global agencies refer to international bodies such as the EU, the UN, the Organization for Economic Development (OECD) and others. Global problem management is defined as the global initiatives that aim to alleviate problems affecting the local community. Waves of such mentions appear to follow an increasing trend, with the exception of global problem initiatives. Although global issues lead in terms of volume, they run parallel to mentions on global agencies.

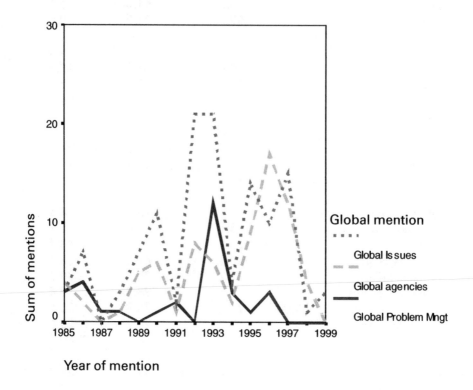

Figure 9.2 *Mentions of global aspects by year (1985–1999)*

Figure 9.3 presents mentions of local and state problem management over the entire period. Other than for 1993, these mentions run in tandem and are of the same magnitude. They appear to follow an opposing trend compared with the global management curve of Figure 9.2. Although there are increases in global issues and agencies, global initiatives to manage problems at the local level do not witness similar increases. State and local problem management appears to remain, in general, at steady levels throughout the entire period.

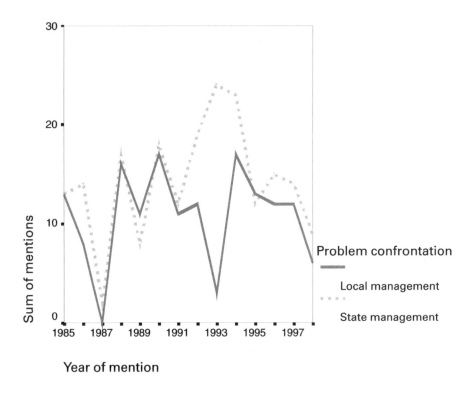

Figure 9.3 *Mentions of local and state problem management (1985–1998)*

Understanding and responding to urban problems

The increasing concentration of inequalities, and consequently deprivation, in cities derives mainly from macro-economic factors. It has been argued (Moser et al, 1993; Moser, 1996), for example, that in a number of countries the negative impact of economic restructuring aimed at international competition (for example, globalization, liberalization) meant that reform measures have fallen disproportionally on low-income, disadvantaged urban people. This is a result of support for tradeables over non-tradeables, price increases, wage restraints, the elimination of food, housing and transport subsidies, and the cumulative impact of declining urban services and infrastructure as a result of poor urban management. Changes in manufacturing production processes have led to an increase in contracting-out; unskilled manual jobs are being converted to insecure part-time jobs due to privitization and sub-contracting. Moreover, disadvantaged urban people are vulnerable within an almost entirely monetized economy and have less robust social networks and fewer buffers against contingencies than do their rural counterparts.

The way in which urban problems are understood in part determines the way policy-makers, planners and practitioners respond to such problems. Nevertheless, urban assessments should not only recognize deprivation

Table 9.5 *Key actors' perceptions on Aegaleo's problems*

Key Actors	Problems	Affected Groups	Solutions
Ex-Mayor	◇ unemployment ◇ transportation ◇ environmental pollution ◇ social services	◇ women ◇ young ◇ Russian expatriates	◇ NOW intiative ◇ HORIZON initiative ◇ ADAPT initiative
Mayor	◇ environmental (waste transport unit, SMA) ◇ powerful central government	◇ labour force	◇ Improve regulatory framework of prefecture
Vice-Mayor (1)	◇ environment (SMA) ◇ ineffective city planning ◇ unemployment ◇ powerful central governmnet ◇ weak municipalities ◇ lack of social services ◇ polluting industries	◇ women ◇ young ◇ Russian ex-patriates	◇ Financial support ◇ Coordination of programmes to combat unemployment ◇ Provision of facilities and infrastructure in neighbourhoods
Vice-Mayor (2)	◇ unemployment ◇ transportation ◇ illegal function of industries (GIOULA)	◇ local labour force	◇ Improve regulatory framework of prefecture for the appropriate use of local land planning

Key Actors	Problems	Affected Groups	Solutions
Office of Environment/ Aegaleo	◊ environment ◊ illegal function of industries (GIOULA) ◊ apathy concerning environmental issues	◊ information provided to all strata of people	◊ Coordination between local and central government
Health representative in Aegaleo	◊ polluting industries in residential areas ◊ lack of social services	◊ children	◊ Coordination between local and central government
OAED ASDA/Initiatives	◊ unemployment ◊ lack of resources ◊ funding, poor communication	◊ migrants ◊ women ◊ Russian ex-patriates ◊ SMEs	◊ Effective policies ◊ Coordination between key managers and decision-making
ASDA/Repatriates	◊ language ◊ adaptation to the Greek reality ◊ unemployment ◊ lack of housing	◊ Russian expatriates programmes to	◊ Coordination of programmes to combat unemployment
Centre of educational training	◊ female unemployment	◊ women	◊ Security of tenure ◊ Lack of funding for the continuation of NOW initiative
Local media	◊ unemployment ◊ environment	◊ SMEs	◊ Environmental awareness ◊ Change of political structure

Source: interviews with key informants, 1998

and social exclusion processes. They should also be consultative or participatory, thus informing policy-makers of the perceptions and tolerance thresholds of disadvantaged people themselves in order that policy can be better tailored and targeted. Accordingly, appropriate policy responses to urban poverty processes fall into four broad categories as extracted from information taken by local key-actor interviews and seen in Table 9.5.

Appropriate policy responses to urban deprivation and social exclusion fall into four broad categories. First, the municipality of Aegaleo is characterized by poor transportation networks and concentrated industrial settings that inhibit the solidarity and the productive potential of local people. This has adverse effects for low-income people, both in terms of employment opportunities and investment priorities with regard to infrastructure and services at the municipal level. For these main reasons, urban deprivation has to be tackled at the central government level, both in terms of local economic assistance and a more coherent institutional framework for targeted delivery.

Second, unemployment still remains an important issue, although it has been addressed in terms of targeted groups (women, youth, migrants) and EU initiatives. It is generally argued that urban deprivation is a function of capitalism rather than urbanism. But as illustrated later on, Aegaleo's target group's well-being, life chances and livelihood opportunities are closely linked and cannot be divorced from either physical or social environments.

This leads to the third category of appropriate policy responses relating to the living environment. Security of tenure or occupation, infrastructure and social services (water supply, sanitation, health centres) can address and thus meet the most pressing needs of low-income or socially excluded groups. Social exclusion is experienced even by repatriates, preventing them from using governmental institutions to acquire information on housing, work permits, etc.

The fourth category of policy intervention as perceived by key actors is again strongly related to unemployment. Implicitly, this means insecurity for many people who reside in Aegaleo. This has had adverse affects on the stability of the local economy, administrative effectiveness, political legitimacy and people's individual and collective security (focus-group interviews). Along with livelihoods and the living environment, physical and psycho-social security should be a focus of policies that address urban deprivation and social exclusion. As Moser (1996) argues, these erode the social assets that form the creative energy on which cities are built. Accordingly, urban deprivation requires a multidimentional approach, as has already been noted by key informants. This involves mutually reinforcing interventions by a broad range of organizations and groups concerned with municipal governance and the creation of secure livelihoods.

This case study, which especially targets the 'disadvantaged' groups of Aegaleo, underscores the multidimensional character of deprivation and the close relationship between unemployment and related processes of vulnerability (Chambers, 1983) and social exclusion (Rogers et al, 1995).

CONCLUSION

Economic globalization is related to global firms, to international competition in new and old markets, as well as to the promotion of capital-intensive products. Global production and marketing have affected Aegaleo's SMEs, which have had difficulty in achieving technological modernization. In Timbaki, intensive agricultural techniques originating in developed countries replaced environmentally friendly traditional practices and led to acute international competition yielding negative impacts on local life (see Moeg and Dijk, 1995). At the same time, free movement of labour has also created many pressures for the new immigrant groups living in Aegaleo as well as in Timbaki.

Global organizations and bodies such as the EU appear to promote but also to hinder sustainability practices through their policies. The Greek state is seeking to adopt sustainability within its constraints. State-funded projects are related to a variety of economic and social EU programmes or policies, such as HORIZON, NOW, ADAPT, integrated pest management (IPM), the CAP and others.

Since the 1970s political territories have become more permeable, consumption appears to be more Westernized, cultural boundaries appear to have become stronger, while – simultaneously – immigration issues are on the increase.

Supranational institutions could better accommodate the transition if they paid closer attention to the needs of the more excluded groups, and not only to the economically and politically powerful agencies. Specific areas and means of assistance have been proposed by target groups and key actors in both Timbaki and Aegaleo.

REFERENCES

ASDA (1994) *Special Development Programme of Western Attiki, 1994-1999*, Development Union of Western Attiki, Peristeri (in Greek)

Chambers, R (1983*) Rural Development: Putting the Last First*, Longman, Harlow

Damianos, D, Dimara, E and Skouras, D (1997) 'Alternative production activities in the less developed rural areas', *Greek Review of Social Research*, pp92–93, 120–137 (in Greek)

Daoutopoulos, G, Pyrovetsi, M and Petropoulou, E (forthcoming) 'Greek Rural Society and Sustainable Development' in K Eder and M Kousis (eds) *Environmental Politics in Southern Europe: Actors, Institutions and Discourses in an Europeanizing Society* , Kluwer Academic Publishers, Dordrecht

Demertzis, N (1990) 'The Greek political culture in the decade of the 80s' in H Lyrintsis and I Nikolakopoulos (eds) *Elections and Parties in the Decade of the 80s*, Themelio Athens, pp70–96 (in Greek)

Demetriadis, F and EPE (1996) *Study of the Organisation of Traffic and Parking in Aigaleo Municipality*, Municipality of Aegaleo (in Greek)

Dodos, D, Kafetzis, P, Mihalopoulou, K, Nikolakopoulos, I and Papliakou, V (1990) 'Political culture in southern European countries: comparative tables', *The Greek Review of Social Research*, special vol 75A, summer, pp107–151 (in Greek)

EMP (1995) *Regenerating Industrial Zones within Cities and Relocation of Economic Activities – Municipality of Aegaleo: the Case-Study of Olive-Grove*, Organization of Athens, Athens

ESDKNA (1984–1985) 'Union of Municipalities and Communes' in ASDA (Association for the Development of Western Athens) (1994–1995) *Special Development Plan for Western Athens* ASDA, Athens (in Greek)

City of Athens (1991) *Population Census, Athens*, Athens (Tables 1 and 3) (in Greek)

Euroform (EC) (1993) *General Characteristics of the Municipality of Aegaleo Survey*, Municipality of Aegaleo

Exousia Free Press (1996) 'Neighbourhoods of Poverty: the case of Aegaleo', 5 November, pp21–23 (in Greek)

Fousekis, P and Lekakis, J N (1998) 'The transition to sustainability in Greece' in T O'Riordan and H Voisey (eds) *The Transition to Sustainability: the Politics of Agenda 21 in Europe*, Earthscan Publications Ltd, London, pp221–240

Getimis, P (1993) 'Social policies and local government' in P Getimis and D Gravaris (eds) *Social State and Social Policy*, Themelio, Athens, pp91–121 (in Greek)

Getimis, P and Gravaris, D (eds) (1993) *Social State and Social Policy: the Contemporary Problematique*, Themelio, Athens (in Greek)

Hellenic Association for Local Development and the Environment (EETAA) (1989) *Environmental Protection Directory for Locally Elected Governments*, EETAA, Athens (in Greek)

Karabelias, P (1989) *State and Society in Metapolitefsi*, Exantas, Athens (in Greek)

Kasimati, K and Pantazidis, N (1988) *Poverty*, GAA, Athens (in Greek)

Kerdos Free Press (1991) 'The Truth about the Olive Grove', 28 April, pp23–28 (in Greek)

Kioukias, D (1991) *Organising Interests in Greece: Labour, Agriculture, Local Government and Political Development during Metapolitefsi*, PhD Thesis, Graduate School of Political Science and International Studies, University of Birmingham, Birmingham

Kokkosis, H (1993) 'Environmental policy' in P Getimis and D Gravaris, (eds) *Social State and Social Policy*, Themelio, Athens, pp361–382 (in Greek)

Kousis, M (1994) 'Environment and the state in the EU periphery: the case of Greece', *Regional Politics and Policy*, vol 49(1), pp118–135

Lekakis, J (1984) *Economics and Air Quality Management in the Greater Athens Area*, Centre of Planning and Economic Research, Athens

Louloudis, L and Maraveyias, N (1997) 'Farmers and agricultural policy in Greece since the accession to the European Union', *Sociologia Ruralis*, vol 37(2), pp270–286

Manesis, A (1986) *The Evolution of Political Institutions in Greece: Searching for a Difficult Legitimacy*, Les Temps Moderne, Athens (in Greek)

Marouli, C (1992) *Urban Environment, Gender and Class: the Case of Athens, Greece*, PhD thesis, Department of Sociology, University of California, Santa Cruz

Marouli, C (1995) 'Women resisting (in) the city: struggle, gender, class and space in Athens', *International Journal of Urban Environment*, vol 19(4) pp534–548

Moisidis, A, Damianos, D, Kassimis, H and Demoussis, M (1994) *Pluriactivity in the agricultural sector and development policy in Greece*, Institute for Mediterranean Studies, Athens

Moser, C O N (1996) 'Confronting crisis: a summary of household responses to poverty and vulnerability in four poor urban communities', *Environmentally Sustainable Development Studies and Monograph Studies*, series no 7, World Bank, Washington DC

Moser, C O N, Herber, A T and Makonren, R E (1993) *Urban poverty in the context of structural adjustment: evidence and policy responses*, TWU Discussion Paper No 4, Urban Development Division, World Bank, Washington DC

Pollis, A (1977) 'The impact of traditional cultural patterns on Greek politics', *The Greek Review of Social Research*, vol 29(1), pp2–14

ESYE (1991) *Population Census, Athens*, Athens (Tables 1 and 3) (in Greek)

Pridham, G, Verne, S and Konstadakopoulos, D (1995) 'Environmental policy in Greece: evolution, structures and processes', *Environmental Politics*, vol 5(2), pp111–129

Rodgers, G, Gore, C and Figueiredo, J (1995) *Social Exclusion: Rhetoric, Reality, Responses*, International Institute of Labour Studies, ILO, Geneva

SODAE (Association for the Organization, Management and Development of the Olive Grove) *Information Booklet*, Municipality of Aegaleo (in Greek)

Stasinopoulou, O (1993) 'Restructuring personal social services' in P Getimis, and D Gravaris (eds) *Social State and Social Policy*, Themelio, Athens, pp271–311 (in Greek)

Ta Nea Free Press (1993) 'Western Athens', 23 October, p6 (in Greek)

Ta Nea Free Press (1996) 'Municipalities of Athens, twenty-one years after: the case of Aegaleo', 21 March, 12–13 (in Greek)

Tsoulouvis, T (1996) 'Urban planning, social policy and new forms of urban inequality and social exclusion in Greek cities', *International Journal of Urban Environment*, vol 20(4), pp718–730

TEE (1982) *Problems of Environment and Quality of Life in One Athenian Municipality: the case of Aegaleo*, Technical Chamber of Greece, Athens (in Greek)

Tsoukalas, N (1986) *State, Society and Work*, Themelio, Athens (in Greek)

Van der Ploeg, J D and Van der Dijk, G (eds) (1995) *Beyond Modernisation: the Impact of Endogenous Rural Development*, Van Gorcum, Assen

ENDNOTES

1   Special thanks to Athena Bogdani and Katerina Vlasaki (for content analysis), as well as to Dimitris Kiourkas and Katerina Vlasaki (for long interviews in Timbaki) for their interest, diligence, sincere work and positive attitudes throughout the data collection process

2   The following account is based mainly on an indepth interview with a key municipality representative

3   This is on the basis of a 66-person targeted sample of long interviews

4   The information derives from a variety of sources using a quantitative approach; sources include published documents, statistics and newspapers, as well as a qualitative perspective via key-actor and focus-group indepth interviews

5   The sewage system in Aegaleo, which was developed before the 1960s by private owners, inhibits the renewal of sewer and water supply systems on a private basis for the increasing foreign population (*Taxydromos*, 22 July 1992, pp10–13; ESYE: 1991 census).

6   Based on an interview with Aegaleo municipality staff

10 LOCAL IDENTITY AND EMPOWERMENT IN THE UK

Heather Voisey, Andrew Walters and Chris Church

INTRODUCTION

The UK has responded relatively well to the call for local action under LA21, the blueprint for implementing the concept of sustainable development agreed at UNCED in 1992. Certainly, there has been a great deal of reported action under the title of LA21 (Voisey, 1998). Many local authorities, community-based organizations and NGOs are doing much more, producing biodiversity action plans, putting in place mechanisms for greater public participation in decision-making and working on areas such as transport, air quality and fuel poverty – namely, the adverse impact on poorer households of higher prices for energy. However, criticism has been levelled at the quality of these initiatives; many only involve a small proportion of the local population, mostly people who already understand environmental principles and concerns (see Levett and Christie, 1999). Activity around LA21 at present is focused on traditional environmental concerns, with rather less attention paid to the issues of economic growth and social needs. This process is usually defined by a small number of usually highly motivated local interests, and is filtered through what is feasible in resource and political terms. This can produce some good work; but looking at the LA21 initiatives alone does not tell the full story about the capacity of people and institutions in any locality to respond to the sustainability agenda or to enter the sustainability transition.

In the UK, two case studies were carried out in very different localities: in the London municipal area of Hackney and within that the area of Shoreditch; and in the largely rural area of Norfolk, eastern England, the city of Norwich and one estate, Mile Cross. The research has looked not only at the LA21 initiatives, but also at the wider context of social, political and economic change in the area. It analyses how local people and institutions are adapting to these changes, how local people feel about them and what they want to see in the future. The idea has been to examine the existing and emerging barriers and drivers to localities moving towards the sustainability transition. This research has been largely exploratory with no preset image of what the sustainability transition will be for that locality. As the analysis in Chapter 2 indicated, each locality and person will perceive, understand and respond differently, based on their experiences, economic circumstances, social–local identity and future needs. Awareness of these aspects is important in understanding the response to sustainable development and how to improve the capacity of people and localities to respond in a positive manner.

For the purposes of the subsequent case study analysis, a brief description of the UK's political, social and economic structure is required. In the last 30 years the economic base of the UK has undergone huge structural change, with the loss of a great deal of its primary and secondary industries and the growth of service-sector employment. There has been a geographical element to this decline and boom, with jobs being lost in the industrial north and in rural areas as fishing and agriculture have been hit by EU quotas and mechanization. Meanwhile, new jobs requiring different skills have increased in the south, close to Europe and transport networks.

In political terms, the country is currently going through huge processes of change to the hardware and software of government. At the level of the nation state, there is a move towards a differentiated polity, away from the Westminster model, with the devolution of legislative power to Scotland and Northern Ireland, and eventually to Wales. At the local level there is an elected mayor of London for the first time, while there are proposals for this to be extended to other local authorities, along with moves towards a more executive form of political management in local government. Changes are emerging for the software of government due to dissatisfaction with the current nature of party-based representative politics. Instead, we have increasing evidence of direct action around single issues such as new roads, greater involvement of NGOs, interest and community groups at all levels, and the introduction of citizenship classes within the national curriculum. Therefore the notion of what politics means is being reassessed, as are the relationships of individuals and groups in society to decision-making and the state.

In social terms, although by many measures the standard of living is relatively high, it comes at the price of some of the longest working hours in Europe, particularly for families where both parents have to work. For example, half of employees work overtime, and among the poorer groups of primary income earners, two-thirds of spouses work at least part-time. A number of social problems exist: the gap between the rich and poor continues to increase. According to the government's first annual report on poverty and social exclusion (Department of Social Security, 1999), the incomes of the poorest 10 per cent of the UK population fell slightly, after housing costs are taken into account, compared with 1979, but the absolute standard of poverty has remained the same. There is no single indicator or definition of poverty, but the unemployability of single or coupled parents is probably the most critical factor. A disproportionate number of the socially excluded are from ethnic minorities, or are disabled, single parent families or the elderly. This social inequality brings with it a host of attendant problems, such as rising levels of crime and drugs; but notably it is often concentrated in certain geographical areas, in particular social housing estates. It is in two such areas that our case studies have been carried out.

NORWICH AND MILE CROSS

Norwich dates back to Saxon times and by the early 16th century had become the second city of England. It remained in a position of pre-eminence until the industrial revolution, at which point it was superseded by towns and ports closer to the necessary natural resources and foreign markets. Norwich is still the regional centre for East Anglia and is keen to promote this image, as well as its reputation for a high quality of life. This latter characteristic is a function of its historical buildings, public parks, garden-city type suburbs, all in proximity to areas nationally recognized for their conservation and landscape value. These aspects have been preserved from the pressures of industrial and residential development because of relatively poor transport links to the rest of the country. However, this high quality of life does hide high levels of poverty and associated deprivation in some areas of the city. Mean household income is around 12 per cent below the national average, with the third slowest rate of wage increase in the nation.

Mile Cross is an area on the northern outskirts of the city. It roughly forms a triangle bounded on the north and east by main roads, and on the south by the River Wensum. It was created in 1923 by the local council to relieve housing need in one area of the city centre after World War I. In comparison to the previous damp, airless and unsanitary conditions, the new housing was designed along garden city lines. This meant well-designed, easy-to-run houses in small blocks and crescents with gardens, representing space and openness. A number of the original residents still live on the estate and remember with pleasure the relocation of the old neighbourhood to these new homes as well as the subsequent changes in the area. There have been two subsequent developments to the east and north of the original estate. The first of these developments was in 1925 and was made along similar lines, with the addition of the first school and a pedestrian link to the city called the Lane, which provides one of the few views of the city skyline. The latter development was in the mid-1960s and built along very different lines, incorporating three 11-storey blocks of flats and blocks of maisonettes which were intended for small families, the elderly and single people.

This area was chosen for closer examination in Norwich for two main reasons. First, it has some of the highest levels of social deprivation in the city and surrounding areas and secondly it was the pilot scheme for democratic innovation in the city. As such, it represents an interesting and instructive case study of the capacity of a socially distinct locality within the larger city to respond to sustainability.

The following sections provide a detailed socio-economic profile of Norwich and Mile Cross, including details of the formal LA21 response within democratic innovation in the city, followed by a discussion arising from fieldwork research. The methodology used in this case study employed a number of approaches: an analysis of documents such as newsletters and council strategies; newspaper articles; existing research; participant observation of meetings; stakeholder and community network analysis; focus groups; interviews with council members, council officers and community leaders.

Socio-economic profile

The resident population of the Norwich area has remained fairly constant over the last 20 years at around 128,000, and for Mile Cross the population is very static at around 8000. However, the age distribution in the city has altered significantly, with an increase in the very elderly population (over 75) of 18 per cent since 1981. The number of households made up of pensioners has increased by 36 per cent, with 80 per cent of all lone pensioner households occupied by women. In contrast, the same period has seen a 40 per cent increase in the 0 to 4 age group. Mile Cross has an estimated 5 per cent of the population with Romany/traveller roots, an ethnic distinction not picked up in official census data collection but one that is important for the area. Mile Cross is an area where 68 per cent of housing remains under local authority control. Another potential indicator of poverty and social exclusion in the city is the significant proportion of households without access to a car: 40 per cent for the city and 46 per cent in Mile Cross, although this is on the decrease.

The economic position of Norwich residents altered between 1981 and 1991, particularly for women. While the number of economically active males remained constant, the number of economically active females rose by 11.5 per cent. During this same period, male unemployment rose by 8 per cent while for women this figure rose by 23 per cent. Significantly, women make up the largest proportion of groups, such as lone parent households, part-time workers, unemployed, long-term ill and lone pensioners, many of whom suffer from poverty and its associated problems. During this period there was a decrease in the number of full-time jobs and an increase in part-time working, mostly by women, and an increase in self-employment by 21 per cent. In Mile Cross, the figures are slightly different with the numbers of economically active men and women remaining broadly static. The unemployment levels did not rise significantly, running at 13 per cent for men and 7 per cent for women. However, there was a notable 119 per cent and 127 per cent rise in the respective numbers of men and women classed as permanently sick, a factor of changes to the way unemployment is classified and calculated. There was also a 77 per cent increase in the number of retired women, although as a proportion of the population older women declined slightly, and there was no corresponding increase among men. In addition, women account for 90 per cent of all part-time employment on the estate.

In 1988 the city council commissioned a skills audit of the city which was carried out in Mile Cross and the adjacent area and subsequently updated (BMG, 1995). Interview data suggest the picture presented by this research largely holds true today:

- At the time of the survey 41 per cent of respondents were unemployed.
- The largest group of long-term unemployed (average length was 35 months) was comprised of ex-workers in traditional manufacturing.
- The major impediments to employment were perceived to be the lack of child-care facilities, training and experience, and age discrimination.
- The greatest area of employment growth was in those sectors employing workers in professional, managerial and related occupations. Many of these jobs have been filled by in-migrants to Norwich.
- Although manufacturing employment for women had declined by 50 per cent in the previous decade, employment in managerial, professional and related occupations had increased by 50 per cent. The increase in related occupations was less for men.
- Most employed people worked in SMEs (25 people or less).
- Over half the women in work were only employed part-time.
- There was a severe lack of formal educational qualifications, with 57 per cent of respondents possessing none, and 34 per cent perceiving themselves to have no marketable job skills. Levels of qualifications for higher education, apprenticeships or specific skills training were also very low.

Local Agenda 21: Norwich 21

It is only since 1996 that a response to LA21 can be perceived and this is in the form of an initiative called Norwich 21 (N21). This was conceived as a general vision of Norwich in the 21st century covering many different facets: poverty, crime, economic development, community development, the environment and democracy. Initial publicity material on N21 used the Brundtland definition, supplemented by the following explanation:

> *Sustainable development is not just about meeting material needs. It recognizes that true quality of life depends on other things as well. So good health, freedom from fear, satisfying work, access to information (and the education to understand it), opportunities for leisure and recreation and the ability to take part in society's decision-making processes are all included.*

This initial integrated vision of sustainable development, rather than starting at the point of the environment and working outwards, has manifested itself in the specific action plans and activities of N21, corporate reorganization during 1998–1999, as well as links with empowerment initiatives in the city.

The first N21 Vision and Action Plan was launched on 21 April 1997. This was the culmination of a series of public meetings, in practice attended by invited representatives of many interests and groups in the city, round tables, surveys and questionnaires. The bias of this exercise was the need for continued and reliable growth, rather than sustainability per se, as outlined in Box 10.1. This process therefore highlighted a narrow range of issues as follows:

- Negative points were: traffic in the city centre; poor and expensive public transport; homelessness; poverty; decline of the small shopping areas servicing neighbourhoods; pollution and litter; the loss of the central library to fire with no replacement.
- It was felt that Norwich city centre should be seen as the heart of the city, focused around people, and should be clean, safe and accessible, enhancing the built heritage and encouraging a multicultural future.
- Communities on the outskirts of Norwich should be able to access services.
- There should be greater involvement of people in decision-making; partnerships between the council and people need to be developed, and there is a general requirement for a more responsible and visionary democracy.
- For the future economy, Norwich should be seen as a 'learning city' with lifelong educational opportunities. It also needs to attract businesses from other areas and Europe, redevelop derelict and empty sites and improve transport.

Box 10.1 summarizes how the N21 Vision and Action Plan addressed these concerns through its themes. The action plan has been reviewed each year through the development of sustainability indicators, and through an annual conference where progress is reported, assessed and new issues are raised. This conference consists of stakeholders, council officers and elected members, representatives of the community and business members of interest groups, as well as ordinary members of the public. Besides encouraging development, transparency and accountability, it also provides, in theory, the opportunity for organizations other than the council to take forward action. However, this has presented only a small window of opportunity for effective participation.

Over the last three years a number of activities have been underway under the auspices of N21:

- The Norwich Area Development Association has been set up to take forward the economic goals of N21.
- Thematic round tables have been set up on transport, city life, young people and the arts.
- A series of citizens' juries have been held on information technology, learning and war pensions.
- The city council now has a European officer to facilitate links between Norwich and the rest of the continent.

Box 10.1 *Themes of the 1997 Norwich 21 Vision and Action Plan*

Sustaining the city

The aim is to develop a vibrant, clean, well-managed and sustainable city that is a regional centre for business, leisure and tourism, and that also provides a good environment and quality of life.

All sectors of the community – business, local government and other public-sector bodies, the voluntary and community sectors, and individuals – should work together in a genuine way to achieve common goals, valuing each other's contributions equally.

Representatives of all sectors should speak with one voice to regional, national and international bodies about what Norwich needs and can offer, with the object of persuading these bodies to support our aspirations.

Environmental protection

It is important to value the city's heritage and find a way to preserve and enhance it by ensuring that it meets present and future needs.

Traffic and other environmental issues should be managed by involving businesses and communities, identifying their real needs, and reconciling these with the needs to reduce waste and harmful processes. This includes reducing traffic and enhancing public transport.

Economic development

Businesses should be welcomed and supported; it is important to help business play its full part in the development of the city.

Business should be encouraged to play its part in the life of the city, for example, by supporting and working with communities.

The concept of Norwich as a 'learning city' should be supported and developed.

Social development

It is important to develop a real sense of civic pride and active citizenship in the city as a whole and in local communities.

The problems of individuals and groups who are most vulnerable and least able to take part in the full range of city life must be recognized and addressed.

- The city is a member of several national and international networks sharing best practice. This includes the European Sustainable Cities and Towns Campaign; Norwich was selected as one of the European sustainable cities of 1999.
- Measures have been put in place to develop N21 into an arm's length charitable trust to take forward sustainable development through partnership and the leverage of external funding.

In terms of LA21's place in the corporate structure of Norwich City Council, a particular strategy has been followed. There is no LA21 officer in the council; instead the operational and strategic responsibilities until very recently have lain with the deputy chief executive. Interviews with senior officers suggest that this has been a conscious strategy not to follow the practice of other authorities where the initiative has been sidelined to junior officers. Rather, the intention has been to keep LA21 central to the corporate structure of the authority. Recent reorganization has created the post of head of environmental strategy. Senior officers claim that this new post will provide an environmental champion in the council to balance the already strong areas of social policy and economic development. The key issue is how far all of these elements will be integrated within a unifying sustainability strategy along the lines introduced in Box 10.1. The answer may lie in the processes of integration summarized in Figure 10.1. The implications of this over time will depend on the effect of Norwich's new award for its work on sustainability, the political will of the leader of the council who chairs the N21 steering committee, and how the overall reorganization of the council plays out in terms of policy-making.

The internal reorganization of the council has sought to integrate policy and decision-making by grouping the committees of elected members around five themes. The central three themes cover environmental, social and economic agendas: the three domains of sustainability, as summarized in Box 10.1 and presented in Figure 10.1.

The aim of this reorganization is to counter departmentalism and to facilitate policy integration through to the 'corporate committee', which draws from the work handled by these three thematic committees. However, it is too early to evaluate whether such integration on paper can be replicated, in practice, in the committee room, and beyond.

These changes are coupled with further democratic innovations (voter turnout is currently 37 per cent and council meetings are poorly attended) as part of an attempt to engender a cultural shift within the council's administration towards joined-up thinking.

The role of the area forums and Norwich 21 in Figure 10.1 represents the participatory role of these forums, and the more detached location of Norwich 21 can be likened to their potential independent trust status.

So far, the idea of sustainability seems to have penetrated the higher policy-making echelons of the city council in several departments such as planning, and has affected the perspectives of some members. However, this is not under the LA21 or even the sustainable development banner. Instead, the N21 term seems to be the 'catchall' for action in this area. There appears to be an eagerness to approach sustainability within the council. This is not just because, as an organization, it does not want to be seen to be slow in undertaking something that has increasing national and international importance, but also because there is some recognition that sustainability draws together several themes and strands which it, and various stakeholders, had already highlighting as needing action. One possible future lies in the development of the arm's length organization for Norwich 21, probably as a charitable trust, with the potential to attract

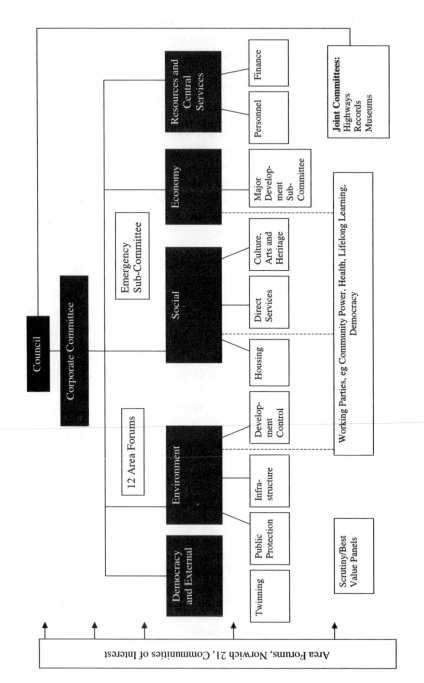

Figure 10.1 *The Norwich City Council Committee structure*

resources, create partnerships with stakeholders and importantly with local people, and provide links to improved community participation in decision-making and implementation through the Community Power (CP) Initiative.

Community Power in Norwich

Interviews with senior officers and council members indicate that sustainability has not been promoted as one of the key objectives of the Norwich Community Power (NCP) initiative. Before becoming leader of the council, Barbara Simpson led the development of the NCP initiative. She is still strongly involved in this area, as well as being the chair of the N21 steering committee. This high-level link between two critical council initiatives is likely to be significant.

The NCP initiative is based on geographical communities, the 12 electoral wards of the city. The intention is for it to complement rather than replace the current system of elected local councillors. The aims of the NCP initiative are to:

- Identify and enhance existing local community resources to improve the ability of people to become involved in issues which affect their lives.
- Carry out that process with the consent and involvement of the communities themselves at every stage.

In the past the council has worked with its neighbourhoods through community centres used by community groups and supported by a network of community development workers. In addition, seven area housing committees were set up on council housing estates in the city to represent the tenants of those areas and to help meet explicit needs. The intention behind the NCP initiative is to build on this work by developing comprehensive area-based strategies through community plans devised by local people. Experience with the area housing committees shows that once people have an avenue for consultation, they want to expand it to deal with issues that they themselves have identified, rather than those promoted by the council. People want to get involved in different ways, and are often not comfortable with the formal committee type of structure. Building a meaningful capacity in the local community to take part in decision-making is the overall rationale for this project. Other intentions involve enhancing the ability of the council to draw in external funding from the government and the EU. These funding sources are increasingly requiring assessments and strategies for involving local communities as a prerequisite for disbursement.

The NCP initiative was piloted in three areas in 1997–1998, one of which was Mile Cross. However, before the pilot study was completed, the council chose to expand the initiative to the rest of the city, with a total of 12 citizen forums proposed. This was launched in September 1997. Each city ward was encouraged to create its own community power structure. The Mile Cross arrangement was as follows:

- Public meetings are open to everyone to air concerns and highlight issues in areas around which a community power forum (CPF) might be organized. People are asked to volunteer as members of a shadow forum to develop the structure and topics of the forum.
- A shadow forum is formed which undergoes a period of capacity-building with the area's community development worker to reach consensus about the best format for the forum and how it relates to the council, existing community groups and the community.
- The shadow forum negotiates its role with the council.
- If the community has an existing area housing committee, the community votes on its continued existence and the formation of a forum.
- Members are elected from the community to the forum, which then becomes a formal council committee.

If the community does not want a forum there is no obligation on them to have one: it may simply extend or vary the committee structure.

> *Community power is not just about local people being consulted. It is about involving people in making decisions about their neighbourhoods and even the way they organize their own forums* (Barbara Simpson, *Evening News*, 11 September 1997).

The NCP initiative is a notable departure in inclusive urban management. It is aided by the introduction of 'best value' as a basis for official targeting of contract government funds to local authorities. Best value is, however, more a philosophy than a budget mechanism. The idea is to improve coordination among official agencies, local authority departments, businesses and civil society. Performance indicators include targets, participatory structures and evidence of involvement and trust-building. Best value allows for cost-benefit appraisals to take into account long-term savings in other cost areas (health care, policing, building repairs) arising from empowerment and constructive community involvement. So the emphasis is on partnerships, performance indicators and on reliable evidence of linkage among budget managers. The final result should be a more integrated performance planning, improved public understanding and support for the final package of services on offer, coupled with transparent procedures for audit.

Mile Cross

As indicated in previous sections, Mile Cross is an area of social housing which features high levels of unemployment, low-income households and a number of poverty's attendant problems such as poor housing, crime, a drugs problem, inadequate health care and relatively high levels of illiteracy.

During the summer of 1998, research for this project was carried out using focus groups made up of teenagers from a youth group, members of a church group parents of a local playgroup, as well as three groups with no sampling other than self-selection. The first three focus groups were carried out to gain access to particular social networks in the locality, identified through interviews and participant observation. All the groups were asked similar questions about Mile Cross, and the findings were roughly similar with almost universal agreement on the problems and priorities on the estate. These include the following:

- Mile Cross was a distinct place with which they could identify. Often the borders were different, making the estate larger or smaller. But the core remained the same: the triangle, bounded by the main roads and the river.
- Everyone felt that the external view of Mile Cross was negative and that this had a damaging affect on the people living on the estate. However, the internal view of the estate was that it was fine; it had problems and could be greatly improved; generally people were not unhappy living there and most did not envisage moving, even the teenagers.
- Youth, and their provision, activities and behaviour, was the central issue for people living there. It was felt that youth boredom causes vandalism, intimidation, petty crime, and leads to drug-taking and worse behaviour in the long run. Almost every adult had a story about problems with young people on the estate. However, many had grown up there and there was a great deal of sympathy for young people.
- The teenagers themselves confirmed most of these criticisms and their causes. They wanted more provision and a greater sense of efficacy as local citizens. The small amount of youth provision that did exist was removed in budget cuts, and they also lost an advocate for their opinions.
- This continual loop of youth crime, vandalism and intimidation in public spaces and drug-taking haunts the estate. The green spaces valued by local residents were seen as largely unsafe for younger children and not pleasant recreational areas.
- It was felt that there is no real police presence on the estate and so there is a great deal of fear of crime, particularly among women and, reportedly, by the elderly. The lack of community policing was confirmed by subsequent interviews with the police service; this has recently been addressed with the appointment of a dedicated officer for the area.
- Unemployment, poverty and economic change were not issues that were often brought up, but the symptoms, in terms of drugs and crime, were. However, generally the problems themselves were interpreted within the status quo. Economic change and its effects on people's lives were only noted in terms of symptoms, not issues that could be addressed.

- In terms of economic regeneration, knowledge of the local urban regeneration project was poor. This largely skills- and training-based project had been running since 1995, funded to the tune of UK£26 million with public and private resources. Although the aim of the project was to increase the economic capacity of local people through a large number of projects, people were only aware of computer skills courses and some housing renovation.
- This urban regeneration scheme highlighted the lack of community participation in making decisions for the areas. People appeared to be unimpressed by its relevance to locally expressed needs or flexibility to meet them.
- The relationship of Mile Cross to the local authority was the dominant external institutional influence on people's lives and the capacity to achieve change. This relationship is dominated by a strong negative perception of the council and a lack of awareness of its role and of local citizens' potential for efficacy within these structures. The community power project appeared to have a low profile.
- In terms of improving quality of life, the most important aspect appeared to be other people's behaviour and consideration. Without that, environmental improvements – such as more trees or better play provision in local parks – were pointless.

Information is currency on the estate and the main networks for its transmission are informal networks. These fluid, yet vibrant, networks are based around parents meeting at school gates, through youth groups, playgroups and churches, and groups with shared leisure interests such as the local pigeon fanciers. They cover an extraordinary range of people and activities and reveal the rich texture of community networks on the estate.

More formalized networks revolve around the community association, the community centre and its café, community development workers and local newsletters (*Chatline*). Figure 10.2 outlines these informal and more formalized networks. The more formal groups and their attendants (shaded in dark) tend to already have good links with institutions of governance, particularly the city council. The lighter shaded groups form the more amorphous social and informal networks described above. Their links with the city council are weaker.

It is this void between the rich informal networking in the community and communication with the local institutions of governance that the community power forum could address in order to improve trust and to empower the local community. However, since the majority of individuals in the community forum are drawn from the inner circle of formal groups, there is a potential danger for 'ring-fencing of social capital' to occur in the neighbourhood. In this scenario, the empowerment potential is not spread out to the rich social networks of the wider community but remains in the domain of those already well connected.

The forum has agreed provisionally to take forward the idea of community planning in the area. These neighbourhood-based strategies are seen as one of the key long-term aims for community forums and potentially a key channel for influencing policy-making. These strategies will be multi-issue and will be drawn up in close consultation with the community. As such, they could potentially be 'neighbourhood Agenda 21s' and could become a vital link for local democracy and Agenda 21/Norwich 21. The link between the two emerging processes has not been explicit, certainly not at the community level, while there is a strong bias for it in the newly structured city council.

In Mile Cross, the forum has yet to engage in community plan consultations. It has taken on the role of consulting with the wider community, which it represents, in order to claim money for local play provision (which would usually feed into a central fund) and to ensure that the money is spent to match local needs. The forum has shown innovation and much energy in this project.

All of these developments will be tested in tackling a community plan with its holistic thinking and multi-issue nature. The research suggested that this is not an approach that suits the nature of local mobilization. The local community has a good record of mobilizing behind single issues as, for example, when the neighbourhood's youth centre was threatened with closure due to educational cuts across the county.

The community power experience in Mile Cross has thrown up several issues for the relationship between formal and new informal community-grounded mechanisms of governance. These issues come under the following areas:

- Representation: there was a potential for conflict between the role of the new community forum and the local elected councillors (who also sit on the forum). However, the councillors' role appeared not to be diminished by the forum, but rather enhanced through trust-building with the forum to establish a stronger mandate for their decision-making on spending priorities and budgets.
- The rights and responsibilities of forum members: the groups are likely to be called on to provide members for discussions at the city-council level on various topics. The burden of time and effort could be huge, causing people to either drop out or to be unwilling to become involved. Councillors receive a small recompense for their work as representatives of the community, but forum members still act voluntarily.
- The procedural structure of community power forums, in order to be taken seriously at council level, could become just as inaccessible as city council meetings in terms of written agendas, minutes and voting. This would continue to exclude from the democratic process those people uncomfortable with, or lacking the necessary skills for, participating in such meetings.
- Capacity-building: the city employs community development officers in most parts of the city who liaise between the forums and the council, and provide specialist information. The training of local people to take part in initiatives such as community planning is now in hand, due to a UK£136,000 grant from the European Social Fund. This initiative from Brussels in an example of outreach governance for sustainability and

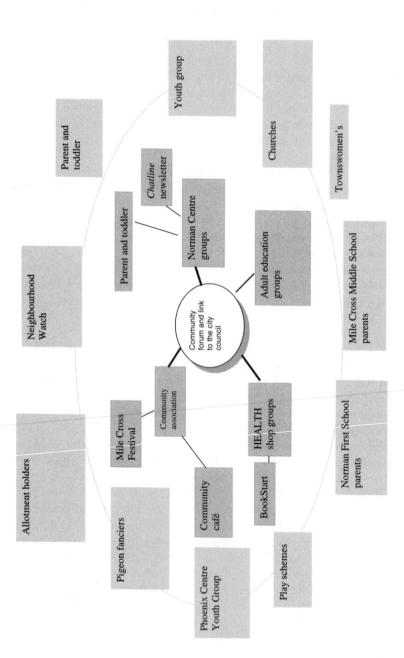

Figure 10.2 *Community networks in Mile Cross, Norwich: many of these have overlapping membership; local–social identity is shaped through this framework*

should boost the confidence of forum members. There is also the possibility that the council, in providing the capacity-building forums, could be unintentionally moulding them towards council procedures, rather than enabling them to evolve from the needs and social dynamics of the local area.

- The relationship to existing community-based organizations is unsure. Often people who are already active in the community, with knowledge of decision-making processes and confident in their ability to interact with professionals, tend to be attracted to new democratic mechanisms such as citizens' forums. That is certainly the case for some members of the Mile Cross forum. If so, these new mechanisms may not create new opportunities but simply re-empower existing organizations or community networks.

Regarding the matter of identity, the Mile Cross study showed that the model of social–local identity presented in Chapter 4 had much merit. There were patterns of security, even within zones of disempowerment, as groups of connected individuals sought safety through self-help efforts. Another example is the formation of neighbourhood watch groups to fight crime and vandalism.

However, insecurities lurk deep in the estate, notably around family violence, loneliness, ill health and abuse of drugs and alcohol. To tap into these feelings, and to assist the disadvantaged to move towards sustainability, is a formidable task indeed. One way forward is to create out of the forum a group of 'facilitators' – local people with detailed knowledge of the estate – who can reach out to the disadvantaged with programmes of skills training and recreational opportunities. Such people could be placed within the framework of performance indicators for best value. Figure 10.3

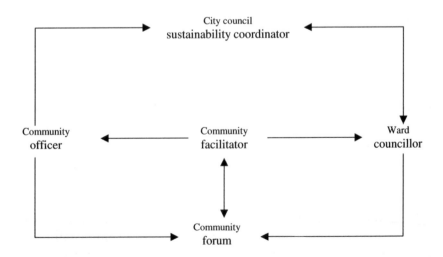

Figure 10.3 *Citizen empowerment and community facilitation*

outlines a possible relationship. The ward councillor is directly involved with the community forum, linked to the strategy committee at council level. The key lubricant is the community facilitator, located in social networks. The facilitator can work with the community official, who seeks out the vulnerable and the community forum; it is the vulnerable who suggest how local councils may prioritize their delivery of services as a whole.

The key to community facilitation is the build-up of real trust and cooperation between the ward councillors, the community forum members and key officers with a strategic social remit for empowerment and identity creation. The facilitators should be forum members, though there is scope for wider representation.

HACKNEY AND SHOREDITCH

Hackney stretches over a total area of 1970 hectares of London's inner-city map from Liverpool Street Station in the south to Stamford Hill in the north, and from the River Lea in the east to Finsbury Park in the west. The London Borough of Hackney comprises the areas of Hackney, Shoreditch and Stoke Newington. These were originally three separate municipal boroughs but were amalgamated in 1965 to form the London Borough of Hackney. Shoreditch is the area of Hackney in the south, adjacent to the City of London, the financial trading area. It is made up of the four electoral wards of Hackney Borough Council (HBC): De Beauvoir, Haggerston, Moorfields and Wenlock.

Socio-economic profile

Table 10.1 *Population by age and sex in Hackney*

Age	0–4	5–14	15–44	45–64	65–74	75–84	85+	Total
Male	8383	13,787	47,796	15,666	5636	2695	567	94,530
(% of total)	50.40	51.83	49.82	48.71	47.71	39.29	23.29	**49**
Female	8250	12,815	48,140	16,493	6288	4165	1798	97,949
(% of total)	49.60	48.17	50.18	51.29	52.73	60.71	76.03	**51**
Total	16,633	26,602	95,936	32,159	11,924	6860	2365	192,479
(% of total)	8.64	13.82	49.84	16.71	6.19	3.56	1.23	**100**

Table 10.1 indicates that the population of Hackney is around 192,000, with most of the population under the age of 44 and a significantly large proportion of children in the population. As age increases, women are increasingly well represented. Table 10.2 indicates another feature of Hackney, a multicultural society.

Table 10.2 *Ethnic minorities in Hackney*

Ethnic Group	Population	Per cent of total population
Black Caribbean	20,370	11.2
Black African	12,240	6.8
Black other	7240	4
Indian	6320	3.5
Pakistani	1750	1
Bangladeshi	3294	1.8
Chinese	1923	1.1
Other Asian	2508	1.4
Other	5168	2.9
Sub-total of ethnic groups	**60,839**	33.6
White	120,409	66.4
Total	**181,248**	100

Table 10.3 *Gross household income in Hackney*

Gross Household Income	Hackney (%)	Inner London (%)	Greater London (%)
< £2500	0	0	0
£2500–£5000	33	17	16
£5000– £7500	22	16	15
£7000–£10,000	11	10	9
£10,000–£15,000	9	15	15
£15,000–£20,000	11	11	12
£20,000–£30,000	8	12	15
£30,000–£40,000	4	7	8
>£40,000	3	12	11
Average Income	**£11,900**	**£19,900**	**£19,700**
Total households (100%)	75,600	1,152,000	2,760,100

Tables 10.3, 10.4 and 10.5 indicate another significant feature of this area: large numbers of households experiencing deprivation.

In order to identify areas of need, an aggregate of seven indicators of deprivation (the Z score) was calculated for all wards in the Greater London area, based on the 1981 census. These indicators represented housing, economic and social conditions. The higher the value of the Z score, the higher the level of deprivation. This showed that 12 of Hackney's 23 wards were among the top 50 most deprived in Greater London. The same exercise was repeated for the 1991 census. It showed that ten of Hackney's wards were still among the most deprived in Greater London, the highest of all the boroughs (although shared with Newham).

Table 10.4 *Household characteristics in Hackney*

Characteristics	Number of Households	Percentage
Households with 1.5 persons per room	3734	4.9
Households with over 1.5 persons per room	1926	2.5
Households lacking/sharing bath and/or WC	2633	3.5
Households lacking central heating	16,799	22.2
Households lacking/sharing bath and/or WC and/or no central heating	17,778	23.5
Households not in self-contained accommodation	3098	4.1
Households with no car	46,674	61.7
Households with two or more cars	5079	6.7
Households with no dependants	40,795	53.9
Households with head of household born outside UK	26,871	35.5

Households with . . .	Number of households	Percentage of total households
One or more persons with limiting long-term illness	20,468	27.1
Dependants only	8,268	10.9
One person living alone	27,314	36.1
Lone parent	6342	8.4
Three or more children aged under 16	4893	6.5
Children aged under five	11,329	15

Table 10.5 *Housing tenure in Hackney*

Household Tenure	Number of Households	Percentage
Owner occupied	23,242	27.0
Private rented or job	20,358	13.8
Housing association	8538	11.3
Local authority	104,943	47.9
Total	**75,631**	100.0

Table 10.6 *Employment conditions in Hackney*

Economic Characteristics	Male (%)	Female (%)
Employment full-time	45.4	36.1
Employment part-time	3.7	10.9
Self-employed	10.1	3.5
On government scheme	1.6	1.4
Unemployed	21.8	11.8
Total economically active	82.5	63.7
Economically inactive	17.5	36.3

These figures are taken from the 1991 census. The August 1993 figure was 25.5 per cent unemployment among the economically active population. These figures are based on the number of people in receipt of benefit. They do not include people who are not in receipt of benefit or who are ineligible for benefit, such as married women, young people on training schemes, under 18s and the long-term unemployed who are not required to register for work.

In the decade leading up to 1991, employment in manufacturing in Hackney fell by more than half. Tertiary industries now provide most of the employment in the area.

Table 10.7 *Employers in Hackney*

Employers	Percentage of total employees
Energy and water supply	0.30
Construction	5.60
Public administration and defence	8.80
Distribution, hotels/catering, repairs	13.0
Manufacturing industries	15.7
Other service industries	26.8
Transport, communication, banking, finance	29.8

The above figures show that Hackney is characterized by many of the symptoms of social exclusion: high unemployment, high levels of deprivation across a number of indices, low levels of income, etc. This is just a brief overview; a more thorough analysis can be found in a poverty profile of the borough carried out in 1996 (Griffiths, 1996). These figures have major implications for sustainable development agendas in the area since the focus is unlikely to be the environment but social policy and urban regeneration.

Shoreditch

Approximately 28,000 people live in this area in 12,000 households. However, there is a different boundary than that for Shoreditch: people in the area take the canal to the north as the natural boundary.

The four electoral wards cover an area that differs hugely. The region extends over the gentrified areas of De Beauvoir and south Shoreditch, the vast concrete local authority-owned estates of most of Shoreditch north of Old Street, and the artist and business area that still exists in south Shoreditch. There are an increasing number of cafés, restaurants and night clubs in the south Shoreditch area that cater to individuals working in the city.

There is conflict between the City of London, a node of the global capitalist economy, and Shoreditch. The city is seeking to expand its boundaries into this area. It is already managing this by default as its high earners move in, taking advantage of factories that have been renovated for high-quality housing. This is causing gentrification of the area. Local people are being pushed out or ignored in favour of the benefits of the city, the global financial markets and the people who have grown rich from them.

The northern area of Shoreditch was redeveloped from terraced housing into local authority-owned tower blocks in the 1950s and 1960s. These are now in a state of disrepair since the local authority has not had the necessary resources to maintain them. As the cheapest form of housing in the area, they have become sink estates for all those people who cannot afford to leave or own housing. With poverty comes a whole host of attendant social problems: crime, vandalism, drug-taking, overcrowding, noise, etc. Among those with the lowest incomes are people representing various ethnic minorities. The ethnic mix in the area is the result of different immigrant populations over the last 100 years; it is an area used to cultural change and, indeed, is the result of cultural change. But these groups in society are often the poorest with the highest levels of unemployment.

Urban regeneration programmes

There are a number of urban (economic) regeneration programmes under-way which are recently completed or imminent in Hackney and, specifically, in and around the area of Shoreditch: Dalston City Partnership, City Fringe, Estates Regeneration, Safer Cities and the Haggerston Single Regeneration Budget (SRB).

New non-governmental, unelected agencies have been created as the focal point of action in order to spend the money brought in for the purposes of urban regeneration. However, the objectives of these new agencies, targets and other measures of progress are not geared to creating capacity among the people of Shoreditch. Instead, the focus is new buildings, office blocks and cleaning areas up. There is improvement to the physical fabric of the area in terms of these new buildings, but the real areas of need, in terms of poor housing, are not being touched. Additionally, the underlying infrastructure has not been upgraded. Despite all this new development, there has been no matching investment in the underlying water, sewage and energy-supply infrastructure. This is only a temporary fix and does little to really change people's lives. The new agencies bypass existing mechanisms of using resources and identifying needs. This means that there is a duplication of effort. It also means that the professionals are running the resource allocation exercise with no say from local people in the area whose needs are supposed to be addressed.

Provision for meeting local needs through these big pots of money, and the timetables for spending the money, have all been worked out in advance according to physical targets and objectives rather than through the creation of opportunities. This is problematic. Local people who are suffering deprivation do not generally benefit from these programmes. Instead, the programmes provide for external people and interest groups. Employment created is often not in relation to the skills of the local workforce. Training courses have been implemented as part of regeneration programmes but are often not tailored to skills requirements.

Training is not what is required in the area. There are a lot of initiatives set up for training but not enough people willing to go on them. What is needed is capacity-building through the positive experience of creating change in people's own circumstances. This would increase people's ability and willingness to go on training courses and expand their skills and involvement in the community in the future. One interviewee remarked that lack of self-esteem is a huge problem: 'this is a very close, unconfident community'. Large capital investment programmes have difficulty in meeting this need.

There are several sources of money in the area. These include the UK government under its SRB programme and the regional development funds of the EU, since the area has Objective 2 status and has won recently a large URBAN project. Consultation has been carried out on very few of the projects that are currently underway, and even then the reported quality of the consultation was very poor, rushed and largely focused on key stakeholders rather than on the population at large. Yet, a high level of meaningful participation is meant to be a prerequisite for funding.

Existing organizations, such as schools, churches and voluntary and interest groups, have not been drawn into the regeneration process. Perhaps this is because they are behind the times, as suggested by one interviewee. But it is also because there is no strategic overview on which everyone in the area agrees. Instead, the council is (along with a number of other agencies) chasing the pots of money for regeneration and lottery funding without any vision or coordination. Consultation is only done at the final stages so that the bid can go through. But this is a cosmetic approach and does not really highlight the problems of the area. The Dalston Community Partnership covers half of Shoreditch, and yet the people of this area have had no input into how that money is spent.

South Bank University undertook a study on Bethnal Green City Challenge and came to the conclusion that mainstream (existing community) organizations were better and more able to respond to community need than these new agencies. This report was so controversial it was not published.

What these successive sources of money have done is alerted people to the fact that change is happening and that their voices are not being heard. The result is a much more vocal community. Local people want progress and changes to be slowed down so that some assessment of the actual needs of the area can be made. Hoxton Trust is eager to get the existing community organizations together to form partnerships and then to access some of this money.

The City Challenge Fund had some money 'ring-fenced' called the Community Chest. This has been used in small amounts for local community projects as a side issue to the big money, and had very successful outputs in terms of changing people's lives. It is hoped that the EU URBAN initiative will have a similar impact as the focus is again very much community-based projects.

There is a great deal of suspicion in the local community about the motives and actions of HBC. Local community groups see themselves in conflict rather than in partnership with HBC. Various policy decisions by the council over the years have been interpreted in the area as neglecting the interests of the community in favour of a grand vision for Hackney. None of the housing estates in the Shoreditch area were included in the huge estate regeneration project: the Comprehensive Estates Initiative. This has been responsible for channelling millions of pounds into five estates in Hackney. The council claims that a housing-condition survey demonstrated that it was not warranted in Shoreditch.

One council decision in particular rankles – the attempt to create a night-time economy, encouraging night clubs, bars and restaurants to become established in the area by selling land and providing infrastructure to enable this to happen. Local people objected on the grounds that it created noise, disturbance and provided entertainment that was outside their income bracket. It was felt to be contrary to the needs and wishes of most of the people of Shoreditch and has created a great deal of bitterness towards the council. The Shoreditch area is cut in two at Old Street, with the old Warehouse area and then the new area of housing estates; they are different worlds. New people moving into the warehouse area are keen for the night-time economy idea to go forward. Money has been spent on providing for this policy; but when nothing is being spent on housing, local people have become upset, particularly since they were never consulted.

General information from interviews

LA21 is not engaging with the people of the area. It is very much a top-down process. Despite being created from consultation with stakeholders (Hackney Borough Council, 1996), it is stuck at policy level. This awakened some concern in councillors who have now tried to take it forward in a different way by putting it together with the anti-poverty strategy of HBC.

Interview data suggest that many community groups feel that the role of the HBC is not what a council's role should be. The perception exists that there is a crucial mismatch of role between the councillors and the officers, with officers very much in control of policy and councillors not doing their jobs properly and taking back control. There is also confusion on the role of officers; they seem to be working across areas but no one is responsible for getting things done. The perception is that HBC is about public relations rather than dealing with issues and asking people what they think. There are no proper mechanisms to bring the community into decision-making.

Currently, there is no strategic view of the needs of the area, making it unbalanced rather than somewhere where everything required can be accessed, even down to food, clothes, banks and leisure facilities. The lack of a strategic view makes decisions and policies concerned very much with the short term. Therefore there is no institutional framework on which sustainability can be hung. Although HBC needs to listen to the community, it also needs to put this information into constructing a strategic view of requirements and solutions in the area. The community itself is good at addressing individual issues but not at assessing the overview.

Since January 1997, there has been a feeling among the community sector and people in the area that it is now Shoreditch's turn in the borough to receive attention and positive change for the future. The chief executive for HBC has chosen to be 'area champion' for Shoreditch – which seems to indicate that the profile of the area in HBC is increasing. In 1999 Hackney was asked to apply for regeneration funding under the government's New Deal for Communities Scheme; the area chosen was Shoreditch. Despite initial signs that the usual mix of economic development was being put forward by the new Not-For-Profit Regeneration Agency, mobilization by the community meant that the final application was largely the outcome of a partnership of community interests. The initial application has been accepted and developed and the area is currently waiting to hear when and how they can take forward their plans.

CONCLUSION

The entrance to the sustainable transition for any locality lies not in creating an LA21 strategy or initiative or a new institution. These can help to refocus or stimulate local activity. Instead, it lies in developing a future from the social networks, institutions and social, economic, historical and political contexts that are already there. These are unique to that area, and will be manifested in a number of concerns particular to that locality and to the lives of the people who work and live there. In the case of Mile Cross, the central issue is the well-being of young people, while in Shoreditch it is having citizen control over urban regeneration initiatives. From both of these areas emerge a whole host of other concerns and problems. Only by starting here, integrating economic, environmental and social concerns, and developing the right political institutions to do so, will the principles and rhetoric of LA21 initiatives and sustainable development begin to become a reality that can be built upon. The sustainability transition cannot be initiated by ignoring the problems and issues that matter to local people. Cosmetic changes do not have the power to engender long-term resilience and proactive approaches to environmental, economic, social and political change.

In both communities, the transition to civic empowerment is painful and slow. It is not at all evident that real civic empowerment is actually taking place, in the sense of embracing in a meaningful way those never before in a position to shape their destinies. Existing patterns of social networks are still in operation and the new organizations still have to gel. In addition, the truly disadvantaged are not yet in any position to be politically effective. None of the funding programmes designed to ensure their participation has actually attained that objective.

Yet, the experience from both communities is somewhat heartening. This is a social–local identity that is finally being tapped. The formerly alienated are now beginning to become truly involved, and local government is opening up its procedures to ensure a greater partnership in effective governance. Skills training in civic responsibility is beginning to have some effect. New alliances are forming, some of which are beginning to merge with the old area. Grievances impel new forms of action and commitment. The scope for overcoming such governances is beginning to be regarded as attainable. The vehicle is urban regeneration and empowerment, not LA21, though an opportunistic LA21 is quite capable of marrying the two.

By the end of 1999 it has become evident that LA21 is being superseded by the higher profile themes of urban regeneration and social inclusion. The push to modernize local government is a serious political agenda. It is geared towards effective service provision, aimed at meeting demonstrable community needs. Those needs, and evaluating the effectiveness of source delivery, must include mobilized participation and indicators of best value. The fact that these programmes are being run through the chief executive's office, and not the environmental planning departments, is a sign of the eclipse of LA21. Urban regeneration is high profile because it may attract European structural funds, and because such areas are perceived to be the heartlands of crime, poverty, violence and drug abuse. Furthermore, it is now recognized that if regeneration is to have any value, then it should contain capacity-building via job training and employment opportunities (see Taylor, 1994, for a review).

Nevertheless, there is a disagreement among regeneration professionals on the scope for sustainability in all of this. Many are happy to support urban greening, but initiatives such as high-quality, low-energy housing programmes are regarded as being too repressive with little short-term benefit. This area of misunderstanding is not being filled by the UK approach to sustainability and may have to wait for more imaginative public–private partnerships.

LA21s do not have the authority, nor the continuity or the resources to deliver both effective participation and prolonged capacity-building. Too many individuals remain marginalized in the local authority programmes of action, and do not follow through early approaches to visioning and participatory involvement. The best that can be hoped for in the foreseeable future is that LA21s may help to 'green' the emerging management framework of best value. Indeed, there is a lively, but incomplete, debate as to how far best-value principles can be incorporated within sustainability. For example, the need to incorporate social housing on brown field sites with integrated transport is still a proposal.

But people need more than homes: they need homes that are safe and homes that they can afford to heat. Affordable warmth should go with affordable homes. It should be emphasized here that 40 per cent of those wanting a home by 2016 may not be able to pay for one. There are many initiatives aimed at improving the quality of housing stock: these include tenants' campaigns aimed at finding workable solutions to the effects of dampness, lack of insulation and the costs of heating. Organizations such as Heatwise in Glasgow aim to improve the fabric of existing property in order to improve dryness, warmth and costs while also providing local employment.

Energy use in homes accounts for 30 per cent of the UK's total energy consumption, so there are climate change implications as well. Redesigning our living and working spaces to demonstrate the viability of sustainability principles in action is the idea behind many exciting new initiatives across the UK. The Sherwood Energy Village in Nottinghamshire links super-insulated typical housing with renewable energy features, while the Hockerton Housing Project is the UK's earth-sheltered, self-sufficient ecological housing development. The houses are at the centre of sustainable development using minimal energy with little environmental impact. There is, however, a long way to go before these new ideas become common practice.

'Urban nature' has become an increasingly important area of work. It includes what we do with gardens, allotments, community gardens and city farms, with parks and recreation grounds, with uncared-for 'inter-mediate spaces' around housing developments, roads and public buildings, and with the few sites of special importance, such as nature reserves, that are still found in every conurbation.

More that ever, green space is under threat in towns and cities. The pressure for new housing and new workspaces, at a time when protection of the countryside around cities is becoming a key issue, means that almost any open space may be viewed as potential development land. This has, in turn, led in some cases to conflicts between those seeking to protect urban open space and those working to save green belts. What is needed here are joint strategies that focus more on the reuse of unwanted and derelict buildings rather than on the easy option of building on open space.

Dealing with problems at a neighbourhood level is at the core of work for more sustainable communities. The importance of working on solutions that benefit an entire neighbourhood has long been recognized in areas with high levels of poverty and exclusion – regeneration strategies now recognize this and also recognize the importance of involving local people in drawing up and implementing plans to improve their neighbourhoods.

This work also relates directly to the buildings, especially in council or housing-association built estates where buildings will share common features and problems. Organizations such as Neighbourhood Energy Action have pioneered work in this field. More ambitiously, the Sustainable Urban Neighbourhood (SUN) Initiative managed by the URBED group is seeking to draw all these issues together and is looking at how our neighbourhoods might work in a more sustainable society.

Getting people to take pride in where they live requires outside support and investment, both to improve the local economy and the housing, and to make the area an attractive and safe place in which to live. Research for the Joseph Rowntree Foundation (1999) has shown how important it is to understand disadvantaged neighbourhoods, including their histories and their assets as well as their problems.

While 'inner-city' areas have tended to be the focus of much work on urban sustainability, most people actually live in areas that can best be described as 'suburban'. There has been much less focus on suburban areas, but many show signs of stress, with declining local centres, deteriorating community facilities and dependence on cars. The more widespread nature of such communities makes wholesale regeneration and rebuilding much harder. Creating sustainable suburbs may be one of the biggest challenges of all, and one where national support for locally-based initiatives that suit local needs will be more important than ever.

REFERENCES

BMG Research (1995) *Skills Audit 1995*, Norfolk and Waveney Training and Enterprise Council, Norwich

Department of Social Security (1999) *Poverty and Social Exclusion*, Her Majesty's Stationery Office, London

Griffiths, S (1996) *The Challenge: A Profile of Poverty in Hackney*, Hackney Borough Council, London

Hackney Borough Council (1996) *Hackney Tomorrow: Shaping a Better Future*, Hackney Borough Council, London

Joseph Rowntree Foundation (1999) *Urban Regeneration and Sustainable Communities*, Joseph Rowntree Foundation, York

Levitt, R and Christie, I (1999) *The Richness of Cities: Urban Policy in a New Landscape*, Demos, London

Norwich City Council (1994) *Norwich Economic Area Strategy*, Norwich City Council, Norwich

Taylor, M (1995) *Unleashing the Potential*, Joseph Rowntree Foundation, York

University of East Anglia (1987) *Norwich Economic Area Strategy*, Norwich City Council, Norwich

Voisey, H (1998) 'Local Agenda 21 in the UK' in T O'Riordan. and H Voisey, (eds) *The Transition to Sustainability: the Politics of Agenda 21 in Europe*, Earthscan Publications Ltd, London, pp221–242

11 Taking the Transition Forward

Tim O'Riordan

The transition to sustainability will not come about through a sustainability driver. If it progresses at all, it will do so because of a changing society and political economy. This will be shaped by the intermixing of the global and local (the centrepiece of this study), the unpredictable implications of the Internet and virtual reality, and reaction to the growing insecurities of the modern economic world. We may have to seek refuge in a more 'social security' through the bonding and connecting that informal economies and local networks create to hold us together.

The first main conclusion from this study is that it is possible to think and act globally and locally at the same time. The spatial differentiation of global and local has gone. We are all global beings, acting out our consumerism and citizenship at a local level. As we move about we carry our locality with us. There is a tremendous need to deploy the visualizing qualities of scenarios and geographical information systems so that people can connect to each other to make local choices that carry a societal as well as a global message. The tools of citizens' juries, of citizens' forums and of virtual citizens' networks are all becoming available. Never before has it been so possible to act as a global–local citizen in the transition to sustainability. It is also unlikely that we will be able fully to grasp the opportunities on offer.

The second key observation is that the onset of community democracy comes at a time of deepening scepticism over politics and political accountability. The Internet has made it more difficult for politicians to prove that they are reliable and trustworthy. Their credibility rankings may drop even further. We may be entering an age of media democracy, where communications through lobbying, through advocacy and through various forms of consensual deliberation become the basis of political decisions. The set-piece political debate and the formal policy framework for disseminating information were never as important as some political analysts would have us believe. Now the lobbying and advocacy are much more decentralized and more fragmented, but also more open and accessible. Decentralized and disjointed democracy will become the muddled medium for accommodating global–local relations in the future.

A third finding arising from this study is the uneasy relationship between central and decentralized units at all levels of policy-making. The EU is steadily facing a period of devolution to a larger group of member states while trying to hold a more powerful centralist policy line, notably on economic and foreign policy matters. Limitations on the veto power of a single member state in Brussels are being sweetened by greater attempts to promote the cause of subsidiarity, moving to the regional and not just the national level. However, central governments are not likely to relinquish power so easily. The multiple layering of government, referred to in Chapter 3, is an important development. It provides a basis for devolution of those elements of power which can be more accessible to local control. This is bound to move onwards, though it is doubtful in the short run that sustainability will be captured by it.

The fourth element of our findings is the vital role that social–local identity may play in this global–local amalgamation. If devolution and subsidiarity do continue to evolve, then social–local identity can become a most important medium for ensuring that those whose needs must properly be met by sustainability can be identified and empowered. The key to this prospect is the role of devolved democracy in translating social exclusion to meaningful social cohesiveness and solidarity.

Now we turn to economic futures. The prospect for reliable employment for the weakest third of the families in Europe is bleak. The rate of upgrading skills is too fast for most of this group to be in a position to grasp. The evidence from the *Sixth Periodic Report* (European Communities, 1999, pp20–21) is that the lagging regions remain slow in their economic transformation. All the peripheral regions to the east and south have wealth per capita of between 60 per cent and 75 per cent of the EU average. It is the city state where the prosperous live. Rural, sparsely populated regions suffer the most, especially the womenfolk. Any sign of European recession hits these vulnerable regions and populations the hardest. We have yet to incorporate a notion of bonding and connecting social well-being as a legitimate and honourable activity for a future state. The average finance minister and social security boss cling to the belief that personally enriching and wealth-creating employment is effectively available to all, irrespective of social background and education.

The case studies reveal that the informal economy is more likely to grow than to decline. This is because it is necessary in order to hold people together. This is especially the case if social–local identity is to be created. The aim must surely be to tap that flourishing informal economy so that it bonds people into supportive activities that ensure empowerment. We are a long way from accepting this as an element of sustainability economics.

Yet, look at the trends in employment and in the nature of a future Western economy. New jobs are less secure, mostly part-time and not fully protected by law. Contractual obligations do not guarantee economic security. Most families can only maintain a viable household if there are two income earners in the home. This is not always possible in the same locality, so the 'second' job may be particularly insecure. At the same time, governments are facing a huge bill for pensions, social security, health care, upgraded education and post-school training courses. They know that they cannot finance these from general taxation and still guarantee a stable economy. This is particularly the case with the single European Monetary Union (EMU). The aim is therefore to place more and more of the cost of social services with the individual. This makes the reward of work less attractive. We are in danger of creating an insecure society that relies on the informal economy for its survival, yet whose identity bonds are being constantly broken by translocation, benefits fraud hassle and sheer economic desperation.

So far, sustainability has not properly entered into the realms of social connectedness – namely, the bonding of trust and accepted rules of behaviour that ensure a society holds together. Sustainability remains driven by the engine of economic momentum. Clean technology, Factor 4 and new forms of negotiated agreements in regulation are the vogue in the current interpretations of the transition. What is still missing are true civil rights, properly devolved democracy, care for the disadvantaged to the point where they can play a role in their own maintenance and hope, and forms of public–private partnerships that target those whose inclusion will also mean empathy.

The case studies try to show that not all is lost. People do form self-help groups in the teeth of adversity. In all the cases studies, with the exception, paradoxically, of the eco-cities of Graz and Linköping, some form of informal social networks have evolved to try to turn the tide of local economic misfortune caused by global economic circumstances, or the capturing of sustainability. What we discovered is that none of these networks is properly understood or adequately incorporated within a useful vehicle for the sustainability transition. A potentially massive resource, and one that has forever kept people from breaking apart, is not fully understood as a vital lubricant for the sustainability transition.

This suggests that the next stage of economic transformation in Europe will display a tussle between the reactionary forces of status-quo growth economics and the more radical drive towards a more decentralized, self-sustaining and localized economy, connected to multiple layers of governance and broad global networks. Such a version will not be at all easy to achieve. It will place enormous strain on conventional patterns of governance and democracy. It will test the resolve of finance and trade ministers to blast away the informal economy. It will challenge the notion that the only good citizen is a working citizen. And it will open up the possibility that social bonding, identity maintenance and constructive socio-economic relationships may become the economy of the future. This is actually the message of a more self-reliant, locally collective sustainability, but linked to global communications and economic opportunity. If we can somehow marry the Internet to social bonding and localized economic entrepreneurship, notably for the currently marginalized groups, then sustainability will have come of age, albeit in another guise.

So the next sequence of work is to attend more to the enormous significance of social–local identity as the best mechanism for social renaissance in a period of growing political economic crisis. The exploding world of globalization can be knitted together through local identities, so long as we realize the goal is about connectedness and security rather than wealth creation as an end in itself. The task for the sustainability transition in the coming decade is to make this linkage work.

REFERENCES

European Communities (1999) *Sixth Periodic Report on the Social and Economic Situation and Development of the Regions of the European Union,* Commission of the European Communities, Brussels

INDEX

Page numbers in *italics* refer to figures, tables and illustrations.